ADVANCED GRAPHOLOGY

TWENTY LECTURES ON SELECTED TOPICS

Volume II

Scriptor Books

To my daughters,

La and Marie-Thérèse

ADVANCED GRAPHOLOGY

TWENTY LECTURES ON SELECTED TOPICS

VOLUME II

Renna Nezos
Principal of The British Academy of Graphology

Edited by
Lorraine Herbert and Kathryn Goulandris

Scriptor Books

an imprint of
The British Academy of Graphology
London

Published in 1993
by SCRIPTOR BOOKS,
an imprint of
The British Academy of Graphology (Limited by gGuarantee)
in association with The London College of Graphology Ltd,
75 Quinta Drive, Barnet, Herts. EN5 3DA

Editorial Office:
1B Limpsfield Avenue, London SW19 6DL

A CIP catalogue record for this book is available from the British Library.

ISBN 0-9513700-6-5

Design and Production by

EuroBuro '92 | Brigitte Froud
London, Tel 081-788 3289

Printed and bound in Great Britain by Coombe Printers & Stationers, London SW20 ORJ

CONTENTS

Introduction to Volume II 11
Preface 13

PART ONE
GRAPHOLOGICAL TECHNIQUES

LECTURE I
GENERAL INFORMATION 17
1. Origins and evolution of writing 17
2. Graphological/psychological analysis 19
3. The process of graphological analysis 21
   A. The Procedure 21
   B. The Definition 23
      B1. Signature 24
      B2. W. Hegar 24
   C. The Synthesis and Resultants 26
   D. Psychological Typologies 28
   E. The Portrait 29
Sources 31

LECTURE II
PRINCIPAL SYNTHESIS OF ORIENTATION 27
1. First Impression 33
2. Organisation 33
3. Spacing 34
4. Harmony 34
5. Formlevel 35
6. Tension 36
6a. Tension (R. Pophal) 40
7. Rapport between Form and Movement 43
8. Structure 44
9. Axes 46
10. Movement 48
Sources 49
Samples 50

LECTURE III

TYPES OF MOVEMENT 57
1. Static 59
2. Floating 60
3. Inhibited 60
4. Controlled 61
5. Flowing 61
6. Vibrant 62
7. Dynamic 63
8. Propulsive 63
9. Obstructed 64
10. Reared 65
Sources 65
Diagram of movements 66
Samples 67

PART TWO
GRAPHOLOGICAL SPECIALISATIONS

LECTURE IV

CHILDREN'S WRITINGS 75
Documents needed 78
E-Scale 80
Evaluation procedure 92
A worked example 93
Process of evaluating a child's handwriting 97
Psychological typologies 100
Jungian Attitudes 100
Hippocratic temperaments 101
Le Sennian characterology 102
Other personality traits 103
Supplementary Notes 108
Dysgraphy 109
Sources 110
Samples 111

LECTURE V

ADOLESCENTS' WRITINGS 115
Fluency 119
Dimension 120
Vertical consideration 120
Curved Strokes 123
Superelevations 124

Horizontal consideration - Spacing 125
Form 127
Oblique movements 128
The Slant 129
The Stroke 130
The letter "t" 131
Signatures 132
Psychological Typologies 132
Sources 133
Samples 134

LECTURE VI
VOCATIONAL GUIDANCE-PROFESSIONAL ORIENTATION 139
Adaptation 141
a) Kretschmer 141
b) Le Senne 142
c) Intelligence 143
d) Degree of rigidity of the Ego 144
Specific qualities for specific jobs 147
General Advice 149
Sources 150
Samples 151

LECTURE VII
PERSONNEL SELECTION 153
Types of vocation 154
Types of intelligence 155
Dimensions of intelligence 157
The Intellectual Process 157
Will Power 158
Moral imperatives 159
Main professional orientation 161
Conditions promoting harmony at work 169
The report 169
Honesty 170
40 Personality elements 172
Sources 184

LECTURE VIII
COMPATIBILITY 187
Compatibility Chart 191
Sources 194
Samples 195

LECTURE IX
GRAPHOTHERAPY 201
Sources 208

PART THREE
PSYCHOPATHOLOGY

LECTURE X
EMOTIONAL AND MENTAL PROBLEMS 211
Neurosis 212
Psychosis 213
Obsession 214
Psychopathy 214
Schizothymia/phrenia 215
Cyclothymia/phrenia 216
Depression 217
Paranoia 218
Perversity 223
The Complexes 224
Homosexuality 226
Fatigue 227
Overtiredness 227
Sources 228
Samples 229

LECTURE XI
CLINICAL GRAPHOLOGY 237
Dyspnoia 240
Cardiovascular malfunctions 241
Intoxications 241
Nervous illnesses 242
Mental illnesses 243
Visual malfunctions 244
Psychopathological constitutions 244
Other malfunctions (arthritis, hyper-,hopythyroidic, etc.) 247
Sources 248
Samples 249

LECTURE XII
PROBLEM WRITINGS 253
Insincerity 254
Samples 257
Aggression 261

Equilibrium 263
The Instinctive-Organised 264
Sources 266
Samples 267

PART FOUR
VARIOUS SYSTEMS

LECTURE XIII

THE PSYCHOBIOLOGICAL APPROACH 271
Graphological Methods 273
Psychobiological temperaments 273
The Harmonic 274
The Melodic 276
The Rhythmic 277
The Complex 278
Their Handwritings 279
Recap of Dominants 282
Sources 283
Samples 285

LECTURE XIV

GRAPHOMETRY 289
Method of research 289
Diagnostic Technique 291
Sources 291

PART FIVE
FURTHER PSYCHOLOGICAL THEORIES APPLIED TO GRAPHOLOGY

LECTURE XV

S. FREUD 295
The Unconscious 296
The Id 296
The Ego 297
The Superego 297
The graphic signs (Id, Ego, Superego) 298
The four stages of development 302
oral 302
anal 303
phallic 305

Oedipus 306
Hysteria 309
Narcissism 310
Sources 312
Samples 313

LECTURE XVI
A. ADLER 317
Sources 322
Samples 323

LECTURE XVII
E. KRETSCHMER & W. Sheldon 325
Samples 328
W. SHELDON 331
Samples 334
Sources 338

LECTURE XVIII
K. HORNEY 339
Sources 344
Samples 345

LECTURE XIX
E. FROMM 347
Receptive type 348
Exploitive type 349
Hoarding type 350
Marketing type 351
Sources 357
Samples 358

LECTURE XX
A. MASLOW 365
Hierarchy of Needs 371
Sources 376
Samples 377

A FINAL WORD OF ADVICE 385

EUROPEAN CODE OF ETHICS 387

INTRODUCTION

Often I have been profoundly touched by the genuine interest and devotion of the students of The London College of Graphology. Looking at their work and watching them progress from year to year makes me more determined to bring them the best knowledge available in any way I can.

In this volume I have tried to incorporate partly what was left out of Volume I due to lack of space, but also to add important new developments in the Science of Graphology. Some of these developments have already been made accessible to the English speaking world during the past eight years thanks to the indefatigable efforts of The British Academy of Graphology and The London College of Graphology which, through their publishing arm, *Scriptor Books*.

This, the sixth publication of *Scriptor Books*, hopefully will add a gram or two to the weight of scholarship the students and all people interested are seeking in order to grasp the essence and intricate complexities of this fascinating search which we call graphology.

It is, of course, physically impossible to put all that I would have liked in this volume. To compensate, I hope and pray that *Scriptor Books* will find the resources to translate and publish many more books, without which English speaking graphology will always trail behind the rest of Europe.

RENNA NEZOS
London, August 1993

PREFACE

GRAPHOLOGY - an Art or a Science?[1]

The word 'science' was first used by the Greek philosopher, Thales of Melos, in 600 B.C. in the sense of 'absolute and exact knowledge of a subject' and it was born of the pursuit of knowledge, understanding and explaining of truth. This concept, however, had been known in Mesopotamia as early as 2000 B.C.

Science is characterised by a search for knowledge, as opposed to a 'belief' (faith) or an 'opinion' (taste). A science, in the modern sense of the word, consists of a body of predictive theories, which must be disprovable through testing whether their predictions come true. These theories cannot be taken as true. They merely are more and more likely to reflect the truth as more and more unsuccessful attempts are made to disprove them.

An art, on the other hand, is defined as the skill developed by habit in doing anything as a result of acquired knowledge of traditional rules and practice. This is not characterised by any search for truth, but rather by an attempt to succeed in performing a task in accordance with aesthetic or practical norms which are neither deduced, nor logically questioned.

The question of which of these two categories graphology fits into is most often raised by those less familiar with the

(1) Article first published in the January 1988 issue of the Journal of The British Academy of Graphology

subject. It is true that a first impression of graphology may be that of a 'mystic art', something rather akin to clairvoyance or fortune telling. A closer inspection of the subject, however, soon indicates that this is not the case.

Graphology is based upon researched laws, deduced and predictive theories whose correctness can be tested by simply observing if their predictions come true. There is no element of belief or unquestioning faith, in the study of handwriting analysis. Graphology is thus not an art, but a science. This is not to say that it is exactly comparable with the natural sciences. It differs from these in the same way as all human sciences do: i.e. in that the terms in which the theories are formulated (the words used in the statement of the theories) are or can be open to more than one exact interpretation. This characteristic, however, does not prevent psychology, sociology, theology or philosophy being classified as sciences.

The only way in which 'art' enters into graphology is in the putting into practice the acquired knowledge and skills. Of two graphologists with equal knowledge, one may put together a good portrait and the other a bad one. The difference between them is art or skill.

This is also true, however, of all other sciences, including the natural ones. A physicist needs not only theoretical knowledge, or rules about how to carry out research, but also art and skill in doing so in order to produce a good publication and be termed successful.

I hope that this makes clear the reasons why I feel that Graphology cannot be classified as an art rather than a science.

RENNA NEZOS
and LA FISCHER, B.Sc., ARCS
London, January 1988

PART 1

GRAPHOLOGICAL TECHNIQUES

LECTURE I
General Information

LECTURE II
Principal Synthesis of Orientation

LECTURE III
Types of Movement

LECTURE I

GENERAL INFORMATION

1. ORIGINS AND EVOLUTION OF WRITING

Man's need to express himself and communicate his ideas, whether religious, superstitious, or simply artistic, goes back into the mists of prehistoric time. It is in the remnants of these early efforts at communication that one is able to appreciate the first manifestations toward graphic reproduction of an object or of an idea.

In many parts of the earth there are engravings on the stone walls of caves, representing images of all kinds, inspired by the need for this expression.

These representations not only expressed the object but also the idea attached to it. For instance a deer, or a bull, could mean "hunting", the sun could mean "daylight" etc. This is why this kind of primitive writing has also been called "ideographic" as opposed to "phonetic" writings, like the Semitic and European writings, in which conventional signs (letters) represent a sound.

Ideographic writings still exist today in the Chinese and Japanese "ideograms" and in part of our own writing; the numbers.

Each nation expresses itself in a different manner, starting from the same premise: to project objects and ideas by signs.

Some nations (the Egyptians), evolved very quickly towards a phonetic writing, whereas others (the Chinese and Japanese) persisted with ideography, simplified and sophisticated, but also increasingly more complicated, since the requirements of progress of the human mind obliges them to use an ever increasing number of signs.

Primitive drawings were transformed into pure hieroglyphics, that is, into a system of abbreviated designs, formalised (schematic), which only the initiated could execute and understand.

Ancient ideographic writings derive from the direct and primitive reproduction of an object, with the purpose of fixing the image and the idea in order to pass it on to other individuals.

Most ideographic writings evolved more or less rapidly into phonetic writings which, being more adaptable, could transmit the notion of the abstract. Egyptians were the first to attempt these new forms. The alphabet signs derived from primitive hieroglyphics, first evolved into "hieratic" (4000 B.C.) - the sacred writings of priests - and then into "demotic" (popular writing) representing the sounds of the spoken language.

This ancient hieroglyphic language remained untranslated for 1500 years, until the discovery of the "Rosetta stone" by the French in 1799. This block of granite upon which there are engraved inscriptions in three languages: Hieroglyphic, Demotic and Greek was decoded when the easily-read Greek characters opened the door to the translation of the two other inscriptions.

In south Mesopotamia, from 3500 to 600 B.C., the Sumerians, Akkadians, Hittites, Elamites, Assyrians and the Persians used cuneiform writing which was at first written from right to left and later from left to right. It was a syllabic writing and was first deciphered by Grotenfed in 1802 and later by Rawlinson, Lassen and others.

All this shows that in prehistoric and ancient times there were already different writings, some of which were quite sophisticated, evolved, as well as artistic, indicative of the people who modified and established them.

It is interesting to point out that graphologists can penetrate with deeper understanding than historians into the soul of these ancient people, who were so different to us and who still remain quite a mystery, despite the remarkable works of the Egyptologists.

Abbé Michon started a study of the mentality of a nation based on the national traits of its writing.

Hieratic Egyptian writing, for example, presents an extremely interesting characteristic in the predominance of curves over angles, whereas the "Moabite" writing (of the Phoenicians of Moab), who adopted the Egyptian script, transformed a lot of these curves into angles. The Phoenicians were instructed by the Egyptians in this form of writing and their intellectual culture was relatively new compared to that of their teachers, but the personality of the hard and brusque Phoenicians who were commercial merchants and travellers, was quickly reflected in the angularity of their written forms, whereas the calm, pastoral life in the rich valleys of the Nile had given to the Egyptian character, and consequently to their writing, a certain sweetness, flabbiness and softness.

2. GRAPHOLOGICAL / PSYCHOLOGICAL ANALYSIS

Today graphology is a recognised science, appreciated not only by an intellectual elite, but more and more by a wider public in many spheres of activity. But, like medicine, it is also an art, and as Keyserling said, "There is no problem in life which does not require art to resolve it."

Like medicine, it is first a science, because for well over a century it has been based on facts discovered through research and experimentation. It has its own laws and from accurate observation recognises elements and produces a diagnosis. It is also an art in that each graphologist, like the doctor, uses the intellectual skills unique to him to interpret and to help where needed.

The skill of the graphologist does not consist only in the knowledge of movement and form in writing, but equally important is the gift of observation, the knowledge of psychology and the general culture of those who practise it.

We know that handwriting is the mirror of all the forces and weaknesses of the writer. The theory of graphology, and even more the practice of it, depend heavily on the study of other so called 'humanistic sciences', since the graphologist must be able to recognise, through the diversity of the stroke, the reasons (physical and psychological) for this diversity, the qualities and the faults, both intellectual and moral, of the writer.

We can no longer separate the physical from the psychological aspect of a personality; each one of these two interacts with the other.

It is up to the graphologist to know how to recognise in a writing heredity, education, and health (physical or mental), since all these put together give the writer his or her special and unique personality .

As in medicine, we must start by knowing and recognising the healthy writer in all his aspects. Only then can we recognise anomalies, uncover their causes, and if possible, try to help cure them.

The most important thing in graphology is to look and to look well, and to look again at the writing. This may sound very obvious, but it is one of the hardest skills to acquire. When a graphologist examines a writing it is easy to see whether it is large or small, low or prolonged, calm or agitated, gross or graceful, heavy or light, etc. A beginner or an amateur can easily do this, and having done so, will be satisfied that he has seen all there is to be seen.

The more accomplished graphologist will never try to deduce anything before he has collected all the characteristics of the writing and interpreted them in correlation with each other..

As Crépieux-Jamin said in his book, *ABC de la graphologie,* "The value of graphological signs is relative, since the same movement may be produced by different causes. The skill of the graphologist is in choosing, among many possible interpretations, the most suitable to the specific writing, the most certain logically and the most necessary psychologically."

The signs in writing are like "syndromes" in medicine, merely indications which will guide us backwards towards the determining cause. Only an accurate definition will allow us to make the correct characterological deductions about the writer, which is the aim of graphology.

3. THE PROCESS OF GRAPHOLOGICAL ANALYSIS

(A) The Procedure *(see Lecture II)*

In summary this consists of:

1. First impression
(General impression) - determines the writer's guiding image, unconscious tendencies and personal choices, his educational level, aestheticism, energy and confidence.

2. Organisation
Organisation of mind and activities (time and money), social/cultural maturity.

3. Spacing
Adaptibility, independence, reflexion, objectivity-subjectivity, contact or lack of contact with reality, security-insecurity, sense of order, aestheticism.

4. Harmony

Logic, intelligence and will, with a balanced personality, in harmony with self and the world (depending on degree of harmony: moral and intellectual superiority - not necessarily creative or productive).

5. Formlevel

Intensity of being

6. Tension

Attitude to life; strong or weak

7. Movement / Form rapport

(a) Dominance of Movement = initial impulsiveness, expressive of psychic contents, difficult control + spontaneity, possible independence from conventions, intense activity.

(b) Dominance of Form = need to structure the personality and to achieve, social values, conformism, conservatism, ethics, need to present the self.

(c) Balance of both = efficiency, acceptance of rules, solidity, patience.

8. Structure

(a) Overstructured = Rigidity. May mask grave and deep inner conflicts, lack of inner harmony.

(b) Good = Maturity, creativity, activity, receptivity, ability to achieve goals.

(c) Poor = Lack of courage, shyness, inhibitions, dissimulation, insincerity.

9. Axes

(a) Vertical = ardour, enthusiasm, confidence, aptitude to play an active part, motivation, authenticity, pride, resolution, presence, affirmation, imposition of ideas, authority, potential.

(b) Horizontal = outside world, avidity, need to assimilate, need to expand, adaptability, need to conquer, action rather than being, enterprising, expansion.

10. Movement

Inner motivation, ability to learn, progression *(see Lecture III).*

(B) THE DEFINITION

To start a definition, we must divide the signs into three stages, according to their importance; this is known as the 'hierarchy' plan :

1. the **Dominant Characteristics**
2. the **Full Definition**
3. the **'Particular Signs'**, that is occasional signs or those of lesser importance.

In every writing there are a number of constant characteristics which allow us to recognise it immediately. We call these *Dominants*. If we take many examples of the writing of a person, the dominants will always be the same. We must be sure, of course, that the writing has been penned freely and that the writer was not hindered by extraneous causes such as cold, heat, illness, emotion, etc. That is why it is always better if we have more than one sample of a writing.

Having established the *Organisation* of the writing, the *Harmony* and *Formlevel,* we assess the *Movement,* and the

Tension and then the *Dominants* which are the most characteristic, the most obvious, the most often repeated signs and which constitute the species, and then we proceed with the more detailed part of the definition, listing the secondary characteristics.

(B1) The Signature

Next comes the assessment of the *signature.* Some people believe that the signature is everything, others that it is unimportant. They are both wrong, of course. The signature is our own personal, free choice. It is our proper sign, our symbol of ourselves.

"The conscious dictates the unconscious writes", said A. Lecerf in his book, *Cours supérieur de graphology.* The text is the dictation of a message from our conscious. It is the *public personality,* whereas the signature is the *intimate personality.* The harmony, or lack of it, between the two will give us valuable information about the writer.

(B2) W. Hegar - assessment of the stroke

The *stroke* is a basic factor of the writing. It is not influenced or lead by the writer's guiding (directive) images (L. Klages). These are expressed through the forms, dimensions, extensions and distribution of the text, and constitute the "representative" function of the writing. The *stroke* constitutes the "expressive" function of the writing and is directly linked to the writer's instincts and mobilising forces.

Walter Hegar's system is based on the observation of the strokes which consists of four characteristics. These are:

1. ***the pressure*** that the pen exerts on the paper in order to trace the letters. This can be *heavy* (active) or *light* (passive) and it manifests the *active* or *passive* response of the writer

towards reality and matter - as represented by the paper and its resilient nature.

2. ***the quality of the resulting stroke*** which can be *precise* (active) or *pasty* (passive). This is influenced by the way the writer holds the pen, by its angle with the writing surface, by the speed and by the movement (curved or straight). The quality of the stroke is guided by the writer's psychological mechanisms (*active* or *passive*), from sensuality to intellectual clarity and independence.

3. ***the movement (of the stroke)*** which can be either dominantly *straight* (active) or *curved* (passive) - (occasionally compatible with the *vertical* or *horizontal* axes) - parallel as well as perpendicular to the surface of the paper, such as *spindles* (concave) or *invisible connections* (convex). The movement is indicative of the ability to take active decisions and hold the reins of one's own life (straight) or imaginative - which considers the paper more as an obstacle than challenge (curved).

4. ***the speed of the stroke*** which can be either *rapid* (active) or *slow* (passive). Speed is never constant in a writing. It depends on the length of the uninterrupted stroke and consequently on the dimension and connectedness of the letters (continuity). It is also affected by the changes of direction during the formation of the letters which can be brusque (angles) or supple (curves). Curves favour speed and vice versa.

The speed of the stroke depends on the intellectual factor of the writer, the ability for abstraction, and on the writer's motivating energy, spontaneity of action, and activity - except in cases of mere professional scriptural virtuosity, which can be detected by the rest of the signs and general characteristics.

(C) THE SYNTHESIS AND RESULTANTS

Now we are ready to proceed with the 'Synthesis', which is made up of combinations of two, three or more elements provided by the previous work. These groupings are known as resultants and provide the means of evaluating the writer's intellectual capacity, emotivity, adaptability, activity, practical sense, etc. This is the passage from the signs to their consequences, from the causes to their effects. It shapes the definition into a more coherent and synoptic form, for which a knowledge of resultants is imperative.

There are **two kinds of resultants** : *graphological*, or *'first degree' resultants* and *psychological* or *'second degree' resultants.* In our definition we have the three hierarchical levels of signs as we have seen. First we take the dominants indicating the same tendency, to form the first resultant. For example: rapid + dynamic = activity (lst degree resultant). We do the same with the other signs of the definition and then we combine these resultants in order to obtain a psychological resultant, which will show us a particularity of the writer's personality, which we could not see through a simple interpretation of signs.

For example:

Signs	1st degree resultant	Secondary resultant
Irregular + Suspended + Light + False connections	= hypersensitivity	
	+	= Crippling sensitivity and inhibitions, lack of confidence, inability to take position and to achieve goals.
Inhibited + Left slant + Slow + Mannered	= inhibitions	

Signs		**1st degree resultant**		**Secondary resultant**
Slow	=	(laziness) +		
Weak	=	(weakness) +	=	Negligence, laziness, lack of vitality
Slack	=	(lack of discipline)		
Vulgar	=	(general inferiority of character) +		
Confused	=	(disorder) +	=	Tendency to monopolise, dishonesty
Complicated	=	(intrigue) +		
Regressive	=	(selfishness)		
Rounded	=	(amiability) +		
Light	=	(delicacy) +	=	Tenderness
Right slant	=	(need of support)		
Slightly rising	=	(ardour) +	=	Zeal
Contained	=	(control)		Self-control
Irregular	=	(emotivity) +		
Contained	=	(reserve) +	=	Impressionability
Closed	=	(discretion)		
Sinuous	=	(flexibility) +		
Closed	=	(reserve) +	=	Dissimulation
Congested	=	(sensuality)		
Irregular	=	(emotivity) +		
Rapid (activity)	=	(activity) +	=	Impatience
Sharp-pointed	=	(causticity)		

These combinations are infinite, of course, since each sign and species has many interpretations, depending on the Harmony, Organisation, the Formlevel, Type of Movement, degree of Tension, Dominance of Axes and Movement/Form ratio and the rest of the species and signs. Each sign can combine with any other sign, or signs, to give its indicative meaning for every specific writing.

When the psychological interpretations of two or more graphic signs of a specific writing are combined, the outcome is a psychological resultant, which indicates a 'characterological trait'.

(D) PSYCHOLOGICAL TYPOLOGIES

Having finished the technical work on the specific writing, we proceed with the *psychological typologies*. These are a great help, but we must not forget that they are only that - a help. They are not the portrait itself. They only give us clues to the writer's tendencies, attitudes, inclinations, etc. They cannot and must not be used rigidly. Many gross mistakes and superficial portraits have been constructed through the narrow-minded use of the typologies. For example, a writer can be lymphatic, but also inspired, or a genius, a genius, but also imbalanced; imbalanced, but also conscientious; conscientious, but also inefficient; inefficient, but also nice, and so on.

One more point of importance is that some writings are more easily assessed with the help of one typology, and others with the help of another. It is not necessary to use all the typologies for all writings.

Le Senne, Jung and Hippocrates are the three most commonly used and most easily applicable typologies for most writings. They are quite basic and elementary and therefore extremely useful.

As you reach the stage of building up the psychological portrait, never forget the extreme importance of *objectivity*.

When we first see a writing we involuntarily form an opinion, favourable or unfavourable. We are influenced one way or the other. We *must* react to that emotion quickly, and whatever it is, try to find the opposite characteristics to those that first impressed themselves upon us. It is one good way to safeguard objectivity.

All personalities may have some aspect which is open to misinterpretation. Graphology is the surest means of penetrating beneath the surface, but as Crépieux-Jamin warned us in his book, *Les élèments de l'écriture des canailles,* "the greatest obstacle to the use of graphology is not in lack of confidence in itself .... but in the great confidence that we all have in our own 'lights'. Pride governs the majority of our mistakes, thus depriving us of the means to put them right".

In time, with a lot of practice and experience, you will understand the writings and their needs more easily.

(E) THE PORTRAIT

The principal components of a personality are as we know: *intellectual ability, the world of emotions, adaptability* and *activity.* The amount of each of these and what results from the combinations with each other, constitutes the individuality of each personality. The range of nuances is infinite. *Intellectual ability,* for instance, can be measured on a scale from imbecility to creative genius. If we add to these the various states of psychopathology, we will have a better understanding of the difficulties facing the graphologist in recognising the right amount of each element present in the writing in order to extract the innermost and true personality of the writer.

Let us briefly look at these four elements:

Intellectual Ability,
which is a collection of 'faculties' that help us obtain knowledge in its widest sense, apart from being either effective, or defective

through an inharmonious development of the faculties, can also be badly balanced. In order to 'acquire knowledge', we must first 'perceive' (through the senses), then 'register' (memory), then 'appreciate' (judgement) and last we must also be able to 'transform', or 'create' (imagination).

We perceive with our five senses and we register, appreciate, transform and create with the faculties of our brain. If the senses are not sensitive enough, we do not perceive adequately. If the memory is bad, we do not retain the information received and consequently we cannot appreciate or transform what we have not retained in the first place.

It is therefore inexact to attribute intelligence to an individual with good memory only. What is the benefit of it if we are unable to combine it with the other 3 elements? However, memory is of vital importance to intelligence, and depends heavily on *attention* and the *desire to learn*.

The emotional world
consists of impressions fed to us by our senses and transformed by our mind.

Inhibitions, anxieties, nervousness, fear, pride, sensitivity, loyalty, kindness, aggression, materialism, and the like, are feelings which derive from the state of our emotional world.

Sensitivity is closely linked to intelligence, as it enhances perceptions and awareness of the environment.

Adaptability
"Healthy" human beings have a natural flexibility which helps them adapt and achieve a certain harmony within themselves and with their environment.

Genuine social adaptability is not easy to achieve. The majority of people either make a conscious effort or have serious difficulty in "fitting in" with what they consider environmental necessities.

Activity
When we speak about *activity*, we mean cerebro-psychic activity. It is the power to act intensively. Graphology can assess the intensity and the quality of activity through the speed and pressure, and the inhibitions and/or dynamism of the writing.

* * *

SOURCES

CRÉPIEUX-JAMIN, J. *Les éléments de l'écriture des cannailles* Ed. E. Flammarion, Paris 1976.

LECERF, A. *Cours supérieur de graphologie* Ed. Dangles, Paris 1947

RIVERE, Dr. J. *Le monde de l'écriture* Ed. Gonon, Neuilly 1958

STRESLETSKI, Dr. C. *Précis de Graphologie Pratique* Ed. Vigot Frères, Paris 1950

LECTURE II

PRINCIPAL SYNTHESIS OF ORIENTATION

There are *ten aspects of writing* which are extremely important for the graphologist to consider in the initial stages of an analysis. These are:-

1. FIRST IMPRESSION

The written page is the product of an effort made by the writer to write the text. At first sight, one way or another, that written page makes an impression on the reader before he/she even starts to read it. This is the ***First (or General)*** impression. There can be no value judgement at this stage, merely an objective observation of the way the writing occupies the space, the way it moves along, its flair or constraint, the way the pen contacts the paper, etc. All these elements indicate the writer's unconscious tendencies and personal choices.

2. ORGANISATION (J. Crépieux-Jamin)

Organisation deals with the evolution of the writing and indicates the general level of education, maturity and 'intellectual milieu'; the cultural level and the organisation of the mind and activities (emotions, thoughts, time, money). Sometimes the writing evolves with age and practice, and not because of new 'intellectual acquisitions'.

Talent in the Arts often helps the organisation as much as intellectual resources and emotional maturity do.

Organised writing shows at least an average intelligence. Simplifications in an organised writing imply development towards synthesis and leads to *combined* writing, which is the agile, personalised (original) and often rhythmic connection of a number of letters in order to facilitate speed. The writing remains correct and legible. This indicates a generally higher culture than simply *organised* writing: good association of images, inventiveness, suppleness, memory and attention. (The opposite does not hold true, as frequently an exceptionally intelligent and cultured mind may hinder emotional development and the writing may therefore remain in an, unorganised, infantile stage). The speed of *organised* writing shows more the liveliness and agility of the mind than intelligence.

3. SPACING

Spacing refers to the distribution of the written parts (black) upon the space offered by the page (white). Spacing is affected by the writer's adaptability, objectivity, independence, orderliness, clarity of mind, security or insecurity, sensitivity and ability to listen and consider, reflect.

4. HARMONY (J. Crépieux-Jamin)

Harmony, which consists of Proportion, Order, Clarity, Simplicity, Sobriety and Flow, is a basic observation which orients the interpretation of all elements and gives them their value. It shows equilibrium, correctness of attitudes, reserve, moral superiority, logic and force, a well-structured personality. The writer is in harmony with the self and the world (confidence). The opposite also holds true. *For example* : an harmonious and typographic writing shows culture, art, whereas an inharmonious and typographic writing indicates ignorance, bad taste.

Harmony is an element of serenity and equilibrium, but also of mediocrity and lack of ambition to attain extraordinary achievements. No great masterpiece has ever been executed by a harmonious individual.

Harmony is a state all humans should strive to reach in old age. It is the brandy of life, the 'digestif' of time.

5. FORMLEVEL (L. Klages)

Formlevel, which consists roughly of the degree of organisation (or "level of culture" (1)), spontaneity, originality (or individuality), dynamism (or intensity) and rhythm, evaluates the intensity and richness of being through the spontaneous originality and dynamic rhythm of the writing.

Rhythm

is created by the spontaneous and natural, consistent reproduction of similar but never identical irregularities. It is an eminently personal movement, particular to each writer. Not all writings are rhythmic. Rhythm indicates the inner intensity of being. The post-Klagesian rhythm is considered in three elements:

(a) *the rhythm of the movement or of the circulation of the stroke* (upon which the *basic rhythm* of Roda Wieser is also founded, which shows the degree of life in the stroke seen in the small letters);

---

(1) L. Klages : *Graphologie,* Stock, Paris, 1975, pp. 92-93.

(b) *the rhythm of the forms*;

(c) *the rhythm of spacing.*

The Crépieux-Jamin equivalent of the Klagesian rhythm is the ***harmonious combination of irregularities.***

Dynamism

or "vital value" or "intensity" (or lack of it) is seen through the ***depth*** (or superficiality of the life*)* of the writing, its ***plenitude*** (or leanness), its ***warmth*** (or lack of it), in the rhythmic ***distribution*** of the written mass and in the "confident"use of space.

6. TENSION (J. Crépieux-Jamin, H. de Gobineau)

Tension represents a constraint, a contraction, a resistance, a pressure, a concentration, an effort. It also represents the degree of impulse towards a goal, the psychic intensity discharged from an affect. In psychoanalysis, tension is part of the action: impulse/ discharge. Tension is a component of the dynamism and the structure of the writing.

"Pressure, being against the surface of the paper, breaks the speed. Stiffness produces a reduction of extensiveness of all the movements. Just as, psychologically, pressure and stiffness are both states of tension, they are also an expression of effort and will. The difference is in the orientation of the effort which conditions the individual's attitude towards the world. Tension is the result of the battle between impulse and obstacle. In the pressure, the obstacle - the surface of the paper - is exterior, and the will is oriented against this obstacle, and the pressure takes the meaning of communication with the world (creative or destructive). The stiffness is an opposition against an inner obstacle; the antagonist muscles put the brakes on the agonist ones. Will acts in the same direction. The general meaning of pressure, therefore, will be activity and/or stiffness, resistance." (R.Pophal, C. de Bose).

Tension is seen in the handling (or 'behaviour') of the stroke through the combination of movement/weight, and is indicative of the writer's attitude to life *(weak, supple, firm, taut [stressed] or rigid).*

Finally, we must remember that although every writing has one or another degree of tension, it is very rare that this degree will be pure all the way through. In the majority of writings, many different degrees may co-exist.

Tension No. 1 - Slack (or Weak) Writing
(Figs. II.1, II.2, II.3)

In a slack writing, the tension is weak. It lacks adequate stiffness or firmness. It has very little rhythm or structure. The movement is floating, pressure usually weaker. Forms are wide and loose, continuity and direction uncertain. The whole looks inconsistent, weak, hypotonic. A slack writing shows little structure of the personality, which lacks consistency, weight and defences: a person who saves energy. Without a real directive axis, without strong convictions, the person is dependent, his level of consciousness is not high, he is emotional and lazy. The writer adjusts to the needs of the environment and often gives in through lack of determination, lack of resistance or through discouragement.

Tension No. 2 - Supple Writing *(Figs. II.4, II.5, II.6)*

A slight firmness gives this writing body without depriving it of its fluidity. The forms are curved and more or less ample. The movement is flowing, elastic without "reactive" gestures or constraint. It is relaxed and comfortable. The pressure is never very strong and the direction is supple (not stiff). There is good co-ordination between flexion and extension (up and down curves). This tension indicates spontaneous adaptability without unnecessary effort, confidence and suppleness. The writer is able to accelerate his rhythm when he needs to, easily regaining his previous rhythm. He has good contact with reality, his energy is channelled. He is laid back and takes life as it comes with a pleasant manner, never seeking to complicate his own or other people's life. This degree of tension is not very common.

Tension No. 3 - Firm Writing *(Figs. II.7, II.9, II.10)*

This writing combines suppleness with tension. There is a very slight stiffness. The movement keeps its easy flow, but the overall appearance is more decisive and firm, less free than the previous two. The strokes are more rigorous, the direction is more consistent, the layout and the structure are relatively proper without stiffness. There is often a mixture of angles and curves. The movement has a controlled freedom and it is usually sober and more resolute and firm. Firm writing indicates a happily blended personality, controlled with quiet determination and well-channelled energy. It shows independence, will power and good balance between instincts and reason. The personality is affirmed and follows its objectives. The writer is in control of his abilities, he is mature, responsible, disciplined and decisive.

Tension No. 4 - Taut Writing *(Figs. II.9, II.12, II.13, II.17)*

The movement, continuity and direction take *definitive*, more *confident* or *dynamic* aspect. The writing may somehow lose its suppleness, but not necessarily its agility of movements. Pressure becomes heavier, the forms become more angular, often narrower and arched. There is evidence of resistance to inner obstacles. This hinders adaptability. The writer is preoccupied with resistance and mobilises his energy excessively in the effort to overcome obstacles. There is little or no elasticity in the writing, whether it is straight or curved. We find this degree of tension in people with a strong personality, who are strong-willed or obstinate, energetic and combative, who rely only on their own abilities to achieve their aims. These people cannot relax, they are always anxious and pressured. The stronger the tension, the more the writer is dissatisfied and stressed in his relationship with the world and the more difficulty he has in affirming his own personality. He is rigorous and vigilant.

The stiffer the writing, the less is the resistance to frustrations, the more the writer turns in on himself.

Tension No. 5 - Over-taut, Stiff, Rigid Writing *(Fig.II.16)*

Excessive tension is marked by general stiffness. There is rigidity and/or mechanisation of the movement, the direction and the forms, or lack of co-ordination through the irregularities that give a splintered look to the writing. Juxtaposition and stiffness impair the continuity of the flow. The texture of the stroke is of bad quality; blurred, muddy, dry or notched and the pressure is exaggerated and spasmodic. These are generally discordant writings. They may indicate a pathological state of any sort, though not necessarily. Over-taut writing indicates anxiety. People with such tension in their writing have great difficulty in mastering their inner conflicts and their emotivity. They usually radiate discordance around them. Or, paralysed by anxiety, they adopt stereotyped behaviour to mask their constant agony. The irregularity of the stroke in an over-taut writing (pressure and movement) and particularly the irregularity of the colour (moiré) indicate emotivity, reactivity and general uncertainty.

Tension No. 6 - Anarchic *(Fig.II.19, II.20)*

Irregularities in the quality of the stroke and consequently of the tension are anarchic since they produce excessive and uncontrolled gestures in the writing (jerky and animated). They disturb the homogeneity of the continuity and the clarity, since the forms and their connections dissolve, the overall speed is reduced and the result is lack of rhythm.

The importance of the association between stiffness-suppleness brings forward the importance of the inner conflicts. The writer has little control over his relationship with the world and with reality. A writing with very irregular tension borders on pathological abnormality, but is very rare. Tension, 6 borders on Tension 1.

6a. TENSION (R. Pophal)

Tension according to R. Pophal is based on the 'physiology of movement' and is divided into *six degrees.* These are:

I (Pallidum) *(Figs. II.1, II.2, II.3)*

Pre-rhythmic writing, similar to J. Crépieux-Jamin's *weak* and to E. Caille's *nEnAP.* Either monotonous, curved, weak writing, or wavy writing, badly co-ordinated without tension, weak, irregular, agitated, rather disproportionate, disorderly with exaggerations, light and pasty, usually large and with negligent, imprecise forms and not very rapid.

It indicates insufficient inhibition resulting in lack of control, lack of backbone, a capricious nature, immaturity, infantilism, lack of discipline, laziness, or inadequately organised activity.

II (sub-Cortical) *(Figs. II.7, II.8, II.9)*

Writing with a supple, gentle rhythm. The ***elegant*** or ***graceful*** of Crépieux-Jamin's species; curved and easy flowing, slightly inhibited, supple, right slanted, in garlands, wide or ample, not particularly precise forms.

It indicates a conciliatory spirit, youthfulness, openness, straightness, empathy, adaptability, general suppleness of behaviour.

III (Cortical) *(Figs. II.10, II.11)*

Similar to firm of Crépieux-Jamin's. More cadenced than rhythmic. Well formed, sober, dynamic movement, firm to taut, angular or angular garlands, without rigidity, legible, usually medium size, rapid, orderly, stable and controlled with regular good pressure.

It indicates good concentration, need for precision and resilience. Reactions are proportionate to the stimuli; good co-ordination of instincts and reason, with good will power and sense of responsibility, efficiency and good self-control. Stylised writings usually have this degree of tension. According to the type of stylisation they show truthfulness (logical stylisation), discipline and often a defensive or a-social attitude (ethical stylisation) or need to valorise the self, resulting in inadequate adaptability (aesthetic stylisation).

IVa (Cortical) *(Figs. II.12, II.13, II.14)*

Regressive and semi-angular writing without much rhythm, inhibited, firm, narrow, rather small, with strong pressure, often rigid forms and baseline, irregular slant, decisive, slow with short finals and a stroke without elasticity.

It indicates strong self-control, refusal to be moved by events, lack of inner freedom and strong self-affirmation, difficulty in exteriorising feelings, inhibition, self-consciousness, gaucheness, insecurity, touchiness, mistrustfulness, dissatisfaction.

IVb (Striatum) *(Figs. II.15, II.16, II.17)*

Disturbed rhythm. Inhibited by sudden disturbances, irregular, hesitant, constrained, not well co-ordinated, imprecise, filiform, often amended, left slanted, often rigid, lacking dynamism and firmness.

It indicates grave inhibitions, weakness of character, inner hardness and fragility, reactivity, difficulty in expressing inner feelings - if the writing is large, it is impressive (representation) rather than expressive - lack of spontaneity and naturalness, vigilance, inadaptability.

V (Striatum with Pallidum) *(Figs. II.18, II.19, II.20)*

A contracted or shrivelled-up writing, jerky, tormented, inhibited, with spasmodic movements, irregular in all categories with imprecise forms, often prolonged up and down, badly co-ordinated, usually small with filiformity and angularity caused by lack of control over the continuity, taut and more hasty than truly rapid, with a *dry* general outlook.

It indicates insecurity, hyper-emotivity, anxiety and fears causing avoidance of responsibilities, decisions and activities and hence laziness (which is one of the points in common between degree V and degree I).

7. RAPPORT BETWEEN MOVEMENT-FORM
(J. Crépieux-Jamin, J. Peugeot)

(a) Dominance of Movement - shows initial impulsiveness, expressive of the psychic contents, difficult control, possible dominance of emotions and instincts, possible creativity and rich imagination. Spontaneity, often independence from conventions, intense activity, when there is firmness of the stroke. The writer has set prospectives. He is adaptable and mobile, but can also be reactionary (with supporting signs). The need for action maybe without adequate control or direction. *(Figs. II.8, II.9, II.19, II.20)*

(b) Dominance of Form - shows dominance of the principle of reality over pleasure. The writer wishes to enhance and highlight whatever increases his value. He has therefore good self-control and will not allow his impulses to take the upper hand. He accepts the rules, he is patient and solid. It also shows a need to structure the personality and to achieve, social values, conformism, conservatism, ethics, need to present the self.

If the *dominance of Form* is excessive, it will indicate a need to construct a personality, an acquired personality (persona). The writer is rigid, too much of a conformist, with attitudes which are very conventional. This may point towards deep-rooted conflicts that the writer unconsciously tries to cover up with a stylisation of attitudes and mannerisms. (*Figs. II.3, II.11, II.14, II.16*)

(c) Balance of both - is an indication of efficiency, acceptance of rules, solidity, adaptability, patience. When there are creative movements and evolved forms with good structure, good spacing and stroke quality, this balance reflects good equilibrium between the motivations (pulsions) and their realisation, good control, acceptance of others, authenticity and a certain independence vis-à-vis conventions. *(Figs. II.5, II.7, II.10)*

8. STRUCTURE (Müller-Enskat, Heiss)

Structure refers to the architectural construction of the writing. This is the materialisation of the abstract concept of the way letters are formed and the way they will look when finished. It is, by extension, therefore linked to the directive images of each writer and, just like architecture, when the forms are realised and become detached from the writer, they will always contain him, his personality, his visions, his sensitivities, his aesthetic sense (or lack of it), his courage, etc. This, of course, presupposes adequate graphic competence, which is normally reached between the ages of 12 and 14 years, some-times later, very rarely sooner.

It is then that the writing starts to become autonomous and to develop a 'personal rhythm'. If the writer is asked what he is thinking whilst writing, he will answer that he is thinking of *what* he is writing, ***not how*** to form the letters.

When the writing becomes autonomous, the mental images are no longer visual. They have become phonetic. Graphic motricity has changed centre and graphic dexterity starts appearing. This is the moment when irregularities, simplifications, speed, combinations, precision, spacing and differentiation of pressure take on a personal style.

In a healthy, autonomous writing, the text must remain legible. When simplified, the simplifications must not occur to the detriment of legibility, since the reason for writing is communication.

Proportion is one of the two most important elements for legibility.

Example:  = element

The main creative element of the handwriting is, of course, the stroke. Its action traces, creates and determines the forms (letters) on the paper. Their ***continuity (spacing)*** is the second most important element for legibility; for example, the reader would have to spend some time deciphering, 'legibility can be maintained in every style' as 'legibility can be maintained in every style'.

The structure once established, in an autonomous writing, remains permanent overall. Its variations are only due to the differences of the nature of the context. ***Speed*** does not modify the structure in any significant way.

A writing with good structure is one which maintains its unity and where the aggregation of forms stays compatible irrespective of speed, pressure and continuity. It contains the notions of rapport, organisation coherence of forms (Gestalt). It is the 'bone structure' of the writing; the solidarity of its elements, irrespective of forms or style.

It is implicit in the above that *Structure* is closely connected to *Movement and Form*.

In general a well-structured writing indicates a well-structured Ego *(Figs. II.6, II.10, II.11, II.17)*. When there is dominance of the vertical axis, the writer has a good understanding of measure. He is adaptable and resistant to his own impulses, thus giving himself a choice and remaining master of his own destiny. His imagination and fantasies do not disturb him and do not affect his behaviour (factor 'k' of Szondi).

Where there is dominance of the horizontal axis, a well-structured writing indicates that the writer is more impulsive, dynamic and imaginative, with little resistance to his impulses. The concept of measure is not strong. The writer's behaviour is supple and fluctuating (factor 'p' of Szondi).

When the writing is badly-structured (ill-structured writing) (*Figs. II.2. II.16, II.18, II.19, II.21)* whether vertical or horizontal, it indicates that the writer does not have a clear concept of his identity. He is not certain about himself and does not make adequate use of his abilities. He lacks landmarks in his life and there is confusion and uncertainty in his behaviour, resulting in lability and influencibility .

Briefly :

(a) good - maturity, creativity, activity, receptivity, ability to achieve goals. Generally it shows a well-structured Ego.

(b) poor - either: illness, old age, illiteracy, or: lack of courage, stress, nervousness, suffering emotivity, shyness, inhibitions, dissimulation, insincerity, stagnation of evolution.

(c) overstructured - rigidity, lack of inner harmony; may mask grave, deep inner conflicts.

9. AXES

Axis is the dominant movement of the scriptural act. People who have dominance of ***vertical axis***, write with an emphasis on the flexion - extension movement of the fingers, producing more emphasised up and down parts of the letters. Consequently the letters become narrower, the ovals acquire an ovoid shape and the secondary connections become shorter and often angular.

People who have dominance of ***horizontal axis***, favour the right-left movement of the hand (progressive-regressive). Consequently the letters are broader, the ovals become round or wider, the high and secondary connections become longer and may even trail on the line. In the extreme, the writing may become filiform. Therefore the horizontal axis is indicated by the width of the base of letters (primary width) and by the width of the connecting strokes between the letters (secondary width). This is the expansion towards the right (when it is wider than the calligraphic norm).

Where the writing with a ***dominance of the horizontal axis*** has a tendency to trail, writing with a vertical dominance does not linger on the baseline. The slant, whether left, right or vertical, is immaterial. What is important is the extend of flexion and extension of the writing figures.

Dominance of the vertical axis points towards expansion of the feeling of self. It shows a need for expansion. This is connected with the writer's general vitality (depending on other concomitant factors such as pressure, tension, stroke quality, speed and rhythm), and is an indication of confidence in one's own abilities and/or *need* to express oneself - for reasons either of natural extroversion or strong natural introversion. *(Figs. II.7, II.10, II.11, II.17, II.18)*

If the writing is also large, it is always an affective sign. If objectivity is influenced by feelings and emotions, then the writer is full of ardour and is able to surpass himself. He does more than he *thinks* he is capable of and surprises himself.

When a writing with *vertical dominance* is also spontaneous, with good proportions and a firm stroke, it indicates the natural ability of the writer to play an active role in life in as large a field as is necessary for him to express himself. At its best a writing like that will show authenticity, resolution, suppleness, freedom in action, affirmation of the personality, the need to take a stand or position, aspirations, motivation and potential. The writer prefers actually to 'be' something rather than appear to be or act as if he were something.

The writer with *dominance of the horizontal axis* likes to expand his knowledge, to conquer and to achieve. He is adaptable and sociable. Unlike the writer with vertical dominance, he prefers to 'act' rather than to 'be'. *(Figs. II.3, II.4, II.8, II.19)*

If such a writing lacks firmness, if it has a bad rapport between form and movement and lacks rhythm, it shows influencibility, precipitation and negligence, emotional instability, inactivity and irregularity in effort.

(a) ***vertical*** - in a +FL it shows ardour, enthusiasm, confidence, the aptitude to play an active part, motivation, authenticity, pride, resolution, presence, affirmation, imposition of ideas, authority, potential, usually Le Senne's EAS.

(b) ***horizontal*** - in a +FL it shows orientation to the outside world, avidity, need to assimilate, need to expand, adaptability, need to conquer, action rather than being, enterprise, expansion, usually Le Senne's EAP.

10. MOVEMENT

(S. Bresard, H. de Gobineau, Crépieux-Jamin)

'*The morphological differences (*differences of the forms*) are of lesser importance than the variations of movement* (J. Crépieux-Jamin: *Les éléments de l'écriture canailles,* p.201). Movement is the graphic gesture caused by the stroke in its endeavour to construct the forms. Only dots have no movement.

It indicates the presence or absence of a wide range of attributes and attitudes : inner motivation, ability to achieve, dynamism, determination, inhibitions, inner contradictions, resistance to frustration, progression, ability to learn, whether inner conflicts have been resolved, and whether there is expansion or control, good or bad utilisation of talents. It reflects the attitude towards others and towards social values. It shows conformity and ethics - or absence of them - and therefore also the need to 'present' oneself, to create a self-image through the act of writing.

* * *

SOURCES

BAOG	Journal No. 9 - July 1989.
de BOSE, C.	"La physiologie du mouvement et son interpretation graphologique d'après l'oeuvre de Pophal", *La Graphologie*, No. 124, Paris, Oct. 1971.
BRESARD, S.	*L'écriture empreinte de l'homme*, ed. Privat, Paris, 1976.
CRÉPIEUX-JAMIN, J.	*A.B.C. de la Graphologie*, ed. PUF, 1976.
CRÉPIEUX-JAMIN, J.	*Les éléments de l'écriture des canailles*, ed. Flamarion, 1976.
FAIDEAU P. PINON, J.	*Dictionnaire Pratique de Graphologie*, ed. M.A., 1985.
GILLE-MAISANI, J.-Ch.	*Psychologie de 1' écriture*, ed. Payot, 1978.
KLAGES, L.	*Graphologie*, ed. Stock, Paris, 1975.
LECERF, A.	*Cours supérieur de Graphologie*, ed. Dangles, 1947.
LEFEBURE, F. van den BROEK D'OBRENAN, C.	*Le Trait en Graphologie*, ed. Masson, 1987.
LEFEBURE, F. GILLE-MAISANI, J.-Ch.	*Dynamique des Pulsions*, ed. Mont-Blanc, 1980.
PEUGEOT, J.	*La Connaissance de L'Enfant par L'Écriture*, ed. Privat, 1979.
PEUGEOT, J. LOMBARD, A. de NOBLENS, M.	*Manuel de Graphologie*, ed. Masson, Paris, 1986.
WITKOWSKI, F.	*Psychopathologie et Écriture*, ed. Masson, Paris, 1989.

HANDWRITING SAMPLES of LECTURE II

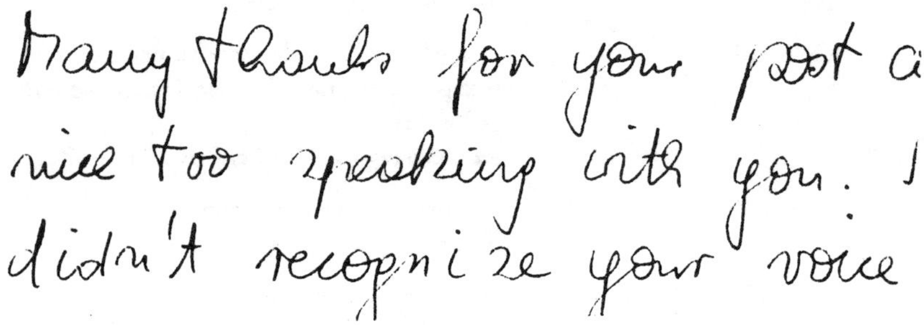
Many thanks for your post a
nice too speaking with you. I
didn't recognize your voice

Fig. II.1
Pressure: light - Woman, 32 years

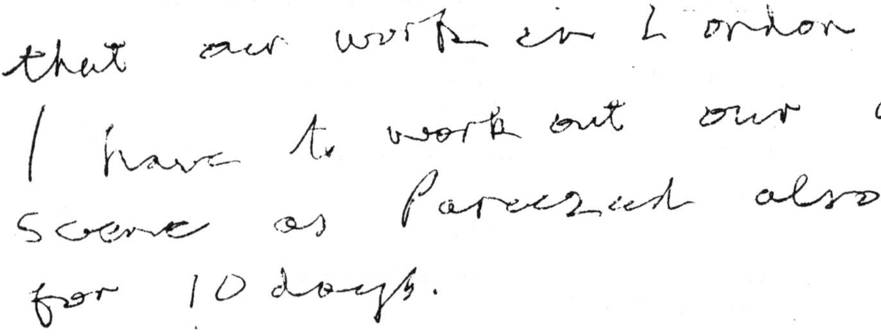
that our work in London
I have to work out our a
scene as Paracized also
for 10 days.

Fig. II.2
Pressure : light - Man, 40+ years

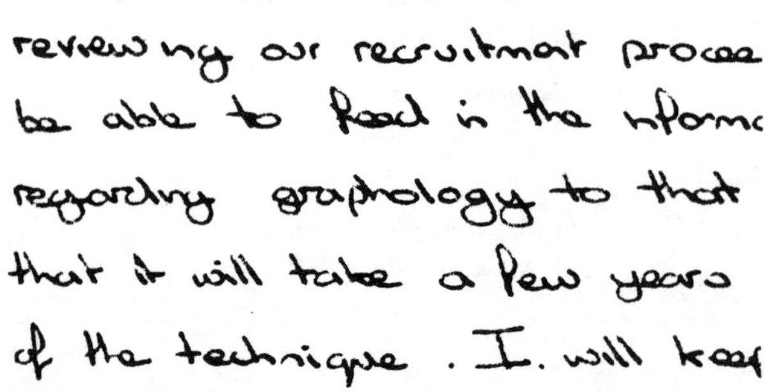
reviewing our recruitment proces
be able to read in the informa
regarding graphology to that
that it will take a few years
of the technique. I. will keep

Fig. II.3
Pressure : light
Woman, 30 years

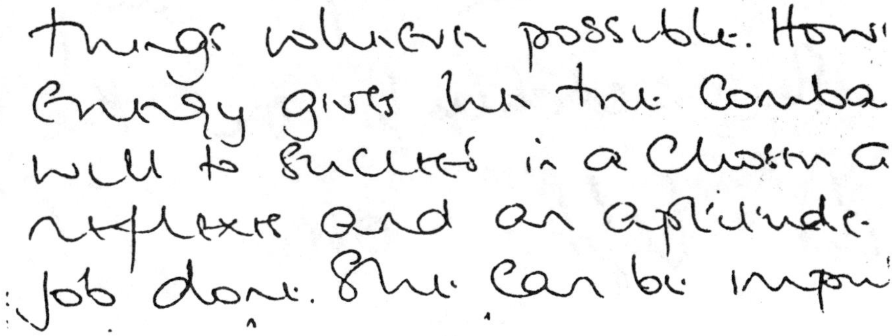

Fig. II.4
Pressure : light - Woman, 37 years

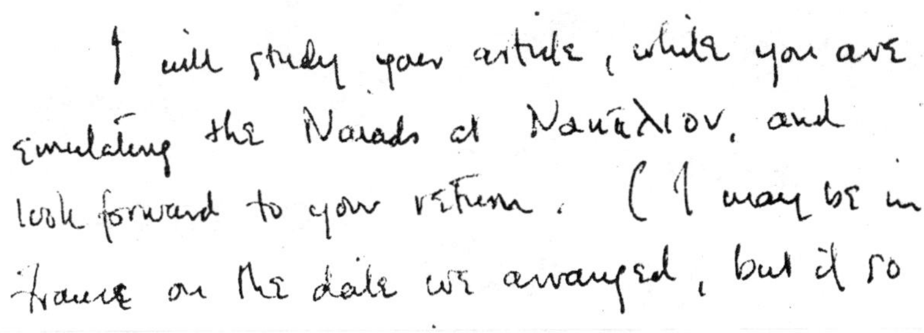

Fig. II.5
Pressure : light - Man, 56 years

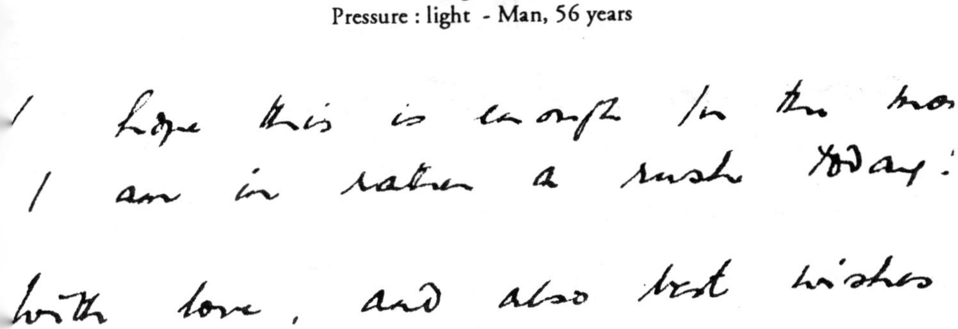

Fig. II.6
Pressure : light - Man, aged 65

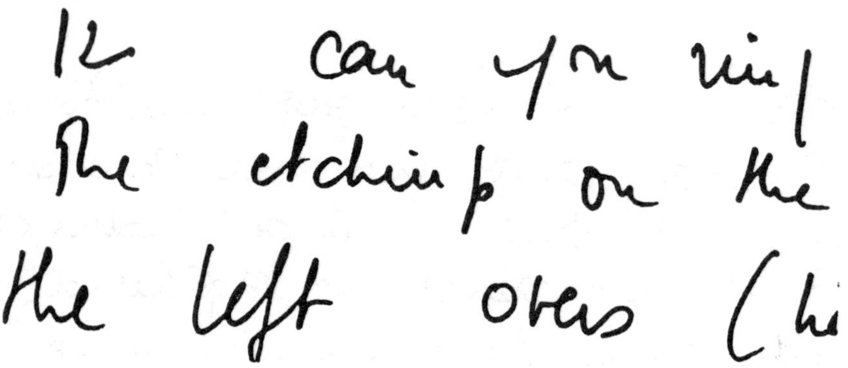

Fig. II.7
Pressure : heavy - Woman, 50 years

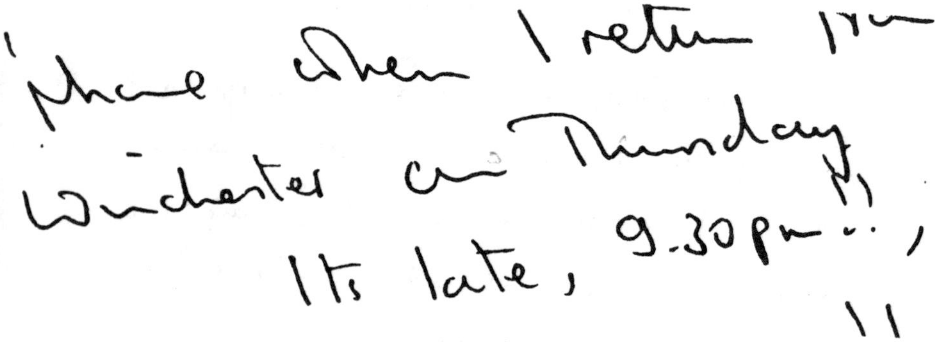

Fig. II.8
Pressure : firm - Man, 50 years

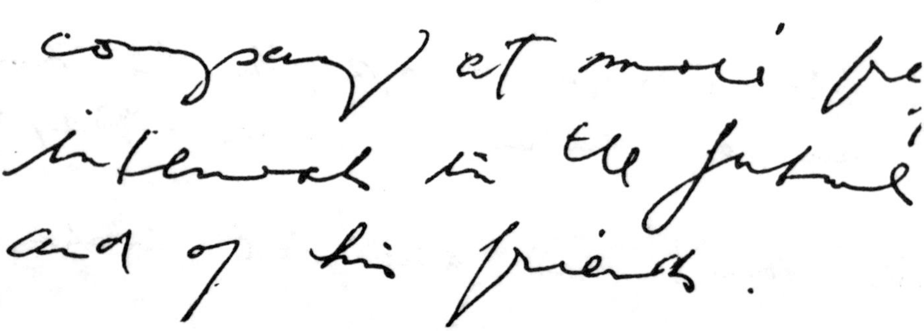

Fig. II.9
Pressure : heavy - Man, 45 years

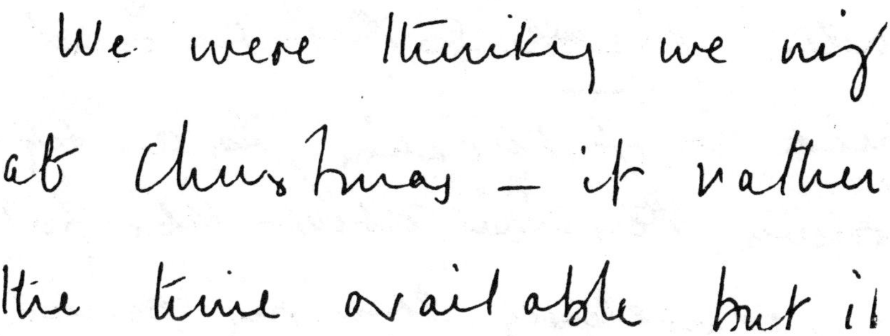

Fig. II.10
Pressure : light +/- Woman, 48 years

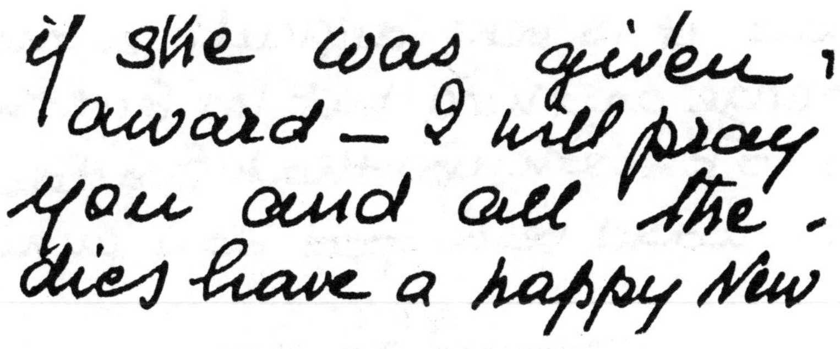

Fig. II.11
Pressure : firm - Woman, 74 years

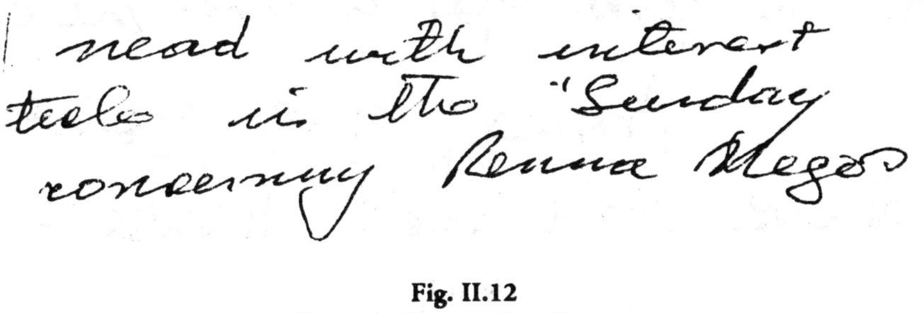

Fig. II.12
Pressure : firm - Man, 50 years

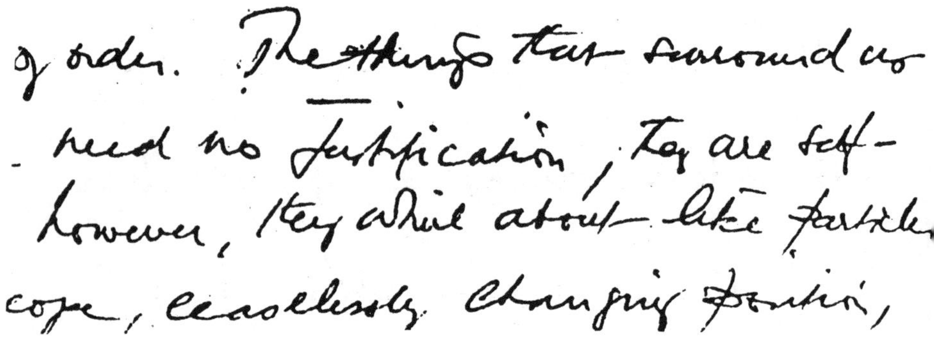

Fig. II.13
Pressure : light - Man 64 years

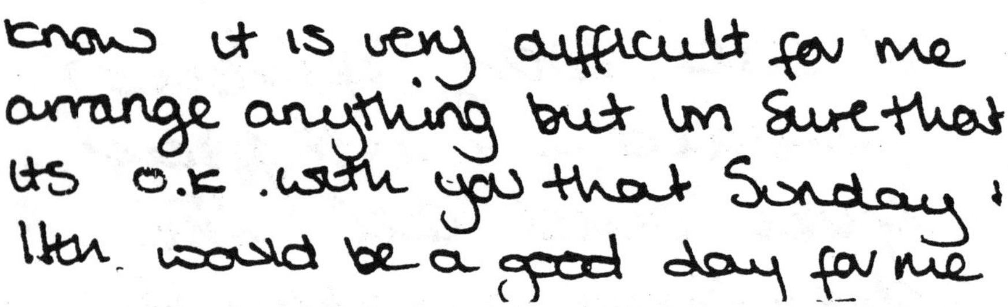

Fig. II.14
Pressure : heavy - Woman, 21 years

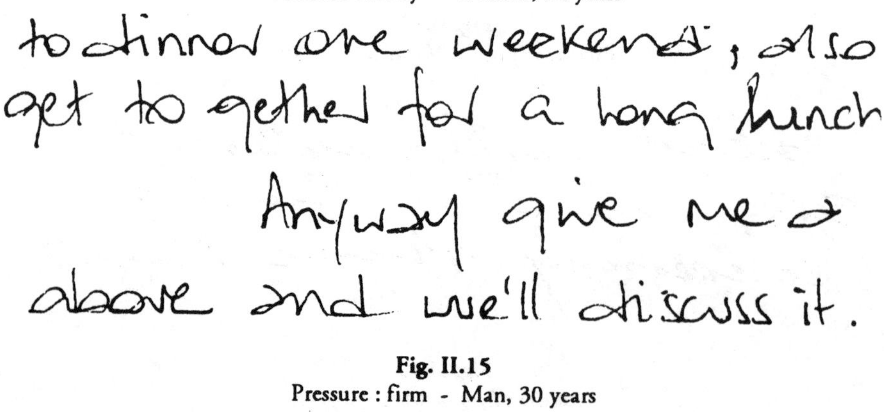

Fig. II.15
Pressure : firm - Man, 30 years

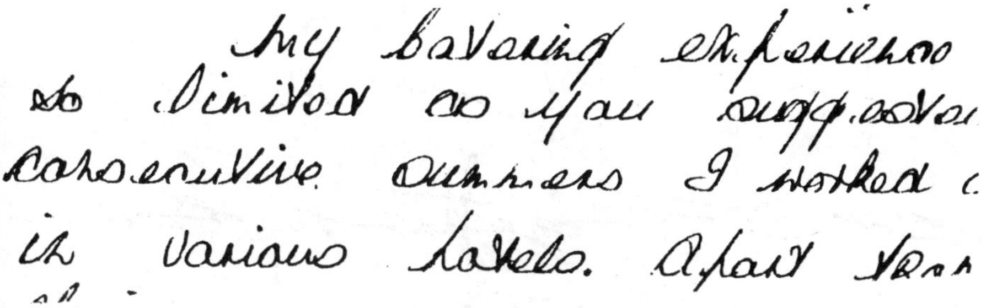

Fig. II.16
Pressure : medium - Woman, 40 years

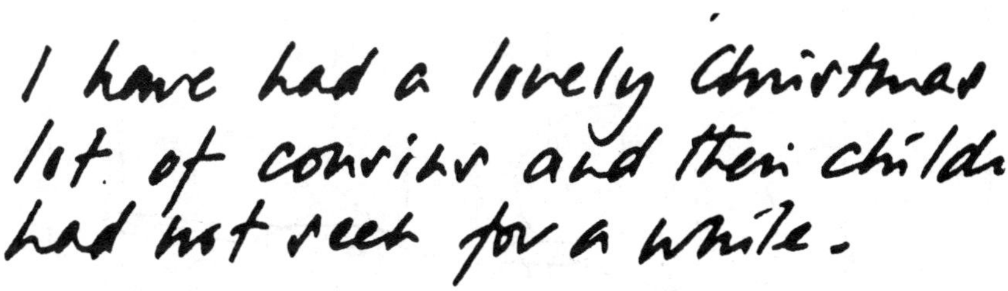

Fig. II.17
Pressure : firm - Woman, 55 years

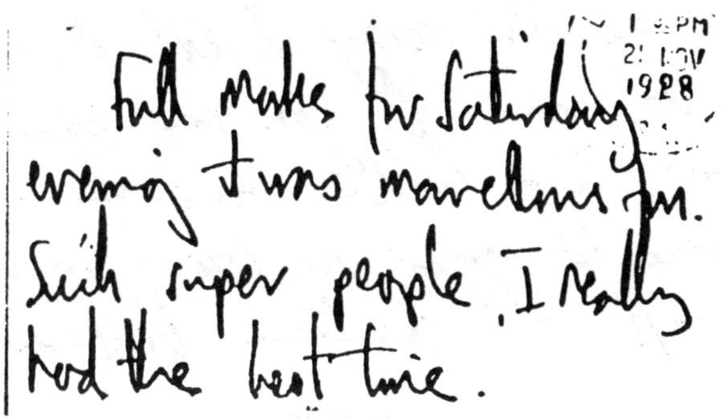

Fig. II.18
Pressure : heavy - Man, 30 years

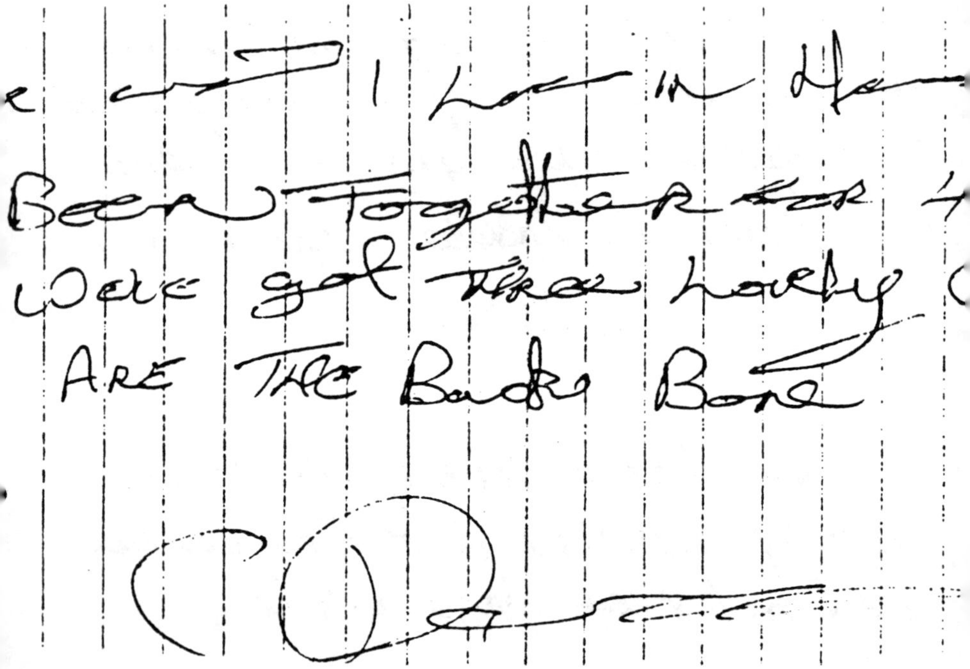

Fig. II.19
Pressure : firm - Man, 35 years

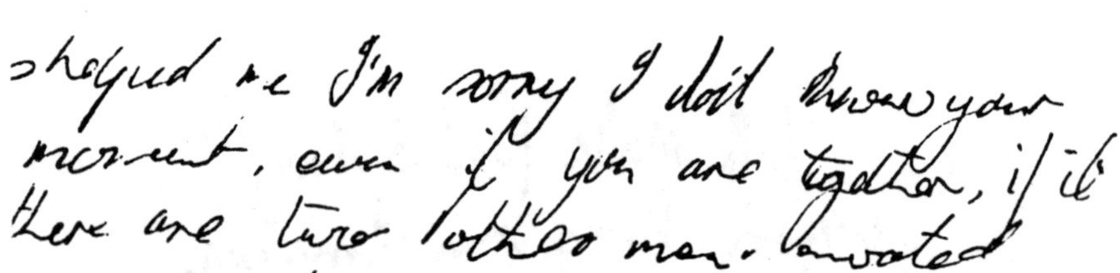

Fig. II.20
Pressure : light - Man, 38 years

LECTURE III

TYPES OF MOVEMENT

Movement is the basic element of handwriting which creates the forms. It is a subconscious component, closely related to motor behaviour and corresponds to the unconscious motivating forces of the personality and to the guiding image. When the emotions and driving instincts are strong, the writing is propelled towards its target and indicates the need for expression, expansion, determination, affirmation and the potential for realisation. *Briefly it reflects the dynamism of the writer. It is an indication of a dynamic attitude in life and/or achievement.*

Suzanne Bresard in her book *La graphologie, Méthode d'exploration psychologique* (Masson, Paris 1990), describes four basic movements :

1. the **propulsive**, which consists of ample, free movements towards the right, often with strong pressure and a certain regularity of dimension (large or small), and which shows a dynamic self-affirmation;

2. the **reared**, which slants towards the left and, depending on the narrowness or width of the script, may show a fear of progress, inhibitions, awareness of obstacles, defensive attitudes and inner blockage;

3. the **rolled-up**, or **coiled** movement, which is the double joined and looped garlands or looped arcades writing, often

shows a cripling sensitivity, vulnerability, impressionability, egocentricity and self-involvement which, when paired up with strong pressure, shows strong vitality without an outlet for achievement, no listening ability and a tendency to dominate, particularly when the coils appear in a writing which is also propulsive.

4. the **disconnected** movement, which can be dynamic or weak depending on the overall vitality of the writing.

The graphic action involves all 7 of Crépieux-Jamin's categories simultaneously. To write with ease one has to integrate forms, dimension, direction, continuity, spacing and pressure with a certain speed.

Movement is the formation of the writing whilst it progresses across the page with its individual speed, pressure, continuity, spacing, dimension and direction, personal to each writer.

The notion of *movement* is an inherent part of handwriting and the most important factor of rhythm.

In order to assess the dynamic potential through the movement, we must always observe it in conjunction with the stroke, both from Hegar's point of view as well as from Crépieux-Jamin's.

(a) Hegar:
pressure of the stroke : heavy or light
quality of the stroke : precise or pasty - i.e. Crépieux-Jamin 'blurred'
movement of the stroke : curved or straight
speed of the stroke : rapid or slow

(b) Crépieux-Jamin:
pressure of the stroke : heavy, light, spasmodic, irregular, deviated, etc.
quality of the stroke : thin, pasty, blurred or precise, taut or slack, etc.
movement : weak, inhibited, effortless, animated, dynamic, carried-away
speed : number of letters per minute

There are about 10 types of movement, indicating various degrees of dynamism and achievement potential. These are:-

(1) **Still, static or immobile** (H. de Gobineau)
(2) **Floating** (H. de Gobineau) or **Slack or weak** (J. Crépieux-Jamin)
(3) **Inhibited, restrained or constrained** (J. Crépieux-Jamin)
(4) **Controlled or resolute** (J. Crépieux-Jamin)
(5) **Flowing** (H. de Gobineau) or **effortless** (J. Crépieux-Jamin)
(6) **Vibrant, animated, effervescent** (J. Crépieux-Jamin)
(7) **Dynamic** (H. de Gobineau, J. Crépieux-Jamin)
(8) **Propulsive,** (S. Bresard),
carried away and flying strokes (J. Crépieux-Jamin)
(9) **Obstructed** (H. de Gobineau)
(10) **Reared** (H. de Gobineau)

Movement is a "*species*", not a "*sign*", nor a "*category*" and modern graphology is moving gently away from the small sign and more and more towards the species which seem to give much richer information about the writer. Of course, small signs are never discarded or ignored.

Very rarely do we come across a writing which has only one movement. Most writings are a combination of two or three movements.

Let us examine them one by one.

1. STATIC (still or immobile) movement

As in most types there are two kinds of static writings: the vital *(Fig. III.2)* and the non-vital *(Fig. III.1)*. In both cases the writing has a repetitive rhythm. It progresses steadily and regularly, it looks uniform and monotonous, and there is, of course, dominance of form.

The writer is preoccupied with his image. He is not satisfied with what he sees. He feels he needs to fabricate a different and better self to show the world (persona).

The personality is unresolved. There are conflicts which neutralise the spontaneous expression, communication, adaptation and development. The Superego is strong.

This type of writer dislikes changes. He is scrupulous, he respects others but has difficulty in establishing relationships. In business he is good at executing jobs where regularity and patience are important.

2. FLOATING movement

This type of writing is similar to the 'weak writing' of Crépieux-Jamin's species. It is irregular and uncertain in its progression. It lacks solid stance on the line. Although not deprived completely of movement, it has no clear projection to the right. It looks as if it moves in place. The pressure is light. The writing is not firm. The structure is insufficient. There are small irregularities of dimension, direction and form *(Fig. III.3)*.

The writer is receptive, intuitive, with good imagination and the ability to improvise. Intelligence and maturity are not relevant in this type of movement, instead, rigorousness, affirmation, strong convictions - and consequently authority - are (in that they are lacking). Heavy responsibilities and strong decisions are not this writer's best qualities. He lacks confidence, has difficulty in explaining himself or in getting involved, and he is dependent on his environment. As a counterbalance he is tolerant and a pleasant companion and partner, youthful, mobile and generally he has few changes of mood. He is easily adaptable and fits into any situation. At work he is pleasant, efficient and a good negotiator. He has a conciliatory personality.

3. INHIBITED movement

Inhibition is an emotional situation. Inhibited writing looks as if it fears to progress across the page *(Fig. III.4)*. It is held back and controlled by apprehension and uncertainty. Inhibited movement may be evident through the narrowness of forms or - the opposite - through forms crushed on the line. There are false connections and suspended letters. The stroke is usually fragile and the pressure is light. The writer is modest, controlled, reserved, even stiff sometimes, constrained, sad, anxious and inhibited.

4. CONTROLLED movement

A well organised and 'controlled' writing, with a steady baseline and supervised progression *(Fig. III.5)*. The writer is conscious of his responsibilities. He is perspicacious and vigilant.

5. FLOWING movement (effortless - Crépieux-Jamin)

The writing flows without constraint *(Fig. III.6)*. It progresses freely across the page with supple use of space and of the baseline. It is usually right slanted, with curved connections. medium pressure, simple forms and a gentle regularity, indicating good control of movement. There is an elastic aspect in this type of movement which results in a supple and rhythmic progression of the strokes indicating equilibrium, maturity and confidence. The writing may also be 'conventional' *(Fig. III.7)*. There is nothing excessive in this type of writing. The irregularities are contained and favour the rhythm. The pressure is medium or rather light. The forms are progressive and there is a controlled horizontality within average dimensions and proportions.

This writer has a supple and open mind. He is adaptable and an easy collaborator. His convictions, whilst firm, do not create barricades. Practical sense, logic and method guide his judgement. His general attitude is progressive, with little or no inhibitions which create brakes. He is a well-adjusted person. He is a resilient personality with healthy resistance to hardship.

He has proportionate reactions to events, good adaptation and collaboration and good common sense.

This type of movement is seen mainly in active and well-adjusted adults. It is never found in mentally ill people or children. It is indicative of confidence and a good equilibrium between needs-motivation and achievement.

6. VIBRANT movement

This is a delicate and discreet writing, where animation and sobriety correspond to the antagonism between movement and restraint. The writing progresses in small vibrant groups discreetly and without fuss. The movement is fine rather than forceful. The outlook - and particularly the middle zone - is generally nuancée *(Fig. III.8)*.

Because of its delicateness, this writing must have unity, good structure, good proportions and good distribution of black and white. The pressure should be gently firm. The less these elements are observed, the more this writing indicates fragility.

The vibrant movement shows great sensitivity and curiosity of the mind. It is the most indicative movement of the great emotives with a nervous disposition.

If this writing is also rhythmic, the writer is supple and most efficient. The writer has the ability to bounce back. He is efficient and modest. At work he tends to be conciliatory, although he may be neither exactly for or against the organisation or the way things are managed. He is vigilant and tends to stay young or/and near young people. He can be good in research.

If the vibrations get accentuated and give the writing a more febrile look, and the irregularities become less discreet or blended with the whole, then the writing becomes ***effervescent*** *(Fig. III.9)*. The emotivity is stronger and less well channelled. There is general amplification; the reactions are stronger and more lively at all levels, even disproportionate to the causes and often unpredictable.

7. DYNAMIC movement

The writing is energetic and aggressive, firm and progressive. There is resolute and dynamic projection of the movement towards the right, vivacity and speed. It is an 'autonomous' writing with right slant and strong rightward projection. The shape of the letters is 'aerodynamic'; they are usually connected with flying strokes and free end-strokes. The movements are efficient, confident and rapid. The words are often wide and connected (or overconnected with tension). The lower extensions are long and there is good differentiation of the three zones. The pressure is often heavy, the stroke precise (firm writing). It is usually a rhythmic writing *(Fig. III.10)*.

The writer has active and rapid perception of situations. His response is confident and usually quick. Depending on the rest of the species (ampleness of movements, proportions, suppleness and diversity of forms), the writer is oriented towards the future, or he may have strong opinions and set ideas (subjectivity).

This type of writer is better suited to a position where his dynamism, his spirit of enterprise and his taste for action will be best put to use. He has the ability to create objectives and to achieve them.

8. PROPULSIVE movement

Similar to Crépieux-Jamin's 'carried away' species. There is great spontaneity in this writing which throws the movement towards the right with speed and vivacity *(Fig. III.11)*. This type of writing has an 'impatient' outlook. Its value will depend on its relative control. The way it occupies the space, its proportions, the quality of the stroke and the tension will be the best guide to its evaluation. Pure impulsiveness should not be the only driving force in this writing. The environment should be taken into consideration, or the writer would risk to lose contact with it and get lost in the realm of illusions and not adapt or achieve his goals.

There is always strong emotivity indicated in this type of movement. Impulsiveness, impatience, imagination, passion, activity, dynamism and ambition, excitability and combativity.The reactions are often intense, and there is a tendency to exaggeration, but also creativity and spirit of enterprise. These people need two or three good personal assistants in order to perform to their full potential.

9. OBSTRUCTED movement

The progression of the movements towards the right are obstructed as if by obstacles. The writing seems to be moving against the current and its energy is concentrated in combating it. This is an 'intense' writing, constrained, as if contradicted. The forms are usually narrow, the strokes are vertical, prolonged and of precise direction (well maintained slant). There are abrupt stoppages and suspensions. Heavy, single down-strokes, wide gaps between words and/or within words *(Fig. III.12)*.

The writer is self-motivated. He has conviction and a need for success. He invests a lot of energy in whatever he undertakes. He takes initiative quickly and decisively. He stands up to his responsibilities with courage and affirmation. His general attitude is usually against rather than for. He has strong principles. He is tenacious and convincing, perseverant, reliable and independent. He does not accept easily other people's points of view. He needs convincing. It is therefore important that his judgement is good. The distribution of black and white should be clear and rhythmic. The proportions should be aesthetic and the layout good. The whole should have no exaggerations of any sort. There should be a sort of homogeneity of the whole. In order to be successful, this strong force of resistance must at all times remain adjusted to the human factor without rigidity.

10. REARED movement

This is a variation of the obstructed movement. There is more constraint. It is a more defensive and less rhythmic writing. The progression is inhibited. There are irregularities and general liveliness of movement. The writing is held back by its left slant. The flow is bridled. Compensatory signs for this type of movement are good continuity, absence of regressive strokes and possible occasionally sobriety *(Fig. III.13)*.

The writer is unsure of himself. He resists in order to prove himself. He takes strong positions. He creates obstacles for himself which only weaken his dynamism. There is potential for revolt in this type of movement.

* * *

SOURCES

BRESARD, S.	*La Graphologie, Méthode d'exploration psychologique.* Masson, Paris, 1990.
PEUGEOT, J LOMBARD, A. de NOBLENS, M.	*Manuel de Graphologie.* Masson, Paris, 1986.
CRÉPIEUX-JAMIN, J.	*ABC de la graphologie.* PUF, Paris, 1976.
de GOBINEAU, H. PERRON,R.	*Génétique de l'écriture et Etude de la personalité.* Delachaux et Niestlé, Neuchâtel, 1954.

DIAGRAMME OF MOVEMENT
Dynamism - Achievement

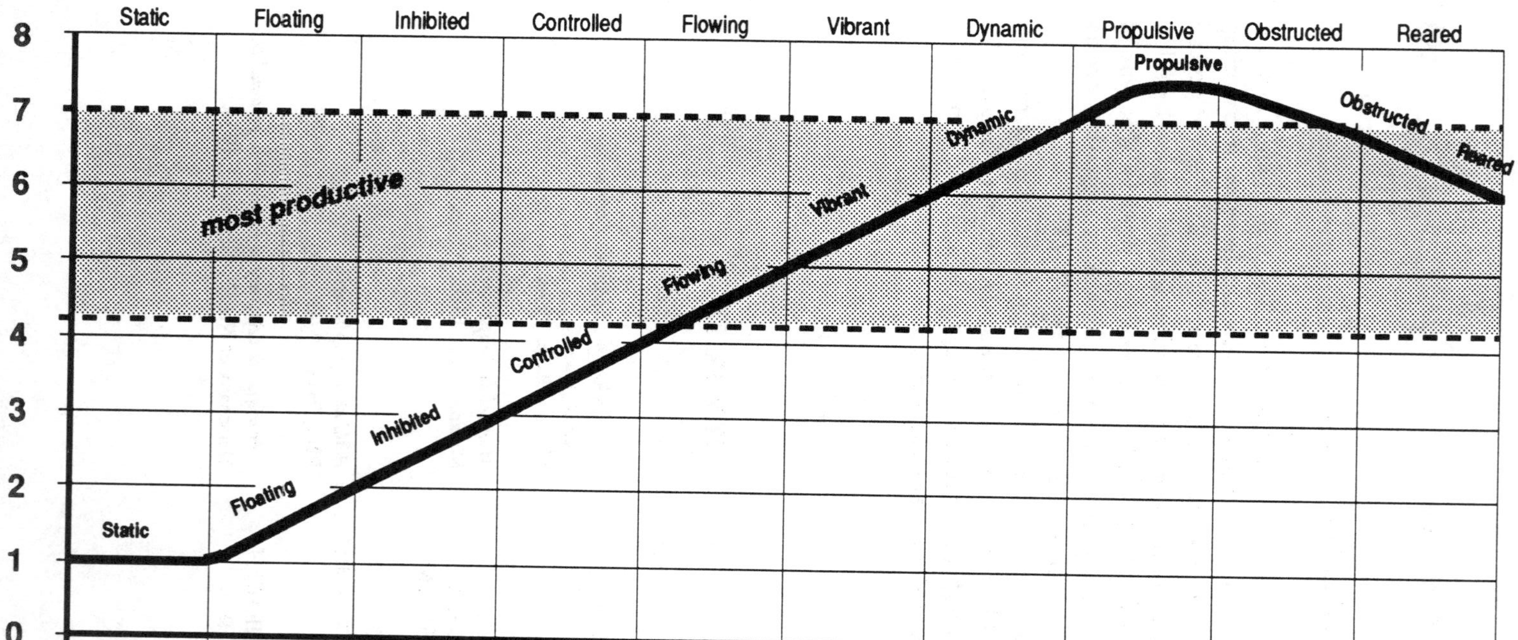

Static	Floating	Inhibited	Controlled	Flowing	Vibrant	Dynamic	Propulsive	Obstructed	Reared
EnAS nEnAS EAS nEAS	EnAS EnAP nEnAP EnAS	EnAS EAS	nEAS EAS EnAS	EAS nEAS EnAS	EAP EAS EnAP	EAP EAS nEAP	EAP EAS nEnAP	EAS nEAP	nEAP EAS EAP
Common Factor: S	nA	ES	S	S	E	A	-	A	A

HANDWRITING SAMPLES of LECTURE III

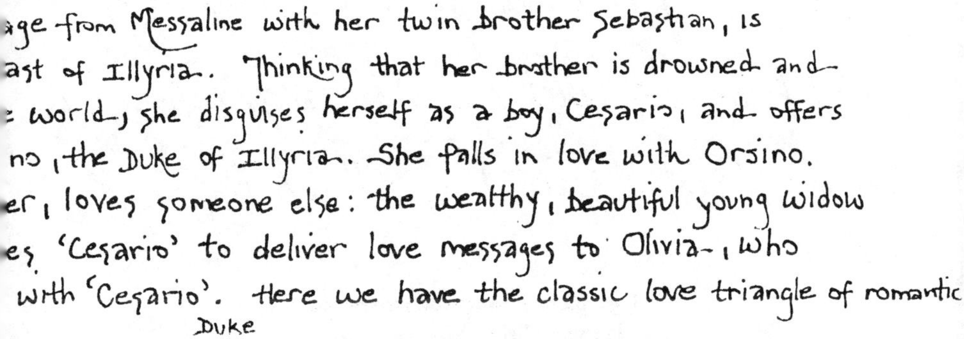

Fig. III.1 - Static, non-vital movement
Pressure : light - Woman, 24 years

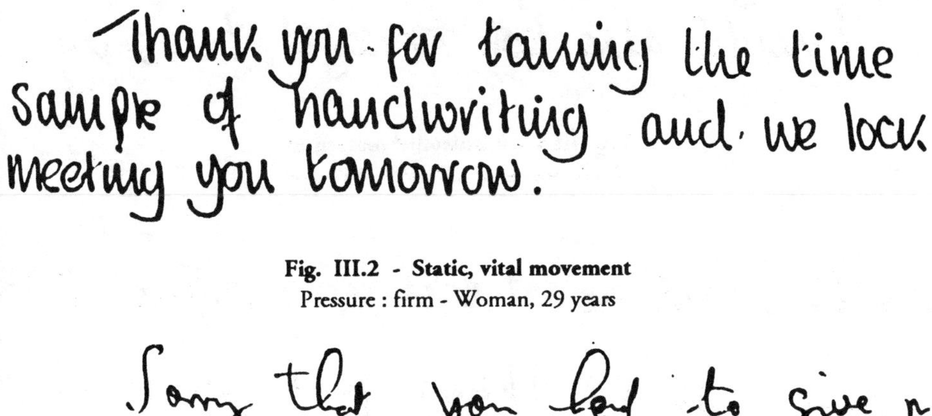

Fig. III.2 - Static, vital movement
Pressure : firm - Woman, 29 years

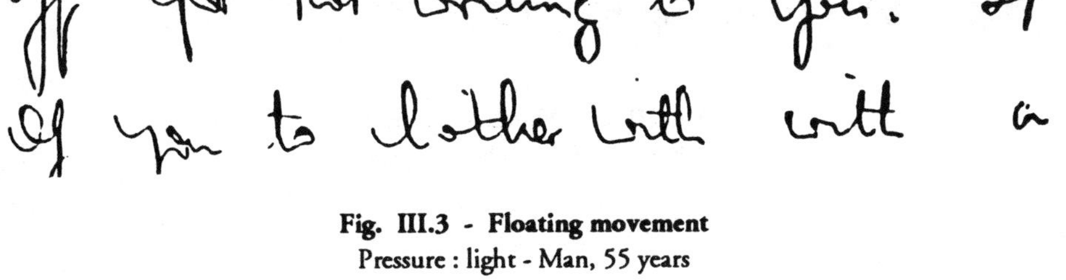

Fig. III.3 - Floating movement
Pressure : light - Man, 55 years

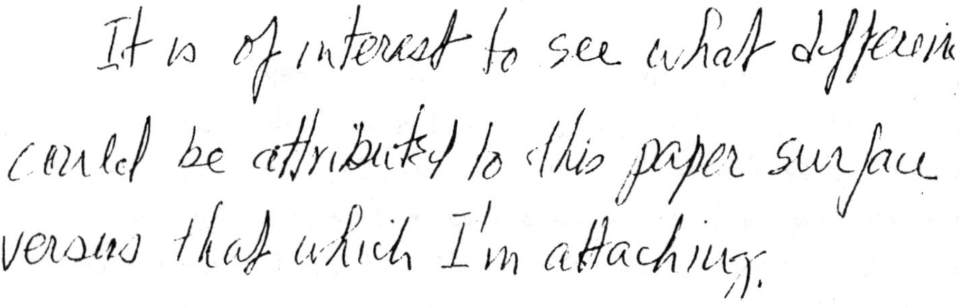

Fig. III.4 - Inhibited movement
Pressure : light - Man, 40+ years

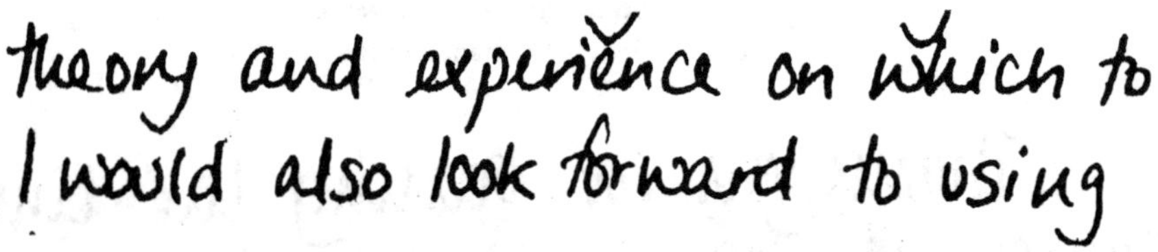

Fig. III.5 - Controlled movement
Pressure : heavy - Woman, 25 years

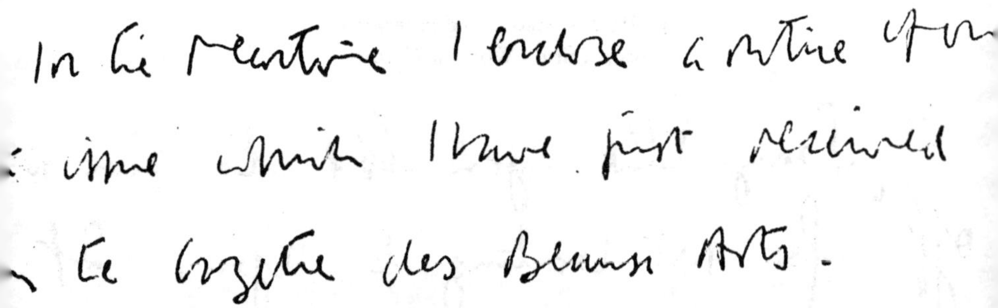

Fig. III. 6 - Flowing movement
Pressure : firm - Man, 60 years

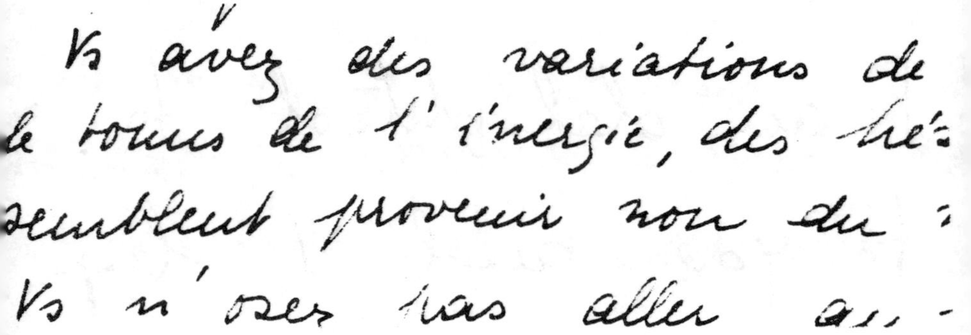

Fig. III.7 - Flowing movement
Pressure : light - Woman, 70 years

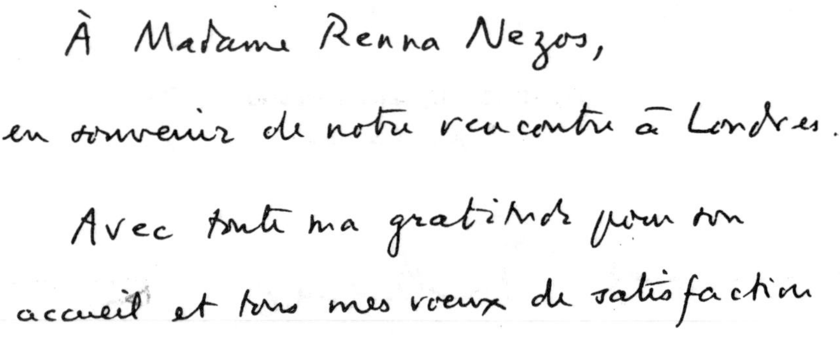

Fig. III.8 - Vibrant movement
Pressure : light - Man, 60 years

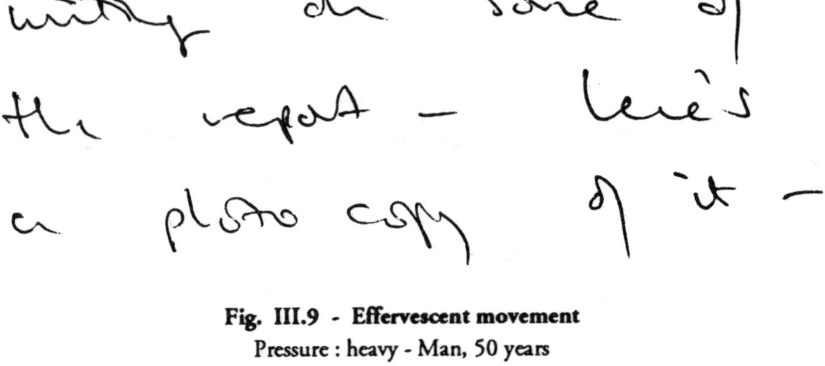

Fig. III.9 - Effervescent movement
Pressure : heavy - Man, 50 years

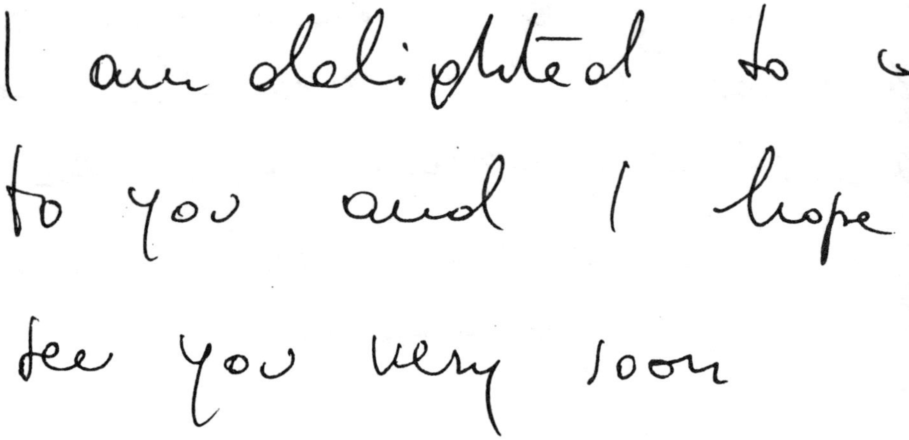

Fig. III.10 - Dynamic movement
Man, 67 years. Graphologist.

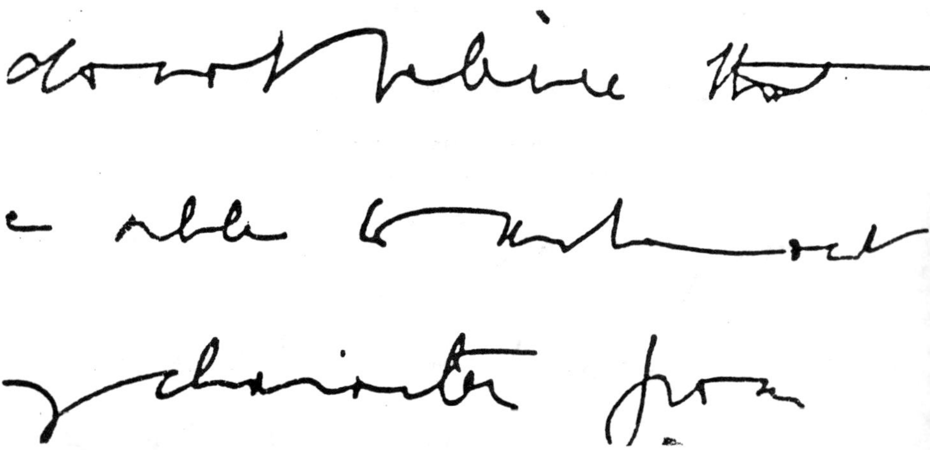

Fig. III.11 - Propulsive movement
Pressure : firm - Man, 55 years

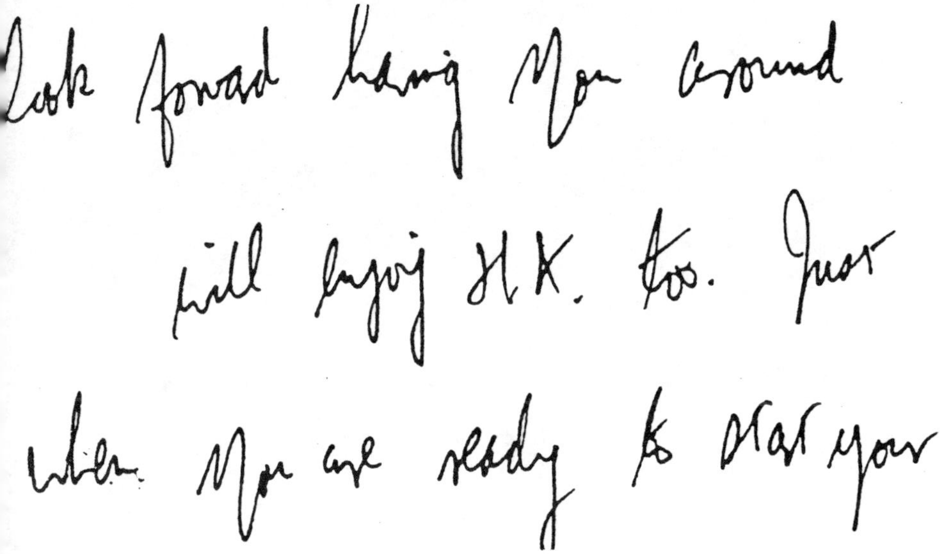

Fig. III.12 - Obstructed movement
Pressure : heavy - Man, 47 years

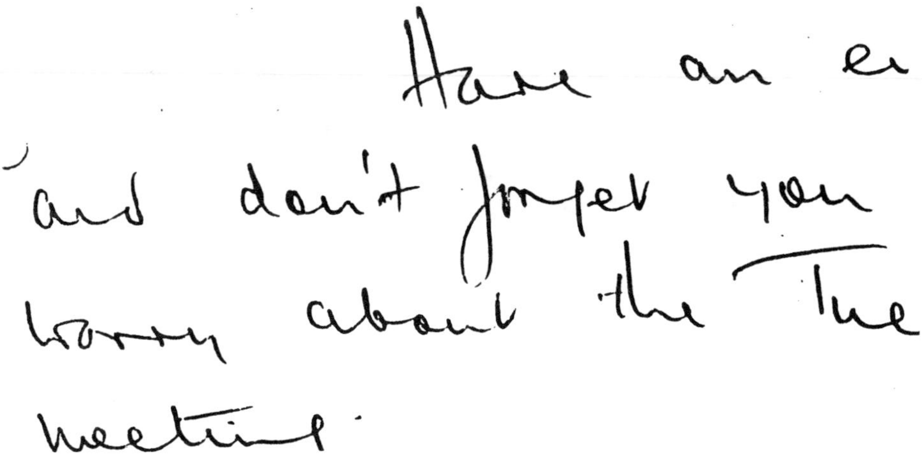

Fig. III.13 - Reared movement
Pressure : heavy - Man, 50 years

PART 2

GRAPHOLOGICAL SPECIALISATIONS

LECTURE IV
Children's Writings

LECTURE V
Adolescents' Writings

LECTURE VI
Vocational Guidance -
Professional Orientation

LECTURE VII
Personnel Selection

LECTURE VIII
Compatibility

LECTURE IX
Graphotherapy

LECTURE IV

CHILDREN'S WRITINGS

Through the works of Michon, Crépieux-Jamin and many others, we have learned that in order to achieve the main objective of a graphological analysis - which is to determine the character and subconscious actions of the writer - we must observe the forms and movements of the handwriting.

The "motivating images" which succeed the "visual images", determine the "muscular contractions" necessary for the accomplishment of the graphic movement.

"Intelligent attention can therefore direct and control the combination of movements, by containing and associating the successive impulses", says L. Manzagol in his book, *Les éléments de Graphologie.*

It is, therefore, necessary to understand the immense difficulty with which a child is faced when he has to see, register and reproduce complicated movements which, being totally new, have no meaning whatsoever.

Crépieux-Jamin, the only one of the great masters of graphology who showed some interest in children's writings, did not believe that graphology could be applied to "unorganised" writings. Although he observed that "from the beginning of learning to write, no one child's writing resembles another's, which indicates that each child has very personal reactions"; he did not pursue this observation further.

He also stressed that children's writings "change all the time with age". This gives an indication of whether, or not, a child is making progress and adapting.

In order to learn to write, the child must go through various successive stages from the first moment when he is given a pencil to scribble with, until the day when he, or she, will produce a cohesive text, clear, regular and harmonious. It will take two or three years from the "primitive stage" (also called "polynesian stage"), to the "Homo Sapiens stage" until the child will be able to communicate his thoughts by writing conventional, complicated signs, in an orderly manner. It is at this point that children first learn to express their personality and their intelligence, or even their genius which may remain undetected and smothered by parents or teachers who only too often, through ignorance, destroy these talents.

From the age of three, and in rarer cases even earlier, the child is interested in writing. Instinctively he, or she, takes a pencil and scribbles - through imitation - lines, curves, or even spirals.

Even at this early stage it is possible for the experienced observer to make a few basic deductions about these incoherent marks because there are no two children who produce the same scribbles.

Since before the last war, there has been a lot of interest particularly in France and Switzerland - in the study of children's writings through scientific experimentation.

As in all scientific experiments, the conditions should be rigourously controlled, i.e. the children should be of the same age, sex and nationality, taught at the same school, by the same teacher, in the same class, at the same time.

It was observed that in a class of 6 year olds, children of the same biological temperament, for example, Bilious-Nervous, would share characteristics which were consistently different from those of children with, for example, Nervous-Lymphatic biological temperament.

Since children of the same temperament share certain similarities, it was apparent that the differences observed in them were more intellectual. *For instance*: X had more aerated writing, the upper prolongments of the letters *l*, *f* etc. were formed with a loop, they were taller and the movement of the writing was more fluent than in Y's writing. X thus had a more lively and clear mind than Y. Ideally, the teacher should apply graphotherapy to Y in order to develop his mind which, in time, would also develop a stronger and more well rounded personality.

A child with strongly irregular and jerky writing would clearly be of Nervous-Bilious temperament. Therefore, to develop calmness in the personality of such a child, the teacher should always treat it with sweetness and understanding in order to achieve more stability in the temperament resulting eventually in a happier state for the intellectual capacities to grow.

But let us examine the problem from the beginning.

When observing young children's writings of the same educational standard and environment, we notice striking differences among them. What are the causes of these differences? The analysis of children's writings is based on the same fundamental principles of graphology as for adult writings, bearing in mind two very important points:

1. the conformity to the school/taught model

2. the lack of scriptural experience of the writer

When they start learning to write, all children have *unorganised* writing. Let us see how we can study such writings.

Unorganised writing is clumsy. A clumsy writing shows signs of difficulty in the driving of the scriptural organ, so characteristic in children and evident in all the genres of the scriptural field (continuity, form, speed, direction, etc.). We must not confuse this kind of writing with *discordant*, or *illegible* writings which, in contrast, show signs of agility in the stroke.

Scriptural fluency requires long experience and it is rarely acquired before 12 years of constant practice. Many educated and otherwise agile people, who don't write regularly, have in consequence a clumsy writing.

DOCUMENTS NEEDED FOR ANALYSIS OF CHILDREN'S WRITING

Documents for analysis should be spontaneous (not written under surveillance of an adult, or knowing it to be for the purpose of graphological scrutiny). There should be more than one document (preferably three or more), written over a period of days or months and these should be in fountain pen or ball point, not in pencil. It also helps if we have some samples of the child's free drawings, scribbles and doodles where the child is not worried about forms and spelling. This will enable us to see more accurately the quality of the stroke, the vitality, the tendencies, etc. We must also know the age and sex of the child and whether right or left handed.

Although the analysis of children's writings is based on the same fundamental principles of graphology, as for adults, the important elements of structure, tension, rhythm, freedom of movement, etc. cannot always be applied. In addition, it must be taken into consideration that all difficulties (intellectual, affective or physical) retard the mastering of the movement, the control of forms and the general evolution of the writing. We shouldn't be surprised, therefore, by the reaction of many great graphologists who announce, when faced with a child's writing, "I can't see a thing".

We must start with a rigourous observation of the writing, and notice first to what degree it is unorganised. Is it normal or excessive for the age? Is it too controlled and constrained, or is it too flabby and slack, or clumsy from lack of control?

In the early 1950s a group of scientific graphologists lead by H. de Gobineau and R. Perron [1] started a research in order to establish a scale of measuring and assessing the mental/ emotional maturity and motricity development of children between 6 and 14 years old.

Writings of 300 children between 6 and 14 years of age were collected, as well as writings of 280 adults of different cultural levels and of 150 mentally ill adults of various types and degrees of intensity[2]. 730 writings in all initially. The research continued on many more writings well into the 1960s, when a finalised scale E (for children) appeared, consisting of 30 components of which 14 refer to the forms of letters and 16 to the movement. This scale allows us to assess the development of the writing of children from 6 to 11 years old.

---

(1) H. de Gobineau and R. Perron : *Génetique de l'ecriture et étude de la Personalité* Delachaux et Niestlé, Neuchâtel, 1954.

(2) J. de Ajuriaguerra et als : *L'écriture de l'enfant*, Delachaux et Niestlé, Neuchâtel, 1964.

THE E SCALE

The E Scale is a genetic scale which allows us to assess the development of the writing for diagnostic purposes. It is made up of 30 components, which are directly linked to the difficulty of co-ordination and *timing* due to the motor difficulties of learning, which in most cases disappear progressively with the age.

This Scale is divided into:

- 14 items of Form concerning the execution of the calligraphic structure of forms and the way letters are connected, and
- 16 items of Motricity which mainly record the difficulties in the movement of the different elements which make up the writing.

The grading is made in accordance with the coefficient of equilibrium, directly linked to the discriminating power of the items in question:

- items with the strongest discriminating genetic power receive the coefficient 3. From the genetic point of view these items express the level of development of the writing age;
- items with average discriminating genetic power receive the coefficient 2;
- items with weak discriminating genetic power receive the coefficient 1.

To summarise:
the items with the coefficient 3 disappear quicker with age and with more certainty than the items with coefficient 2 or 1.

CHART 1

SCALE E

Mark: 0, 0.5 or 1 to multiply by the coefficient of equilibrium

		Mark	Eq.	Total
F1	Handwriting on surface		2	
F2	Plump		1	
F3	Absence of movement		2	
F4	Large writing		2	
F5	*m* and *n* school type		2	
F6	T-bars school type		2	
F7	*p* school type		1	
F8	*a* in two parts		3	
F9	*d*, *g* and *q* in two parts		2	
F10	Clumsy capitals		3	
F11	False connections		3	
F12	Solderings		1	
F13	Irregular space between lines		3	
F14	Poorly differentiated zones		2	

Total EF

		Mark	Eq.	Total
M15	Lower extensions amended (written in several strokes)		3	
M16	Amended letters		3	
M17	Altogether the impression is muddy		3	
M18	Arched stems of *d*, *t*, *p*, *q*		1	
M19	Dented round middle letters		3	
M20	Bad outline of the looped upper and lower extensions		2	
M21	Trembling strokes		3	
M22	Fading strokes		2	
M23	Jerky		2	
M24	Telescopic		2	
M25	Broken lines		2	
M26	Fluctuating lines		1	
M27	Descending lines		1	
M28	Words dancing on the line		2	
M29	Irregular Dimension		3	
M30	Irregular Direction		1	

Total EM

Total E

CHART 2

Chart of the evaluation of the graphomotor age of children between 6 and 11 years old

	EF			EM			E			
Age years:months	Q1	Q2	Q3	Q1	Q2	Q3	Q1	Q2	Q3	
6	23.5	26	27	15.5	30	31.5	44	55	58	
6:6	20	24	26	14	22	27	35	47	53	
7	17.5	22	25.5	12.5	17.5	24	29	39	47	
7:6	15.5	19	22.5	11.5	15.5	20.5	27	34	41	
8	13.5	17	21	10	13.5	17.5	25	29	35	BOYS
8:6	13	15	18.5	8.5	11.5	16.5	22	27	32	
9	12.5	13.5	16.5	7.5	10	15.5	20	25	29	
9:6	12.5	14	17	7.5	9.5	14.5	20	24	30	
10	12	15	17.5	7	9	13	20	23	30	
10:6	10	12	14.5	5.5	8	10.5	16	19	25	
11	8	9	11.5	4.5	6.5	8	13	16	20	
6	22.5	23	26	17.5	23.5	25	41	48	51	
6:6	18.5	20.5	23.5	14.5	18.5	22	34	40	45	
7	16	18	21	12	15	17.5	28	33	39	
7:6	13.5	16	18.5	10.5	13	16	26	30	35	
8	12	14.5	16.5	9	11.5	14.5	24	27	30	
8:6	11	13.5	15.5	8	10	12.5	21	24	27	GIRLS
9	10.5	13	14.5	7	8.5	10.5	19	21	24	
9:6	10	13	14.5	6.5	8.5	10.5	18	20	24	
10	10	12.5	14.5	6	8	10.5	17	19	24	
10:6	8.5	10.5	13	4.5	6	8	14	16	20	
11	7.5	9	11.5	3	4.5	5	11	13	16	

The chart shows:

- a ***horizontal reading*** which situates a child in his age group, comparing his/her performance with that of children of the same age;
- a ***vertical reading*** assessing the performance of a child in relation to a child of a different age.

Q2 divides the children into two halves (50%)
Q1 represents 25% of the best writers
Q3 represents 25% of the less able writers

CHART 3

SCALE D

Mark: 0, 0.5 or 1 to multiply by the coefficient of equilibrium

	Mark	Eq.	Total
Organisation of the page			
D1 Altogether the impression is muddy (M17)		1	
D2 Broken Lines (M25)		1	
D3 Fluctuating lines (M26)		2	
D4 Descending lines (M27)		1	
D5 Squeezed words		1	
D6 Irregular space between the words		1	
D7 No margins		1	
Clumsiness			
D8 Bad quality stroke		2	
D9 Amended letters (M16)		2	
D10 Congested bows		1	
D11 Arcaded *m, n, i, u*		1	
D12 Angularity of *m, n, v, u*		1	
D13 False connections (F11)		2	
D14 Solderings (F12)		1	
D15 Telescopic (M24)		3	
D16 Jerky (M23)		2	
D17 Flying away end-strokes		2	
D18 Irregular dimension (M29)		2	
D19 Poorly differentiated zones (F14)		1	
D20 Stunted letters		2	
Form and Proportion			
D21 Letters either over-structured or slack		2	
D22 Bad forms		1	
D23 Writing too large or too small		2	
D24 Bad proportions of the three zones		2	
D25 Writing either too wide or too narrow		1	

Total ______

Explanations to the E Scale

Items F (Form)

F1 Handwriting on surface

Dominance of curves at the expense of straight sticks due to incapacity to make firm and confident strokes.

- inability to produce straight and firm sticks .... 1 point
- inability to produce straight and firm sticks, but with some curves of good quality in the middle zone .... 0.5 point
- straight and firm sticks, fewer curves, with a few simplification .... 0 point

F2 Plump writing

The copybook norm tends to broaden the round letters and loops of the upper and lower zones. The letters are wider than they are high. The general aspect of the writing is inflated.

Plump writing necessarily implies Handwriting on surface. It is only taken into account if F1 is present.

- writing definitely plump in the middle and upper zone .. 1 point
- slightly plump in 2 or 1 zones .... 0.5 point
- no inflation .... 0 point

F3 Absence of movement

The school type writing is usually cursive. The flow of the movement is helped with a right slant, connections and a certain simplification (no bow ties, no little loops). The letters are just put down on the line.

- straight writing or right slanted, disconnected, with solderings or false connections .... 1 point

- the writing may be connected but without suppleness in the progression .... 0.5 point
- the cursive movement with a few modifications of the forms and combinations .... 0 point

F4 Large writing

The school type writing prescribes the dimension of letters in the middle zone to 2.5 mm.

- half the words are more than 3.5 mm or if all the words have this dimension .... 1 point
- half the words are more than 2.5 mm but are lower than 3.5 mm .... 0.5 point
- all the words or nearly all the words are 2.5 mm .... 0 point

F5 'm' and 'n' in school type form

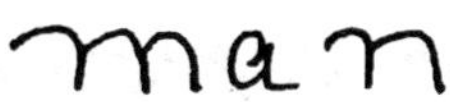

In the school type form the *m* and *n* are in arcades. The child has the tendency to make the arcades heavy, to dent them.

- if the *m* and *n* are heavy or dented .... 1 point
- if a few ones are personalised .... 0.5 point
- the majority are personalised .... 0 point

F6 T-bars school type

In the school type writing the t-bars must be small and placed two thirds of the way up without crossing the vertical stroke. The position of this bar requires quite an effort for the beginner.

- clumsiness in producing the t-bar .... 1 point
- if the t-bar is well placed .... 0.5 point
- if the t-bar is personalised .... 0 point

F7 'p' school type

The *p* is made with a stick and an arcade. It can be made in one or two parts.

- if the *p* is in two parts or with an added connection .... 1 point
- if all *ps* are in one movement .... 0.5 point
- if all are personalised .... 0 point

F8 'a' in two parts

- if all in two parts .... 1 point
- if half of the *as* are in two parts or with added connections .... 0.5 point
- if no *a* is in two parts or with added connections .... 0 point

F9 'd', 'g', 'q' in two parts

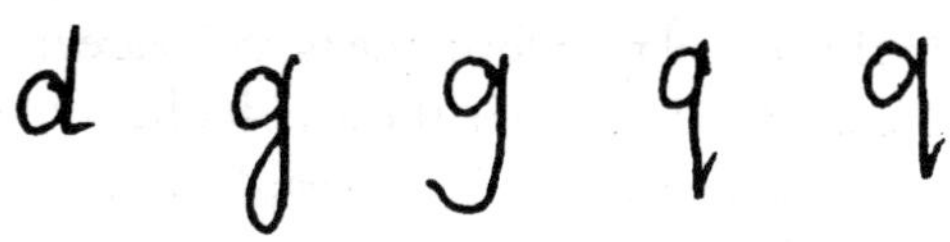

The same as for F8.

F10 Clumsy capital letters

- if all are clumsy and dented .... 1 point
- if slightly clumsy .... 0.5 point
- if they are all well executed .... 0 point

F11 False connections

The child is unable to connect the letters. "Momentary stops in the flow of writing. The writer starts again exactly from where he stopped reconnecting the stroke" (R. Nezos)

- 10 false connections in the first four lines .... 1 point
- not so many .... 0.5 point
- very few .... 0 point

F12 Added connections or soldering

The following letter is pushed back to touch the end stroke of the previous letter.

- 10 or more solderings in the first line .... 1 point
- 4 to 9 solderings .... 0.5 point
- 3 or less .... 0 point

F13 Irregular spacing between lines

What we must look at is the distances at the beginning of each line.

- if all are irregular .... 1 point
- if 2 identical spaces .... 0.5 point
- if all spaces are equal .... 0 point

F14 Poorly differentiated zones

= element

In extreme cases of irregularities, all *'e'*s can have the same size as an *'l'*.

- a few occurrences in several words .... 1 point
- 1 or 2 occurrences .... 0.5 point
- no occurrences .... 0 point

* * *

Items M (Motricity)

M15 Downstrokes of sticks amended (written in several strokes) - for example in ‘d’, ‘p’, ‘q’, ‘t’.

Inability to produce a vertical stroke in one go due to lack of firmness in the handling of the pen.

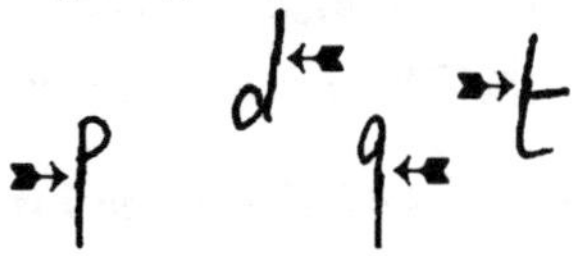

- a few amended straight lines (3 or more) .... 1 point
- one stick amended .... 0.5 point
- none .... 0 point

M16 Amended letters

These are not spelling amendments.

- at least two occurrences .... 1 point
- 1 occurrence .... 0.5 point
- none .... 0 point

M17 Altogether the impression is muddy

Smeary aspect (congestions, sometimes the child goes twice over the same strokes).

- very muddy.. 1 point
- muddy .... 0.5 point
- clean script .... 0 point

M18 Curved stems of ‘d’, ‘t’, ‘p’, ‘q’

The stick instead of being straight is bent and shows deviations.

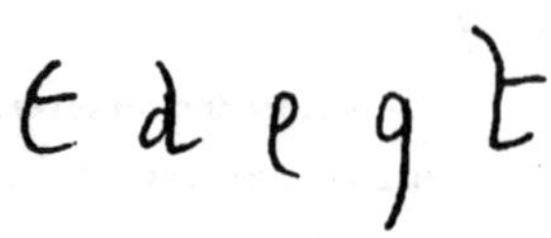

- more than half of the sticks are bent .... 1 point
- a few are bent .... 0.5 point
- none are bent.. 0 point

M19 Dented round middle zone letters

Imperfect curve, badly placed angles, dented aspect of the letters.

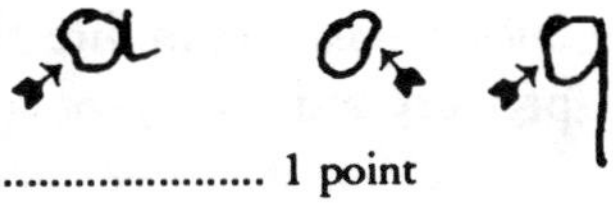

- if there is a majority .... 1 point
- if only half .... 0.5 point
- if none .... 0 point

M20 Bad outline of the looped upper and lower extensions

Inability to make a curve at the top and bottom of the loop. Presence of angles, narrow letters and dented letters.

- if at least two thirds of the loops are angular or dented ... 1 point
- if a few are decidedly so or all of them slightly so .... 0.5 point
- no trembling.. 0 point

M21 Trembling strokes

Small oscillations, detectable with a magnifying glass which can be amplified by irregular deviations.

- trembling on most letters .... 1 point
- obvious trembling on a few straight sticks or discreet and frequent .... 0.5 point
- no trembling.. 0 point

M22 Unstable strokes

One seldom comes across them. Anomalies in the quality of the stroke due to difficulties in pressure. The writing as a whole gives the impression of having been executed in a moving vehicle. The stroke is thin, the letters are badly structured. There is irregularity of dimension, direction and of the baseline.

- if the writing is very unstable .... 1 point
- if the writing is slightly unstable .... 0.5 point
- if there is no instability .... 0 point

M23 Jerks

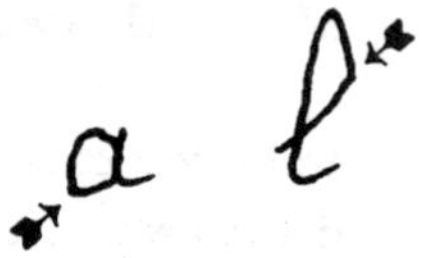

Sudden changes in direction, dimension, pressure and form producing unwanted angles.

- 3 or more obvious occurrences .... 1 point
- 1 or 2 obvious occurrences or discreetly occurring throughout the text .... 0.5 point
- none .... 0 point

M24 Telescopic letters

Difficulty of progression that a child tries to control. The letters are suddenly squeezed together irregularly.

- a few occurrences .... 1 point
- 1 or 2 obvious occurrences or slightly occurring throughout the text .... 0.5 point
- none .... 0 point

M25 Broken baseline

The line goes down then comes up again at an angle and not in a curve.

- at least one .... 1 point
- a beginning of a broken line .... 0.5 point
- none .... 0 point

M26 Fluctuating baseline

Wavy lines but without sudden angles.

- all .... 1 point
- 2 or 3 .... 0.5 point
- none .... 0 point

M27 Descending baseline

They make a 6° angle with the horizontal.

- one line over 6° .... 1 point
- one line under 6° .... 0.5 point
- none .... 0 point

M28 Words dancing on line

Each word has an irregular baseline (at least 5 letters and connected)

- all .... 1 point
- few .... 0.5 point
- none .... 0 point

M29 Irregular dimension

The height of the middle zone varies in the text.

- big variations in height in at least three long words .... 1 point
- frequent variations but smaller .... 0.5 point
- slight irregularity of dimension .... 0 point

M30 Irregular direction

Variations of slant within the word and within the text.

- if there are very pronounced variations in 3 long words .. 1 point
- if frequent variations but not too big .... 0.5 point
- if slight irregularity of direction .... 0 point

* * *

Evaluation procedure

Each estimation is multiplied by the *coefficient of equilibrium* (as per Chart 1) which is the statistical figure obtained as a result of a research carried out by Ajuriaguerra's group during the 1950s and published in his book *L'Écriture de l'enfant* (Delachaux and Niestlé, Neuchâtel, Switzerland, 1964).

After applying *Items F* of the Scale, we add up the figures obtained in the third column (Chart 1). The total is compared to Chart 2 according to the age of the child (1st column) and we find the proper quota. Considering the age and the sex of the child, we find whether the child is ahead, normal or behind his age.

We do the same with *Items M* and find whether the motricity is ahead, normal or behind the average age.

Then we add the total of *F* and *M* and we look up the nearest figure in the third column (column E) of Chart 2, considering again the age and sex of the child and we find out the *overall development* of the child compared to the average development of other children of the same age and sex (preferably of the same school, the same teacher and the same year).

The *Items of Form* seem to depend more on practice, training or *"talent"* in handwriting, whereas the *Items of Motricity* seem to be more connected with the motor development of the child.

Indeed, the evolution is quicker for *Motricity Items* than for *Form Items* in both sexes: this means that the *M Items* disappear more quickly than *F Items.*

If the *Items of Form* are dominant, they give the writing a more infantile aspect; the *Items of Motricity* give an appearance of movement in the writing.

The resulting values obtained from dividing *EF* by *EM* signify the following :

if $\frac{EF}{EM} \geqslant 1$ the child is well within its age group if $\frac{EF}{EM} \geqslant 3$ it is consequence of a dominance of *Items of Form* which is a possible indication of emotional retardation

if $\frac{EF}{EM} \geqslant 0.5$ it is the consequence of a dominance of *Items of Motricity* and we can suspect a dysgraphy which ought to be confirmed or disproven by using the **Scale D** (the scale which measures dysgraphy). (N.B. **Dysgraphy** is a problem in the organisation and evolution of the graphic act).

Scale E stops at 11 years old as this is the age of learning to write stops and personalisation should start. But it may start earlier or later.

Note: pre-calligraphic stage .... up to 6-7 years
calligraphic stage .... from 8 to 11 years
post-calligraphic stage .... from 11 or 12 years

* * *

A WORKED EXAMPLE

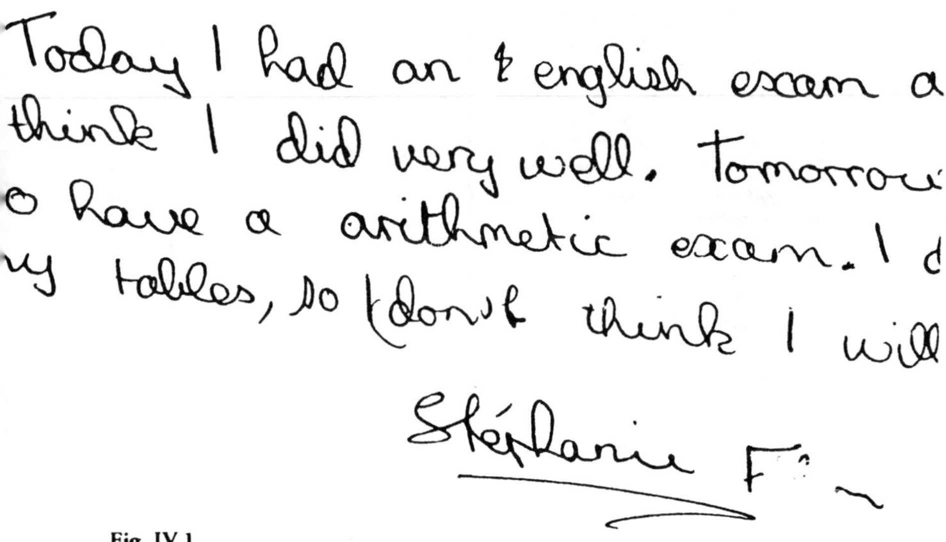

Fig. IV.1
Girl, 8 years

CHART 1

SCALE E - Sample : Girl, 8 years
Mark: 0, 0.5 or 1 to multiply by the coefficient of equilibrium

		Mark		Eq.		Total
F1	Handwriting on surface	0.5	x	2	=	1
F2	Plump	1	x	1	=	1
F3	Absence of movement	0	x	2	=	0
F4	Large writing	0.5	x	2	=	1
F5	*m* and *n* school type	0.5	x	2	=	1
F6	T-bars school type	0.5	x	2	=	1
F7	*p* school type	0	x	1	=	0
F8	*a* in two parts	0	x	3	=	0
F9	*d, g* and *q* in two parts	0	x	2	=	0
F10	Clumsy capitals	0.5	x	3	=	0.5
F11	False connections	0	x	3	=	0
F12	Solderings	1	x	1	=	1
F13	Irregular space between lines	1	x	3	=	3
F14	Poorly differentiated zones	0	x	2	=	0
		Total EF				9.5

		Mark		Eq.		Total
M15	Lower extensions amended (written in several strokes)	0	x	3	=	0
M16	Amended letters	0.5	x	3	=	1.5
M17	Altogether the impression is muddy	0	x	3	=	0
M18	Arched stems of *d, t, p, q*	1	x	1	=	1
M19	Dented round middle letters	0.5	x	3	=	1.5
M20	Bad outline of the looped upper and lower extensions	0.5	x	2	=	1
M21	Trembling strokes	0.5	x	3	=	1.5
M22	Fading strokes	0	x	2	=	0
M23	Jerky	0.5	x	2	=	1
M24	Telescopic	0.5	x	2	=	1
M25	Broken lines	0	x	2	=	0
M26	Fluctuating lines	1	x	1	=	1
M27	Descending lines	1	x	1	=	1
M28	Words dancing on the line	0.5	x	2	=	1
M29	Irregular Dimension	0.5	x	3	=	1.5
M30	Irregular Direction	0.5	x	1	=	0.5
		Total EM				13.5
		Total E				23

CHART 3

SCALE D - Sample : Girl, 8 years

Mark: 0, 0.5 or 1 to multiply by the coefficient of equilibrium

	Mark		Eq.		Total
Organisation of the page					
D1 Altogether the impression is muddy (M17)	0	x	1	=	0
D2 Broken Lines (M25)	0	x	1	=	0
D3 Fluctuating lines (M26)	1	x	2	=	2
D4 Descending lines (M27)	1	x	1	=	2
D5 Squeezed words	0.5	x	1	=	0.5
D6 Irregular space between the words	1	x	1	=	1
D7 No margins	0	x	1	=	0
Clumsiness					
D8 Bad quality stroke	0	x	2	=	0
D9 Amended letters (M16)	0.5	x	2	=	1
D10 Congested bows	0.5	x	1	=	0.5
D11 Arcaded *m, n, i, u*	0	x	1	=	0
D12 Angularity of *m, n, v, u*	0.5	x	1	=	0.5
D13 False connections (F11)	0	x	2	=	0
D14 Solderings (F12)	1	x	1	=	1
D15 Telescopic (M24)	0.5	x	3	=	1.5
D16 Jerky (M23)	0.5	x	2	=	1
D17 Flying away end-strokes	0	x	2	=	0
D18 Irregular dimension (M29)	0.5	x	2	=	1
D19 Poorly differentiated zones (F14)	0	x	1	=	0
D20 Stunted letters	1	x	2	=	2
Form and Proportion					
D21 Letters either over-structured or slack	1	x	2	=	2
D22 Bad forms	0.5	x	1	=	0.5
D23 Writing too large or too small	0	x	2	=	0
D24 Bad proportions of the three zones	0	x	2	=	0
D25 Writing either too wide or too narrow	1	x	1	=	1
	Total				17.5

In this eight year old girl's writing the Scale shows EF 9.5 which indicates that the child has a well above average graphic maturity. In Chart 2, in Q1 (25% of the best writers) she equals the 10 year olds and in Q2 (50% of all children) she almost matches the 11 year olds. Indeed this girl grew up to become an artist. However, the Motricity measuring of EM 13.5 shows her to be nearer the 7 year olds in Q2 which indicates a possible need for testing for dysgraphy, although the 23 overall (column E of Chart 2) puts her just over her age in Q1 and near the 9 year olds on average (Q2).

In fact, if we divide EF 9.5 by MF 12, the resulting 0.79 calls for an assessment in Scale D (Chart 3). This gives a total of 17, which is a confirmation that there is kinetic difficulty. (Anything over 14 shows dysgraphy according to the research done by the Ajuriaguerra team[(1)]).

One in 19 children between the ages of 7 to 9 year 6 months suffers from some type of dysgraphy. The causes of dysgraphy lie usually in the field of emotions. Pressures from parents, from school or strong demands upon the child can cause dysgraphy.

A child's writing tells more about its environment than about its proper personality.

---

(1) Page 245 of *L'écriture de l'enfant,* Vol. 1., *L'évolution de l'écriture et ses difficultés,* by J. de Ajuriaguerra, M. Auzias, F. Coumes, A. Denner, V. Lavondes-Monod, R. Perron, M. Stabak. Ed. Delachaux and Niestlé, Neuchâtel, Switzerland, 1964. Coll. Actualités Pédagogiques et Psychologiques. Published under the auspices of the Institute of Sciences and Education of the Geneva University (Institut J.J. Rousseau).

PROCESS OF EVALUATING A CHILD'S WRITING

In order to assess a child's writing we must try to capture the general "trend" of the movement; the force, the vitality, the dynamism. Does the writing have a certain harmony or at least show an indication of effort to achieve neatness or some aesthetic appearance?

We must look for any conventional, basic signs applicable, (direction, dimension, form, etc.). Although the basic outline of interpretation is still the same, with children's writing it should be modified, watered down and reduced to mere indications. Remember the golden rules: *"One sign has no value unless it is within context, repeated and supported by other concordant signs in the same sample"*, and that *"the same sign can have a different significance from one individual's writing to another's"*.

So, when it comes to children's writings, what matters most is the general aspect, the general impression of the ensemble.

We then proceed with the dominant characteristics (the essentials). We start with the general ***layout*** which will show us the child's organisation within his environment and his adaptation to it. For instance, a simple and well presented page will show a child who is orderly and knows how to organise himself.

The ***dimension*** of the writing will give us an indication of the position the child occupies, or believes he occupies, or desires to occupy in life. You may find large writings of egocentric children, very young and spoiled (usually a first child) or minute little writings of timid and fearful children who regress within themselves, or who become suspicious and cunning by way of reaction to their environment.

The ***pressure*** can be heavy and thick or light and fine. It may have relief. The quality of pressure shows the affirmation of the personality but, particularly in children's writing, it also indicates dynamism, vitality and whether or not the child has the ability to receive impressions and react to people in a direct or lively manner. Artistic tendencies will also be revealed by writings that are vividly coloured and in relief.

Speed cannot be seriously considered when assessing a child's first efforts at writing. However, one can detect early on a certain movement, mainly through the co-ordination of the various directions, and whether it is well balanced or not. If the writing tapers, it is a sign of some speed indicating nervousness and agitation.

Slant will show the child's attitude in his contact with others. If the writing slants *towards the right*, the child has an open attitude, an ease of communication, adaptability to circumstances or his environment, and he will usually be more extroverted. If it slants *to the left*, the child is introverted, timid, fearful and attached to the family. He or she may be negative. If it is *vertical*, the child may not respond easily to friendship or may be undemonstrative or may simply lack interest in contact.

Direction - (it will help if we can obtain a sample written on unlined paper in order to assess the true direction of lines). If the writing *rises*, it shows dynamism and enthusiasm. If it *descends*, it is probably because the child is tired or disappointed. If it progresses *horizontally* (on unlined paper), it indicates that the child has good equilibrium, unless the rest of the signs indicate otherwise and/or the horizontal movement is too rigid.

Form is not very revealing in young children's writings as they copy the teacher's model. It is very rare to find organised, personalised or original forms. However, the three main forms of movement, when appearing as dominants, are quite expressive. *Garlands* will show an open-hearted and adaptable child. *Arcades* will show a more closed character, probably introverted, but also possibly constructive. Finally, a dominance of *angles* shows energy, activity but sometimes also aggression and lack of adaptability.

Continuity, like Form, is difficult. Children rarely connect their letters when they start learning to write, but we can still observe the movement. If it is *continuous*, without many interruptions of the stroke, the child is more actively adaptable and may have some continuity of thoughts (ideas) and actions. If there is *juxtaposition* of the letters, there is lack of ease in adaptability and often lack of continuity in action, or possibly even in thought.

Irregularities in children's writings are a general trait. They can appear in any of the genres. If they are excessive (always by comparison with an average, a "norm"), they will indicate nervousness, and if they are in all the genres, they will indicate extreme instability.

The 3 zones - Dominance of the *middle zone* will show an affectionate child, adapted to reality and conscious of his own personality and his environment. Dominance of the *upper zone* will indicate imagination, a taste for intellectual things, or sometimes pride. Dominance of the *lower zone* will indicate that the child is practical with instinctive tendencies.

The ***quality of the stroke*** can also be studied in children's writings, but it is wiser to do this from scribbles and drawings rather than from writing, as children tend to press much more heavily on their paper than is necessary.

If the stroke is:
heavy - it is a sign of authority and will power
light - it is a sign of impressionability and sensibility
straight - the child is able to impose his or her personality
curved - it is a sign of adaptability
precise - it shows clarity of mind and intelligence
pastose - it shows sensuousness and possibly weakness
rapid - the child is active
slow - it will indicate hesitation in action.

PSYCHOLOGICAL TYPOLOGIES

Psychological typologies can also be applied to children's writings. The signs can be quite clear, but more often than not they are very uncertain and confused.

We must never try to rigidly classify a child (or an adult) into one character to the exclusion of all others. Personalities are infinitely varied and are differentiated from each other by a complexity of innumerable, fine nuances. Very few people indeed are of one clear character or temperament, or are, for instance, totally extrovert or introvert etc. All typologies are merely a rough guideline towards a better understanding of people.

JUNGIAN ATTITUDES

By nature children are either dominantly introverted or extroverted, but their environment may well develop or alter their attitude. So an extrovert child will not necessarily grow into an extrovert adult and introverts may also change. However, the graphic signs are similar to the adult's as follows:

Extrovert
The writing is clearly oriented outwards, towards the right. It is well spaced between letters and words and altogether progressive. The signature is generally placed on the right of the page, often underlined. The stroke is more elastic and communicative.

Introvert
The direction of the stroke is vertical or slanted leftwards. The writing is small or very small and the ovals are well closed or double joined. The signature is modest, or small, occasionally encircled and/or followed by a full stop.

Functions

Thinking the writing is clear, well organised and rather small.

Sentiment right slant, light pressure, rather large middle zone with garlands.

Sensation often pastose, in relief, well nourished with ink, rather full, occasionally compact (when introvert), mostly with right slant.

Intuition the writing is of reasonable size, light, fine and irregular.

HIPPOCRATES' TEMPERAMENTS

The ideal would be for all four temperaments to be harmoniously developed, but this is rarely the case. Children, like adults, have a hierarchy of dominance of temperaments and this dominance can be seen in their writing.

Bilious

- in adults it is usually the firmness of the stroke which gives us the first clue for a Bilious temperament, but all children when learning to write tend to press hard with their pen. So, in order to recognise this temperament in children, we have to look for other signs: a certain sobriety of the movement (with no unnecessary strokes), more angles than curves and more regularity in all genres. The stem of the letter 't' is straight and firm and the bar often crosses the stem. The letter 'x' also forms a cross.

Nervous

- is fairly easy to recognise. The writing is irregular in form, dimension, slant, continuity, etc. It is agitated, jerky, hopping; the stroke is thin and rather light in weight.

Sanguine

- shows in supple and rounded writing. It has many loops; it is expanded (occupies more space), the capital letters may have ornamentations. There are all sorts of unnecessary little movements and the pressure, although irregular, is usually well nourished.

Lymphatic

- lacks firmness; is often round and weak, calm and rather regular in dimension.

LE SENNIAN CHARACTEROLOGY

Characterology is not easy to apply to children's writings. However, the three components E, A, P/S are not impossible to assess.

Emotivity

- is seen in the irregularities. Often the forms in all 3 zones are of different sizes despite the discipline of regularity imposed by the teacher. The same applies to slant which may vary from right to left within the same word. The pressure is generally light but not consistent. When written on unlined paper, the lines are not parallel, when written on lined paper, the letters, or whole words, do not always touch the line. Often, when the child is very emotive, the writing is shaky and has many amendments.

Non-Emotivity

- the writing is more or less regular and much more stable. There are no interruptions in the movement. The pressure is more constant and generally the writing is much less amended and disturbed.

Activity

- the writing is well pressed down and gives the impression that the child squashes the pen on the paper, particularly with regard to accents, which are usually ahead of the letter, and the t-bars which may be thrown ahead of the stem. The final strokes of the letters are short.

Non-Activity

- the writing is light, often unfinished, badly formed and careless. Accents and i-dots (or even t-bars) are often missing.

Primarity

- the writing is fast and irregular. There are many breakages in the movement. It is rising and directed visibly towards the right. The ovals are open and there are some - or many - sharp pointed endings.

Secondarity

- the writing is poised and more controlled. It is taut, connected, vertical, or at times with left slant and the ovals are closed.

OTHER PERSONALITY TRAITS

We have talked about the signs and the basic typologies of children's writings. Let us now look at some more specific traits of the personality.

Vitality

It is very imprudent to diagnose the state of health of children, or of adults, from their handwriting. However, it is possible to recognise tiredness or the beginning of illness or of some serious nervous disorders.

Not only does a person's physical condition deteriorate with illness, but it also affects the communication between the brain and the central nervous system which, in turn, affects the writing action. This should not be confused with the writing of naturally "clumsy" people who have difficulty in co-ordinating or timing their movements in many of life's everyday activities such as sport, play, dancing and also writing. If the clumsiness (or lack of adequate co-ordination) is very accentuated, it produces a disorderly writing, with breakages, false connections, stains, etc, and the writing shows signs of dysgraphia or dyslexia *(Fig. IV.4)*.

In cases of tiredness (physical, emotional or mental), *or* illness, usually the graphic signs are a constant tendency for letters, words or lines to fall beneath the base line. Horizontal movements (t-bars and final strokes) also slant downwards and the stroke becomes light and inconsistent.

A normally grouped or connected writing may lose its continuity. The forms of the letters become imprecise, unfinished and the whole writing loses its unity. In such cases we can only say that there is a crisis pending, whether this be moral, mental, or physical, in most cases we cannot tell with any certainty. We can only see the alarm signs.

Intelligence

As in adults, children's intelligence varies in intensity and quantity. Clarity, originality and combinations in writing generally show high intelligence.

As in adults, generally speaking, it is the spontaneous individualisations (personalisations) of the writing which will show intelligence. In children, naturally, it cannot be so, not before adolescence at least. It is therefore almost impossible to assess intellectual abilities in a child's writing, up to the age of 12 or 13. Since the mind is the directive force of behaviour and of the whole personality, the qualities evoked by the various intelligences can be seen more easily in those children who are lively, expressive and communicative, than in those who are timid, closed, shy and do not exteriorise their thoughts, conceptions, imagination, feelings, etc.

From a child's exercise book and letters we can tell whether his intelligence is slow or quick, orderly or disorderly, constructive or destructive, productive or not.

The lay-out of the page, the clarity and neatness of the general distribution of the text and of the writing, the curviness of the forms, the upper extensions, will all give an indication of intellectual tendencies.

Lack of balance in the forms, general weakness of the writing, mingling letters, messy or squeezed writing, will show a disorderly, uneven, or unproductive intelligence.

Will Power

There are many different ways in which *the will* combines with other elements of the personality. Some signs of this are easy to see in a child's writing, while some are almost impossible. There are active children with strong will power who are creative and there are inactive children with strong will power who are stubborn and uncreative.

A well organised and regular writing, firm and pressed down, with straight, and strong t-bars, and with good balance between starting and ending strokes, shows signs of a well balanced and constant will power. These same signs, when paired up with falling t-bars and a slight left slant will indicate stubbornness, but when the ending strokes are strongly pressed down, the writing is regular and progressive, then the will power can be aggressive and nasty. Finally, a weak, slack writing, with light pressure and weak, very small, light or missing t-bars, indicates weakness of will.

Adaptability

The margins, in particular, give a fair notion of a child's need for security or for adventurousness. Rigidity of the stroke and all signs tending towards the left, lassos, leftward directed paraph of the signature, etc. will show difficulty in adapting outwards, and attachment to parents. The same signs directed rightward in a supple and curved writing, will indicate easy adaptability.

Egoism
Regressive writing, with hooks, little spirals, dominance of the middle zone, and ends of m/z letters turned towards the left, will indicate egoism.

Altruism
Openness of the writing, soft right slant, curves and all the signs which indicate altruism in adult writings, are also true of children's writing.

Aggression
Sharp pointed endings, often diagonal in direction, or horizontally towards the right are the main signs of aggression in children.

Sweetness - softness
Openness of the writing, dominance of curves, absence of sharp points, right slant and general suppleness of the movement indicate softness.

Pride
Large, full signature, accentuated personal pronoun, even disproportionate, capital letters distinctly more important than the rest of the text show pride.

Modesty - simplicity
No exaggerations; the writing is sober, harmonious and simple.

Disorder
Lack of general order in the text with numerous irregularities and amendments in all 3 zones, lack of clarity and tangled lines.

Order

Good lay-out, regularity, correct placement of i-dots, t-bars, commas and full stops.

Discipline

Similar signs to the above, combined with order and simplicity, no signs of aggression and soft, supple strokes indicate a child who is easily controlled.

Introverted and secondary children are more readily disciplined than extroverted or primary children.

Indiscipline

All kinds of irregularities; *i*-dots missing, ignoring the rules of the copybook style and signs of aggression, will show lack of discipline.

Lying

Children normally do not lie. If they do, it will be out of fear. In young children, strong imagination (when the borders between reality and dream are not clear) may give the impression of lying.

When *lying* is caused by extreme introversion (hiding the self), the writing shows all the signs of introversion and the basis of this form of lying is again fear (exposing his innermost feelings).

When *lying* is caused by weakness (fear and instability), or by frustration (vindictiveness), then the signs are: imprecise writing, covering strokes, hidden amendments, numerous irregularities, discordances (rigid angles mixed with flabby garlands), very open ovals mixed with tightly closed ones, mixed slant, narrow, centripetal movements (fear), hooks, arcades (hiding), spirals, complications, double bows and bow ties, ovals, open or closed underneath, missing letters, irregular pressure ranging from extremely heavy to extremely light (instability), ink spots in the letters, resting dots in the upper and/or lower extensions, exaggerated ornamentations, signature totally different from the text, and whatever else compromises the clarity and legibility of the text, all these may raise doubts as to the emotional happiness of the child.

It is, of course, never one sign alone, even if repeated many times, which will indicate lying, in any writing. It is absolutely necessary to interpret many concomitant signs before any deductions can be made as to lack of honesty. Lack of honesty is not natural in children.

*

SUPPLEMENTARY NOTES ON CHILDREN'S WRITINGS

- Small children do not have spontaneous writing.
- Spontaneity can only be found in scribble (scrawl).
- Without 'model' everything is authentic.
- Disorders are normal from the beginning of scholastic years up to the point when graphic maturity has been achieved.
- School models inhibit the writing movement because the effort increases the pressure and the tension, and produces shakiness, blockages and false connections.
- From the age of 10 the best criteria of appreciation is the tension of the stroke. Before then, we need to comprehend the scribbles as well as the handwriting.
- In children's writings do not look for the malformations. Look for the good elements and develop them.

DYSGRAPHY

In Holland, Helen Schneider suggests:

"Motricity, and a combination of physical, neurological, sociological and social elements, play a big part in the dysgraphy of children". She points out the consequences that dysgraphy may have on the development of the personality. As a solution she proposes the use of a better school-model alphabet based on the researches of Prof. Thomassen and his collaborators.

- The desire to draw is awakened in a child through a harmonious atmosphere and loving attention. The structure of the letters must be constantly observed; they must be simple and clearly differentiated.
- Slant and dimension should be freely chosen, but the graphic movement should be exercised through the combination of the short varied letters.
- The child, whilst writing, should pronounce the word simultaneously.
- Since writing is a means of communication, it should meet the conditions of legibility.
- There is no autonomous writing before the age of 15 (and often even later).
- Two factors authorise and motivate the development of the writing : (a) practice, (b) 'motor' development.

(a) All practice benefits the control and guidance of the writing instrument. So do drawing and painting. When all conditions are equal (age and psycho-motric level of development), the child who has written much will have a more fluent writing than the child who hasn't. Same stands for adults.

(b) Development is not achieved only through practice. For example an adult who first learns to write will achieve in months a better graphic level than the child will in many years.

Writing reflects the motor development of the writer as much as it reflects the troubles of motricity.

Since writing is the combination of an extremely complex psychomotric activity, many factors are involved:

i) the general maturity of the nervous system sustained by an ensemble of various movement exercises,

ii) the general psychomotric development; the tonic support and movement co-ordination,

iii) the development of the fine movements of fingers and hand.

- There are three stages of graphic development:
  1. The pre-calligraphic
  2. The calligraphic
  3. The post-calligraphic

* * *

SOURCES

de AJURIAGUERRA, J — *L'écriture de l'enfant,* ed. D et N. Neuchâtel, 1964.

CAILLE, E — *Le caractère et l'écriture de l'enfant,* ed. Fleurus, Paris, 1972.

le GALL, André — *Caractérologie des enfants and des adolescents,* ed. PUF, Paris, 1973.

de GOBINEAU, H and PERRON, R. — *Génétique de l'écriture et étude de la Personalité - Essais de graphométrie,* ed. Delachaux et Niestlé, Neuchâtel, 1954.

LESOURD, M — *Votre enfant: son écriture,* ed. L. Hachette, Paris, 1965.

La Revue de la SFDG — Nos. 121, 144, 157.

PEUGEOT, J. — *La connaissance de l'enfant par l'écriture,* ed. Privat, Paris, 1979.

STRELETSKI, Dr. C. — *Précis de graphologie pratique,* ed. Vigot Frères, Paris, 1950.

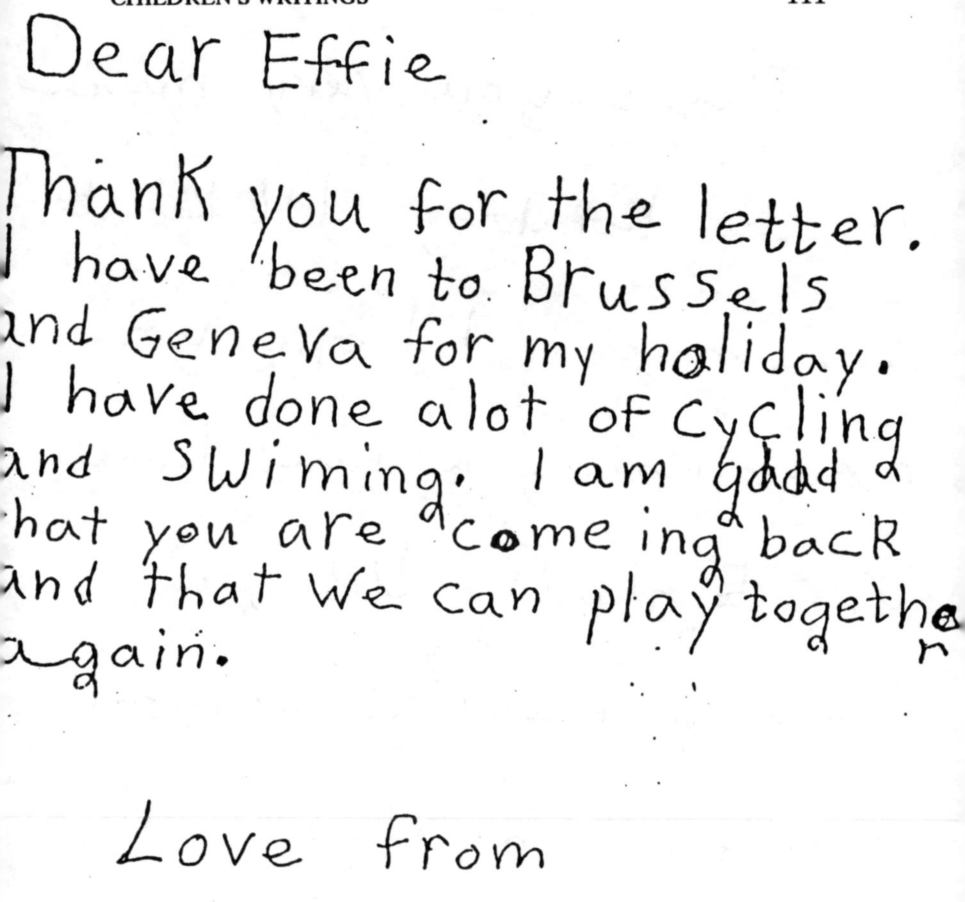

Dear Effie

Thank you for the letter.
I have been to Brussels
and Geneva for my holiday.
I have done alot of Cycling
and Swiming. I am glad
that you are comeing back
and that We can play togethar
again.

Love from

Anne-caroline.

Fig. IV.2 - Girl, 7 years

Blue ball-point on white unlined paper. Rough under-surface.

Pressure: precise, slightly irregular, rather heavy.

Anne-Caroline's writing is calm, firm and precise, moderately heavy and well laid out in a typographic style. She is obediant, consciencious and calm. She is well adapted to her school environment and she is in the average level of studies. Her Lymphatic/Sanguine temperament gives her benevolence and imagination, and order in her activities and her thoughts. The little pecularities in the lower zone are rather common at the beginning of the school years. A slight anxiety and uncertainty.

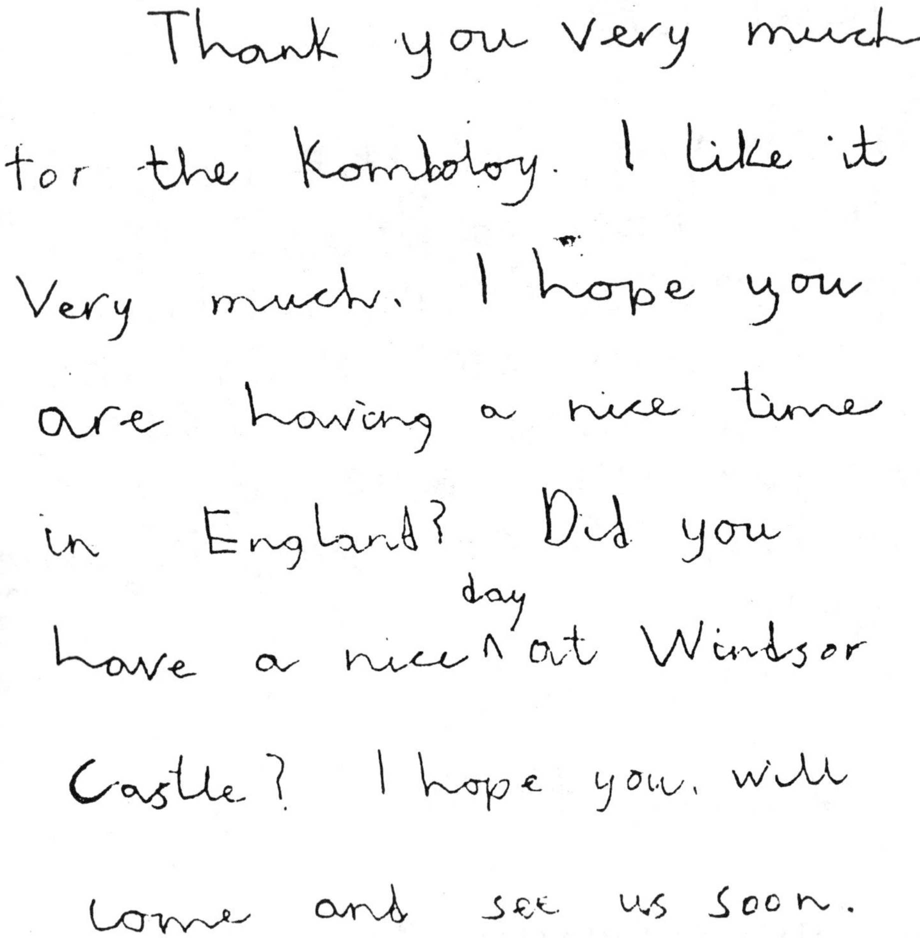

Thank you very much for the Komboloy. I like it Very much. I hope you are having a nice time in England? Did you have a nice day at Windsor Castle? I hope you will come and see us soon.

Fig. IV.3 - Boy, 7 years

Pencil on lined light green paper. Pressure: light, irregular, precise.

A wide writing with tendency to filiformity at the age of 7 is already an indication of flexibility and niceness. There are also sharp-pointed endings in diagonal direction. He is of Lymphatic/Nervous Temperament (lymphatism is common to all at the beginning of our life. We are born in water). There are no exaggerations in his writing. Everything contained and controlled. The wide spaces show respect for the reader, but also an imposed discipline which is rather strict and starts to create a certain emotional isolation towards the social adaptability. The continuity of the strokes and the little movements in reverse indicate already an intelligence above the average, a fact confirmed by his teachers at school.

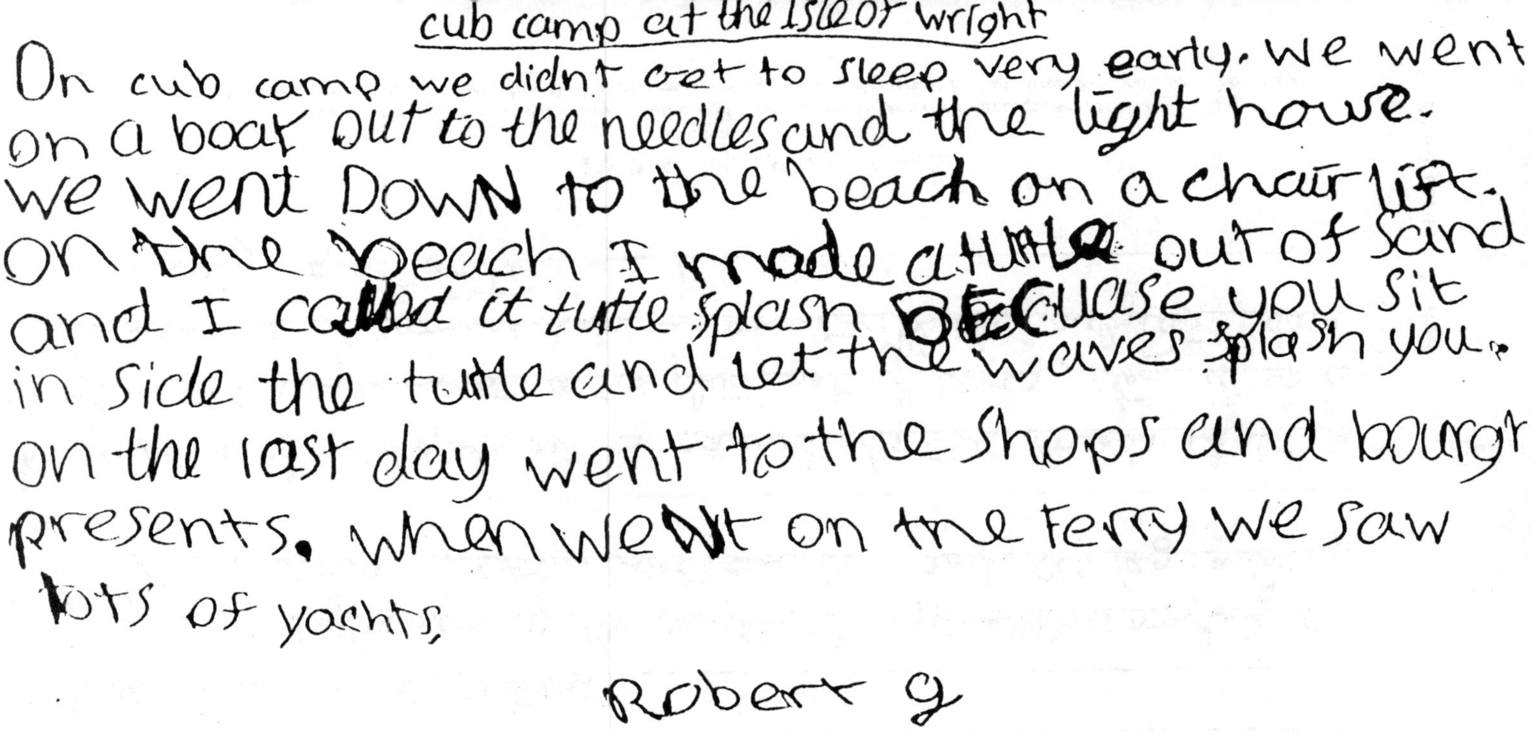

Fig. IV.4 - Boy, 9 years

Ball-point on white paper. Pressure: heavy, spasmodic.

This young boy's writing is tormented. It is heavy and very amended. The dimension and direction of the strokes are not well controlled. The distribution of black and white is inadequate. Many ovals are closed on the left. The upper and the lower extensions are contained within the middle zone. He is a profoundly sensitive boy with a very rich inner world, uncertain and insecure, who is constantly trying to comply with the image imposed by his family. He is trying but he doesn't feel he succeeds. He is very unhappy. His psyche is suffering. His personality is slowly becoming complicated without inner harmony.

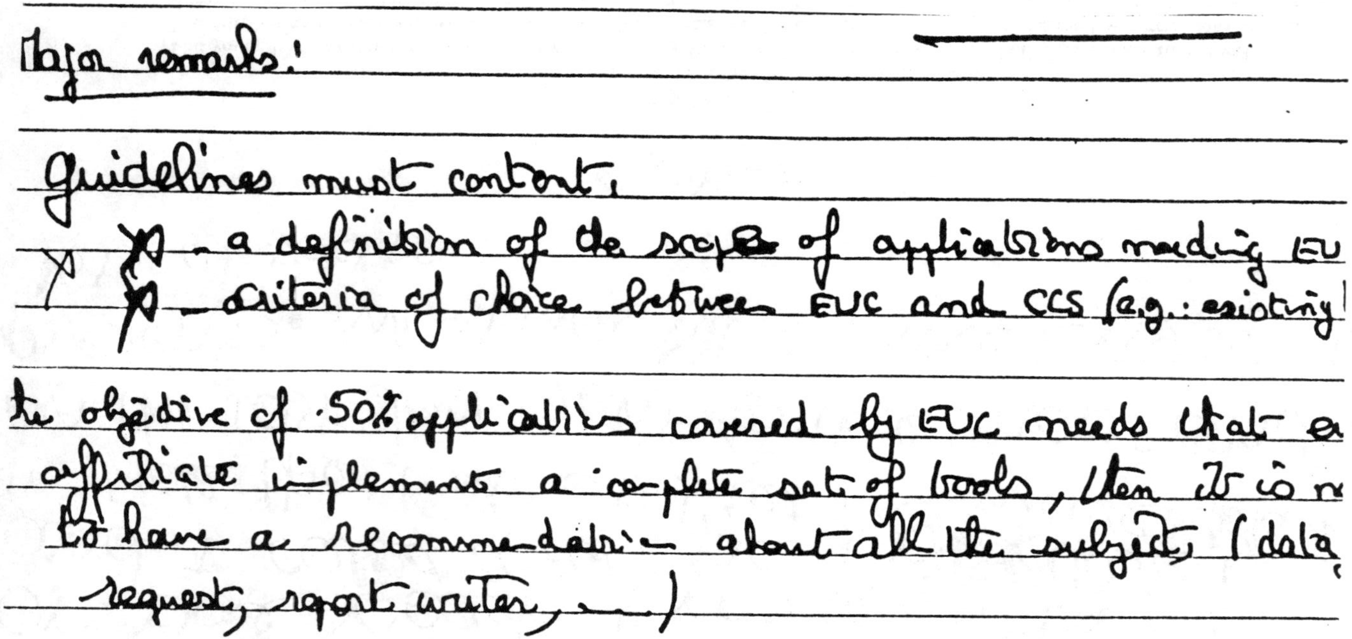

Fig. IV.5 - Man, 33 years - Chemist
Blue biro on white paper.
Hegar: heavy + pasty + curved + slow. **Synthesis of Orientation:** *Organisation* - unorganised, *Harmony* -, *FL* -,
Tension: Crépieux-Jamin - slack, Pophal -IVa, *Movement* - weak, floating, *Rapport M/F* - bad, *Structure* - poor, *Axis* - horizontal.

LECTURE V

ADOLESCENTS' WRITINGS

Adolescence is a period of deep psychological transformations. These transformations are likely to cause a temporary imbalance in the emotional and mental state of the individual. It is a natural process of inner evolution, starting around the age of 13 or 14 and finishing around 18, 19 or even later.

The sudden, rapid growth at this time needs room to expand. For the young adolescent, the family circle may become either an 'oppressing obstacle' where he (or she) thinks they don't understand him or they suffocate him. This can cause him to become aggressive, impatient and short-tempered, or the family may become a shelter from the wild world he is suddenly forced to face, compete and survive in, in which case he regresses and refuses to grow up. In either case, a combination of affection, intellectual stimulation and proper nourishment is the only way to help the child come through this unpleasant and delicate biological upheaval.

Lack of proper care and understanding at this period may have grave consequences which can endure throughout life. Insufficient intellectual growth, acquisition of unfortunate attitudes (aggressive or defensive), which remain in the soul creating nothing but problems and unhappiness for the individual and those around him, may be some of the results which can ensue.

Adolescence is the period when we prepare for the rest of our life intellectually and emotionally. The need for independence and for personal affirmation demands distance from the parents and the rest of the family.

This concept of separation is not necessarily physical; it is in the mind and the soul of the young person and takes the form of either violent crises alternating with periods of calm and obedience, or of a steadily progressive and discreet alienation between the child and his environment. In both cases, it is dangerous to ignore the physical necessity of this separation.

Adolescence is also an age of extreme sensitivity, whatever the outward appearances may be, and only affection, understanding, devotion, patience and intuition can help to ease the transition into adulthood.

Many parents understand, only in retrospect, the problems of adolescence that their children went through, while teachers, who face the same problem each year with large numbers of children, have no time to apply their experience to each individual child.

Modern psychological techniques, tests, questionnaires, etc., although quite helpful for some, are very difficult, time consuming, and often totally ineffective for the introverted adolescent. They are useful for only a small number of children whose behaviour may be obviously worrying. Introverted children with serious inner problems can remain undetected.

The careful and competent use of graphology is the only means by which problems can be detected, without wasting the time of the young person, and which can also be used to follow his evolution through to adulthood. It will show the conscious and unconscious tendencies, the attitudes and the basic structure of the personality. It can be used to advise teachers and parents how to direct the young person towards constructive activities, more in line with his natural inclinations and talents, where he, or she, stands a better chance of success.

Graphology should not of course be the only means of getting to know a child. Observation of his behaviour, the friends he chooses, his results at school, his reactions to events, etc., are all indicative, helpful and necessary, and given consideration, they show the personal pattern and aptitudes of the individual psychic structure. Along with graphology, this will help parents and teachers to guide each individual child towards the path most suitable to his/her character, temperament and general personality.

Teachers and careers advisers would be better able to help the adolescent achieve his independence if they could orient him in accordance with his talents and inclinations. In this way, he would achieve success and this would give him the real self-confidence so very much needed as this difficult age. It would also progressively produce individual maturity, which together with confidence, is the best hope for building today's societies into a better organised and more adaptable world. The young individual, with the help of prudent graphological advice, can be helped to achieve creativity, success, productivity and, hence, self-fulfilment instead of crippling inhibitions, frustrations and dogmatism.

We know that handwriting is a very complicated psycho-motivated activity, which is different from the reflex actions and which takes a long time to acquire fluency. Eventually it becomes, more often than not, an automatic and spontaneous movement.

It has been proved that writing acquires fluency through progressive substitution of a system of images. The formation of the letters is at first represented by the forms which serve as models, then by the concept of the movements necessary to copy them, and finally by the 'kinaesthetic' sensation attached to these movements. So the writing movement gradually becomes independent of the writer's conscious will, and the 'cerebellum activity' is liberated from the brain's control.

The reasons for this, embodied in the laws of writing, are evident in the *movement* stemming from the unconscious, in the attitude (subconscious or conscious) and in the design (conscious) of the writing, all three are symbolic and under the influence of the temperament. As we know, our conscious dictates *what* we write, our unconscious dictates *how* we write.

Among all the factors necessary for learning to write, the two most important are the ***intellectual level*** and the degree of ***emotional maturity*** of the child.

It is often surprising that an intelligent child, healthy and gifted, still has an unorganised writing at the age of 15, 16, or even later. This is not so uncommon as one might suppose, as it is caused by lack of emotional maturity.

There is a genetic relation between emotivity and psychomotor functioning. All emotional disturbances reverberate on the psychomotor processes and vice-versa. Whatever happens in the soul has its effect on the body just as whatever happens in the body affects the soul.

What though is ***emotional maturity***? It is *the autonomy of emotions, together with respect for others and the ability to co-operate.* In other words, it is *the acceptance of other people's rights as being equal to one's own; an adaptation to the principles of reality and a control of the need for pleasure.*

As in young children's handwritings, we use comparative graphology in studying adolescents' writings. We have to take, as a standard, the *normally* developed adolescent - of *average* intelligence - to be able to assess and understand the variations in development of others.

Around the 12th year of life the items of Scale E (*see LECTURE IV*), which are related to the difficulties in learning how to write, should start to disappear. This is an indication of the natural development of writing skills, and H. de Gobineau and R. Perron devised the Scale A (Autonomy)[(1)] which consists of 31 components and measure the beginnings

(1) For further information on this Scale A see ***Génétique de l'écriture et étude de la personalité***, by H. de Gobineau and R. Perron, (page 165 onwards), D & N, 1954.

of personalisation and freedom of writings in relation to the development, intellectual, cultural and emotional of the writer.

Fluency

The *fluency* of the writing is the best indicator of a good equilibrium between basic intelligence and emotional development (*see Fig V.1*).

An average, intelligent child, whose emotional maturity has not developed normally, or adequately, between the ages of 9 and 12, will show signs of psychographic dysgraphy as opposed to calligraphic dysgraphy, the latter being physical rather than psychological difficulty in writing. The writing will lack spontaneity and originality, conforming to a conventional style (copybook, typographic, Palmer or whatever is taught at school) (*see Figs. V.2a, V.2b).*

The balance between the intellectual and emotional levels of development is the springboard of healthy maturity and the graphologist must orient himself by establishing these two main lines of evolution in the writings of adolescents.

What is most striking in the writings of adolescents is their unending diversity. The global aspect of the writing gives us the first impression of the variability of maturity from one individual to another.

Take the writings of several adolescents of the same age, class and school, and observe the differences. You will find that some are puerile, some are clumsy or simple, whereas others may be simplified, harmonious, or will have acquired some scriptural fluency. Adolescent writing thus falls broadly into two main categories : those showing childish tendencies and those showing more maturity.

Puerile writings are not necessarily unoriginal and they may belong to students who are achieving good grades in their studies. For this reason, extreme prudence is imperative in the use of graphology.

Dimension

Another observation is very important here. The *size of the middle zone* can vary enormously from 1mm to 4mm or even more. The upper and lower extensions may also vary. Anyone's writing can vary in size according to the circumstances, which may not necessarily be visible, and the degree of variability can differ from one adolescent to another, as do the reasons which lie behind it. The most common reasons for this inconsistency in size are variability of self-confidence, inhibitions, susceptibility, nervousness and sensitivity.

The consistency, or variability of the size must be considered in relation to the general maturity of the writing, the pressure, speed and movement (angular or curved).

It is more important still to consider the rapport between the height of the small letters and the long letters and their relationship to the format of the paper used. The rapport between letters "cannot be voluntarily modified except with great difficulty, and this modification cannot be maintained" (Klages), therefore great care should be applied in the interpretation.

From experience we know that the stability of the rapport of dimension between the 3 zones belongs to a certain period in the life of a person. Usually this comes with emotional maturity and, in some cases, may never appear at all. We must also consider the origin of this distribution which lies in the psychic movement. It is the only way in which we can formulate a principle of interpretation applicable to many cases, since it will be founded on the psychological motivation behind the movements.

Vertical consideration

The distribution of strokes in the 3 zones of writing is due to the differences in length of the vertical movements, rising and descending (upstrokes and downstrokes). When the downstroke is predominant, the lower extensions are long and the middle zone letters tend to hang under the base line - (sign of dominance of materialism, of instincts, or, in a less *primitive* level, of need for self-affirmation). This is very rare in school children.

More often, we see upper prolongments which are an indication of dominance of the matters of the mind; of learning, of art or of spirituality.

We must remember, of course, that *the dominance of these prolongments, upwards or downwards, gives no indication of the quality of these tendencies*, and that *prolonged upper extensions do not indicate great spirituality, but only a great interest in the mind and in the intellect* (Pulver).

Everyday life is expressed in the middle zone through the alternations of the up and down movements. It is, as Pulver put it, *the empirical zone of self*; the activity in the family, the fluctuations of the sentiments - a more personal domain than that represented by the U (upper) and L (lower) extensions. Here the movements become amplified during periods of euphoria or excitement, or reduced due to fatigue, disappointment, or due sometimes to intense concentration. That is why it is helpful to know the conditions under which the sample in hand was written and also to have samples from different periods at intervals of 6 months or so.

Dominance of the middle zone indicates, as we know, the influence of the sentiments on the behaviour in everyday life. The length of the upper and lower extensions is considered in accordance with the size of the middle zone.

In Europe, the extensions, according to the rules of *calligraphy*, should extend by 1.5 times the height of the middle zone, and i-dots and accents should be placed directly above the relevant letter at a distance of half the height of the letter *i*. These proportions vary according to the general size of the body of the writing, in a small writing the prolongments will be longer and in a large writing they will be shorter. What matters most is the variations of height in the same writing, even in the most regular writing. Nothing, however, should be too precise. Absolute regularity produces automatism which indicates lack of 'life'.

The same rules apply to the Anglo-Saxon writings, except that the proportions of the extensions should be equal to once the height of the middle zone letters.

After many years of research into the writings of many thousands of adolescent children in various schools; the average proportions were found to be as follows:

Good balance of U and L extensions	-	45%
Dominance of U with average L	-	25%
Prolonged U and L	-	18%
Low writings (U and L atrophied)	-	10%
Dominance of L over U	-	2%

The general size was found to be:

Medium writings (2mm to 2.5mm)	-	50%
Large writings (over 2.5mm)	-	40%
Small writings (1.55mm or less)	-	10%

It is usually normal for writing to diminish in size as a child develops intellectually. However, it is not uncommon for writing to increase in size around the end of adolescence - particularly in girls. The change in the size of the writing, as the adolescent reaches maturity, is less indicative than the variations in dimension during other periods.

The size of the writing indicates the importance the writer attributes to his (or her) 'self', and this is quite understandable in the adolescent. The 'affirmation of self' - and also its deviations which may lead to 'worship of self', or to the desire to 'impress' and to be 'different' - appear in modifications of the writing and particularly in complications in the signature. (M. Debesse).

These interpretations should always be considered in accordance with the general attitude - introvert or extrovert - of the writer.

The need for expansion, which is projected in the space of the paper, is most spontaneously manifested in the largeness of the writing. (*Fig. V.3*). There are, of course, many variations regarding this dimension. The extrovert will have not only a high middle zone writing, but, also, wider and fuller letters, although the spacings will be normal. On the other hand, introverts with a high middle zone will have narrow letters, squeezed within words, but wide spacings between the words. This indicates that the child feels misunderstood and closes up more and more. Another manifestation of the combination of need for expansion on the one hand and introversion on the other, is found in large writings with a *left slant*.

Curved Strokes

Normally downstrokes should be straight, but often, particularly in young people, downstrokes curve, forming a small vertical bulge ( = h). This *twisted* form is more common in children under 14 and indicates lack of self-affirmation. If it persists after that age, it shows a fault in development: hesitation and difficulty in self-affirmation, but as it has been observed in adolescents whose aptitudes, application and intellectual progress are otherwise normal, it would not appear to indicate a severe hindrance in development.

Twisted downstrokes appear mostly in vertical or slightly left-slanted writings, which is understandable since the twist is not compatible with the interpretations of the right slant.

Generally, curved downstrokes indicate a more supple attitude than do straight downstrokes. The writer will have a personal force of character capable of modifying the effects of instinctive forces.

Superelevations

Superelevations in adolescents' writings, particularly in the down strokes of the letters (= p = m), are usually a sign of 'exaltation', when supported by general amplitude. When it causes tanglements with the lower extensions of the zone above, it will indicate false judgement caused by exaltation. It is also a sign of juvenile enthusiasm and interest in things of the mind. This may be so in small writings as well.

According to Crépieux-Jamin, all superelevations - including the *t*-bars as ( ) and letters with superelevations occurring at their base (usually the capitals), e.g. (= L = D) indicate pride, pretension and the like. Dr. Carton, on the other hand, makes a distinction between the two. He differentiates the first as a "desire to raise the concept of self" and "selfish tendencies", and the second (the letters pushed upwards from their base) as "the real exalted individuals" which does not involve pretension or pride,as he considered these were mainly shown by high placed t-bars; this individual can be timid and quite sensitive.

It is an interesting fact that we rarely find the two kinds of superelevations co-existing in the same writing. Superelevated capitals are rare in adolescent writing, whereas they are much more common in adults.

When the second degree of superelevations is not exaggerated and is combined with a normally developed lower zone, it may show a sense of reality and efficiency in action,but since affirmation of-energy is shown from the middle zone to the lower zone,when the descending strokes originate in the upper zone, then the length and quality of the lower zone part of the stroke will need to be taken into consideration for the correct interpretation of this kind of superelevation. If, for example, the lower zone is weak or stunted, this will not indicate efficiency in action.

If the writing shows signs of exaltation and, at the same time, the middle zone letters *m* and *n* hang down into the lower zone, which is a sign of psychic excitation, then the interpretation of the superelevation of the second degree should be interpreted unfavourably. This is very rare in young girls' writings.

Horizontal consideration. Spacing

The progression of the writing towards the right does not generally follow any strict rules of calligraphy. On average, the distance between two consecutive downstrokes in the same letter ('m' or 'n'), should be equal to half its height. The same applies to the distance between the vertical strokes of consecutive letters. The distance between words should be equal to the width of the letter 'n' or 'm' (as it appears in the same writing). Of course, in a small writing the spacing, for reasons of legibility, will be wider, and in a large writing may be narrower, yet still not affect the legibility.

Variations on the above, or the consistency of spacings in the same writing, is what interests us.

Spacing between words is caused by the progression of the writing instrument towards the right and not by the progression of the stroke. Spacing, therefore, has nothing to do with the progress of the writing.

Generally speaking, a writing is *progressive* when it is uncomplicated and the leftward movements necessary to form the loops (be it with a downstroke as in  etc., or with an upstroke as in 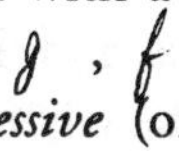 etc.) are reduced to the minimum. A writing is *regressive* (or with leftward tendencies) when the rightward movements are diminished and the necessary leftward movements are amplified 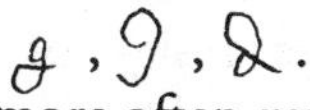.

A *spaced out writing* is more often *regressive* than progressive. The exaggeration of white spaces between words is common in people who tend towards isolation.

Progressive writing favours speed and generates dynamism.

Insufficient leftward movement symbolises an absence of

psychic substance, imprudent confidence and a nervous tendency to "run away".

Insufficient rightward movement indicates an inability to make contact, inactivity, pessimism or a fixation on the past.

Extremes of either of the above show mental imbalance or alienation from reality. In a well balanced individual, we see signs of equal manifestations of extroversion and introversion and an equal balance between physical, intellectual and emotional activities.

Since interpretations of the various horizontal movements are so numerous, few conclusions can be drawn from them alone.

In general, the writing of adolescents, particularly girls, shows a good number of signs of extroversion. *Narrow* writings are as rare as exaggeratedly *wide* ones.

Narrow writing in young people signifies inhibitions, it is opposed to dynamism, spontaneity and joie de vivre, which are natural in youth. It is not a sign of introversion, it is a sign of refusal. As Pulver said: "movement towards the right is the road which takes us far and wide (we can take it or refuse it) into the joys of discovery and of self-development, or in the opposite case, a constraint, a self-conservation and reserve .... Joy of the world is opposite to the ideal of complete discipline or a secret fear of facing life".

Moderately *wide* writings are the most common; this width, of course, is always relevant to the size of the writing, which depends heavily on the fullness of the ovals, and should therefore be judged by the general impression of the whole.

Little deformations of progression, when lacking in adolescents' writings, are a sign of puerility. *Simplifications*, except in very rare cases, do not start before the end of adolescence.

Progressive movements in the lower zone are a sign of maturity and also of intelligence (together with supporting signs from the vertical axis).

Another sign indicating resistance to rightward tendency is seen in *short final strokes. Long final strokes* (on the horizontal axis) have been observed in adolescents with an uncontrolled tendency to talkativeness. Reserve and self-control are indicated when moderate final strokes appear in a wide writing, whereas suspended final strokes are not indicative of moderation,but of an inability to achieve.

When the text is squeezed on the left of the page, leaving a wider right margin, indicates timidity, hypersensitivity, fear of contact, a refusal of, or opposition to all things symbolised by the right, unless this is imposed by the teacher for the purpose of corrections. This tendency to place the text on the left usually is accompanied by signs of inhibition in the rest of the writing.

When the text leaves no margins either side, it indicates an invasive self, egocentricity and a demanding personality who has a lot to say and never enough time to say it. Also lack of adequate organisation and consideration if it is also compact, or illegible out of speed and weak in tension.

If there is a wide right margin (wider than 2.5cm) we can think with some confidence in most cases that the young writer has started to be aware of his individuality and is not trying his wings.

When the text is gathered at the top of the page (very common in children and adolescents, often also in adults) it usually indicates dependence on authority which is natural in children and early adolescence, but should start to disappear at around 16 years of age. It may also be a sign of lack of organisation and foresight or simply lack of aesthetic taste.

Form

An *artificial writing* may indicate lack of spontaneity usually caused by external factors related to the family or the social circle. In rare cases this writing may indicate serious disturbances of the psychic equilibrium. On the other hand, however, a stylised writing may indicate artistic inclinations (*Fig. V.4*).

Leftward tendencies in the upper and lower zones and in the capitals is found in 30% of adolescents' writings and should be examined and interpreted as *regressive movements*.

Exaggeration of the lower loops is usually interpreted as eroticism. This is an oversimplification. More often than not, it is a sign of imagination in the physiological field, quite common in girls of Sanguine temperament. Large leftward projections of the lower zone loops which do not return sufficiently towards the right to close the loop, are usually found in young people whose attention has been drawn towards their physique through an illness or a malfunction, sexual or not, and in some cases they are, or have been, under some sort of therapy or medication. In some schools in the U.K. this form is taught as an obligatory style of writing.

Triangular lower loops are a regressive movement but also brusque, since it involves angles, (sharp changing of direction), either two angles or one. This shows unconscious opposition which may be hidden under amiable manners.

Leftward movement in the upper zone is also portrayed by the lyrical 'd' which shows intense inner life, although this is not often found in adolescents' writing. When it curves sharply towards the left, it is a caricature of the lyrical 'd' (). When the stroke is connected to the next letter (e.g. *do*), it may have favourable indications (reflection and action).

All *big loops*, as well as the i-dots drawn as circles, delay progression of the writing. They indicate deep inhibitions and submission. In Lymphatic and Sanguine temperaments, it shows coquettishness and behaviour relevant to this attitude.

Oblique Movements

Diagonal movements appear mainly in t-bars (), disconnected starting strokes and/or in end strokes (*Figs. V.2a,*

V.2b). It is an impulsive and independent movement showing impatience and aggression without a specific aim. Despite its progressive character, it does not always indicate a spirit of conquest or a tendency towards the future. It may be a sign of aggressive rejection of the past, of childhood. It is a sign which usually disappears with maturity.

When diagonal movements are concentrated in the starting strokes, it indicates systematic opposition and impertinence, while if it is in the middle of words it indicates more serious aggression, in adolescents as well as in adults.

This movement in the signature has been seen in the writings of mentally ill people with a tendency to self-destruction.

The Slant

According to the rules of calligraphy, downstrokes should be parallel. According to different models, they should have a slant of around 55° for a right-slanted writing or 90° for a vertical style. If the slant is *30° or less*, the writing is called 'very slanted to the right' and at *120° or more*, it is called 'very slanted to the left'.

Regardless of the style taught, it has been observed that students usually choose their own personal slant.

Slant is not necessarily the same in all 3 zones. In a right-slanted writing, although the downstroke is consciously directed towards the left, the initial upstroke is directed out away from the self (even if invisible) and is therefore interpreted as a rightward slant, i.e. a leaning towards people.

On average, young adolescents' writings are:

Very slanted to the right - less than 30°	- 1%
Slanted - between 30° and 90°	- 10%
Vertical	- 60%
Slightly left-slanted - between 90° and 100°	- 10%
Very slanted to the left - between 100° and 120°	- 1%

The remaining 18% were extremely variable and the downstrokes were very curved.

A strong right slant shows impulsiveness and dependence; the greater the slant, the more impulsive the writer.

A left slant, if it is accentuated, shows active resistance with negative impulsiveness and a reaction to authority. It may also show a need for independence. More information will be provided by considering this sign in relation with the rest of the writing - its width or narrowness, and its pressure and stroke.

According to Pulver, variability of slant is generally interpreted as *ambivalence.*

But what is *ambivalence* and is it necessarily always a negative trait?

Ambivalence is an indication of indecision. Depending on the zone in which the irregularities appear, they show which part of the personality is involved. In general, it is a sign of vivid inner activity, of discordant dynamism, but it can also be a stimulant to personal development.

"It is good if it contributes towards the construction of the personality and it is bad if it paralyses the individual with its polarity of tendencies", said Pulver.

Crépieux-Jamin sees in the irregularity of slant *animated* writing, which indicates imagination and activity, provided the irregularities are frequent and controlled. If they are not, then we have a *discordant* writing which shows inconsistency.

The Stroke

As in physics, where the energy of a body in motion depends on the factors of its mass and speed, in handwriting, energy is expressed by the thickness of the stroke and its speed.

In a *thin writing,* speed is achieved with less effort and less expenditure of psychic energy than with a thick stroke of the same speed.

Irregular thickness of the stroke is more expressive and more active than regular thickness, which indicates passivity and a mere need of representation. Irregularities of the stroke and pressure, are more likely to occur with rapid writing.

"The alternation in the flexion and extension of the fingers, which corresponds to the natural muscular movements, is much less tiring than constant pressure - be it weak or strong" said Saudek.

These *variations in the weight* of the writing create relief which is a sign of energy and originality; the concave arc in space (*spindles*) and the convex arc in space (Hegar's "invisible connections") ("broken" strokes).

Many adolescents change pressure and speed when they are free to choose their own pen. Therefore, great prudence is needed in the interpretation.

There are 4 main qualities of the stroke; *thin, medium* (which covers the 85% of writings), *thick* and *very thick* (which is only found in 1% of writings.

The stroke quality too must be interpreted in the normal way, in correlation with the rest of the signs.

We have considered the writings of adolescents in a different light to conventional graphology; through the stroke and the movement. This system of observing writings helps us to uncover more readily their most constant and important characteristics.

The Letter 't'

The letter *t* is the most important single letter of a writing. It is a synthesis of many signs of the highest importance. It is the expression of the nuances of the intellectual life, of the imagination, of strong or weak will power, of aggression, of strong or weak energy, of affirmation and of egocentrism or allocentrism. It must always be considered in correlation with the whole of the writing. It is interesting, however, that what the *t* alone indicates is also seen in the rest of the writing

Signatures

Children only start forming a signature around 11 years of age. At this stage they are usually imitations of the father's or the mother's. As from 13 or 14 they start searching for a personal style to suit their own personality. It is then that the signature begins to give some information about the writer. It indicates how the adolescent feels his position in the family and his intimate circle. The relationship between his/her own name and the family name will show his/her personal feelings about his status. If the surname is larger than the first name, it show inadequate self-confidence and dependence. The same if it is altogether smaller than the text or crossed out.

The signature of adolescents can be interpreted along the same guidelines as the signatures of adults[1].

Psychological Typologies

Psychological classification is important and very helpful in assessing young people's writings.

The three main typologies - of Hippocrates-Carton, Jung-Teillard, and Le Senne-Caille are the most commonly used. In some cases, where there is evidence of possible problems, Freud, Adler and Horney can also be applied and will help direct the researcher towards a deeper understanding of the problems. (see PART 5).

The same rules and the same dominant signs apply here as for adults' writings.

* * *

(1) For more information on this subject see the relevant chapter on page 196 of *Graphology, Volume I* (by Renna Nezos, *Scriptor Books*, London 1992).

SOURCES

CARTON, P. — *Le Diagnostic de la Mentalité par l'écriture,* Librairie Le François, Paris, 1973.

CRÉPIEUX-JAMIN, J. — *L'Écriture et le Caractère,* PUF, Paris, 1960.

DUBOUCHET, J — *L'écriture des adolescentes,* Librairie le François, Paris, 1967.

le GALL, A. — *Caractérologie des enfants et des adolescents,* ed. PUF, Paris, 1973.

de GOBINEAU, H. and PERRON, R — *Génétique de l'Écriture et étude de la Personalité - Essais de graphométrie,* ed. Delachaux et Niestlé, Neuchâtel, 1954.

KLAGES, L. — *Expression du caractère dand l'écriture - Technique de la graphologie,* Delachaux et Niestlé, Neuchâtel, 1953.

A. LOMBARD — Revue 164, 165

PULVER, M. — *Symbolisme de l'écriture,* Librairie Stock, 1953.

SAUDEK, R. — *Experiments with Handwriting,* W. Morrow & Co., N.Y., 1929.

La Revue de la SFDG — Nos. 144, 157.

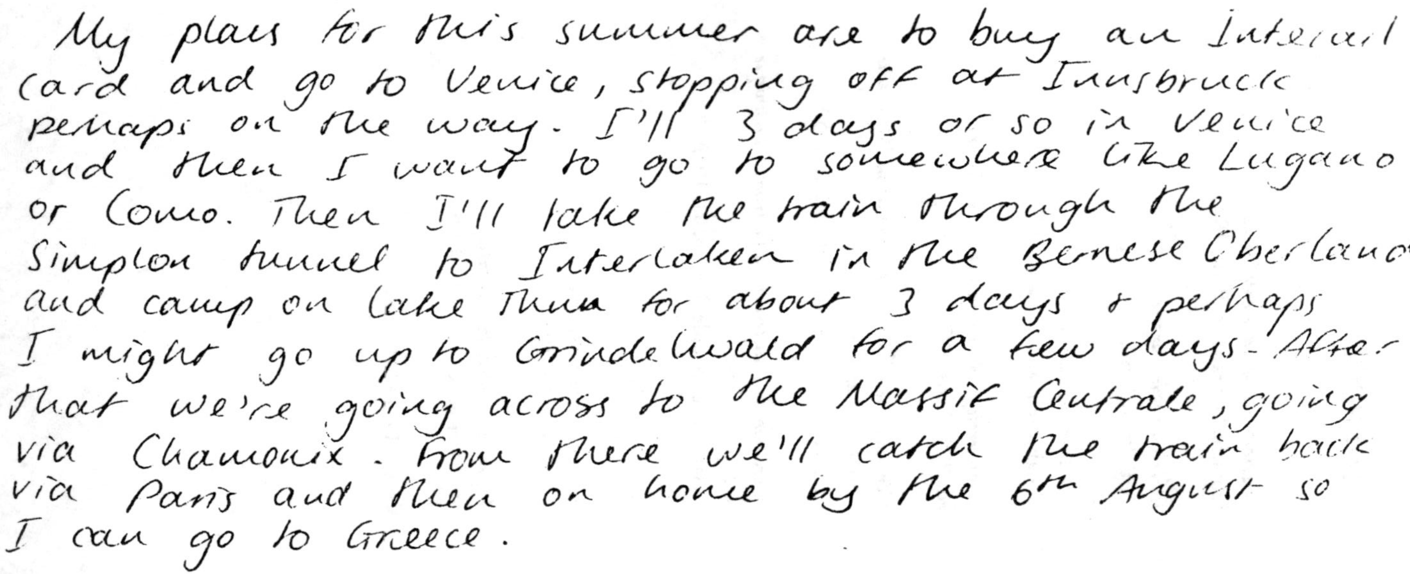
My plans for this summer are to buy an Interail
card and go to Venice, stopping off at Innsbruck
perhaps on the way. I'll 3 days or so in Venice
and then I want to go to somewhere like Lugano
or Como. Then I'll take the train through the
Simplon tunnel to Interlaken in the Bernese Oberland
and camp on Lake Thun for about 3 days & perhaps
I might go up to Grindelwald for a few days. After
that we're going across to the Massif Centrale, going
via Chamonix. From there we'll catch the train back
via Paris and then on home by the 6th August so
I can go to Greece.

Fig. V.1 - Boy, 15 years old.

Blue biro on white paper. Pressure: light. Stroke: precise, curved, rapid, supple and elastic.
Good balance between Form and Movement.

The writing is compact, simplified, progressive, vibrant and animated. The slant varies in degrees, but remains consistently right. It is a sober, grouped script with some combinations. The boy is intelligent, logical and communicative, with a well centred personality.

Not much is happening up here apart from that I never realised the English countryside could be quite so dull and I really wish I was back in London.

Well I hope you can read the writing and the bad spelling. I'll see you soon.

Fig. V.2a (20% reduction)

Boy, 12 years, in boarding school.

Blue felt pen on white paper. Pressure light, spasmodic, stroke pasty (runny, muddy), curved and slow, without much differentiation.

This writing is infantile. The letters are connected without ease or fluency. There are many vast spacings between words, superelevations and prolongations. The clumsiness of the forms, the twisted arcades, the jerkiness and shakiness and the covering strokes, all point towards dysgraphy and show great inner anxiety, (the drawings speak for themselves), fear and secretivity caused by the environment (no-one is born in that state).

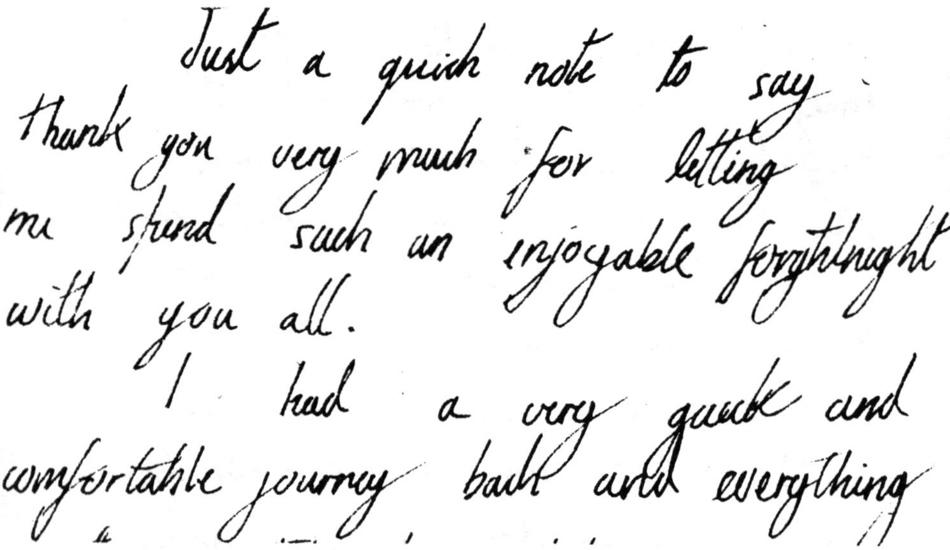

Fig. V.2b

The same boy 2 years later and now 3 years in a boarding school.

Blue felt pen on green paper.

Pressure - light, stroke pasty, straight and slow, no differentiation.

The spacing between words is less wide. In places almost aerated but the dysgraphy is persisting. The spacing between letters is squeezed and the letters are narrow and tall. They have lost their suppleness and whatever adaptability they had. They have become prudent and mistrustful, bitter and touchy. The maturity is advancing slowly but not smoothly. There are superelevations (see letter *p*) and many exaggerated and weak prolongments without differentiation between the down and the up-strokes, oblique tendencies (*g, y* and *t*-bars), amendments, false connections, messed up words (see 'fortnight' particularly), solderings, ambiguous letters, crenellated and bruised ovals, double curves and covering strokes. The writing is large, regressive, static, tormented and false. "Not a brainy chap, but he blunders his way through anything", say his classmates. His behaviour is very "extrovert", argumentative (oblique and sharp-pointed ends) and very "self-assured". He is also very artistic. He draws beautifully.

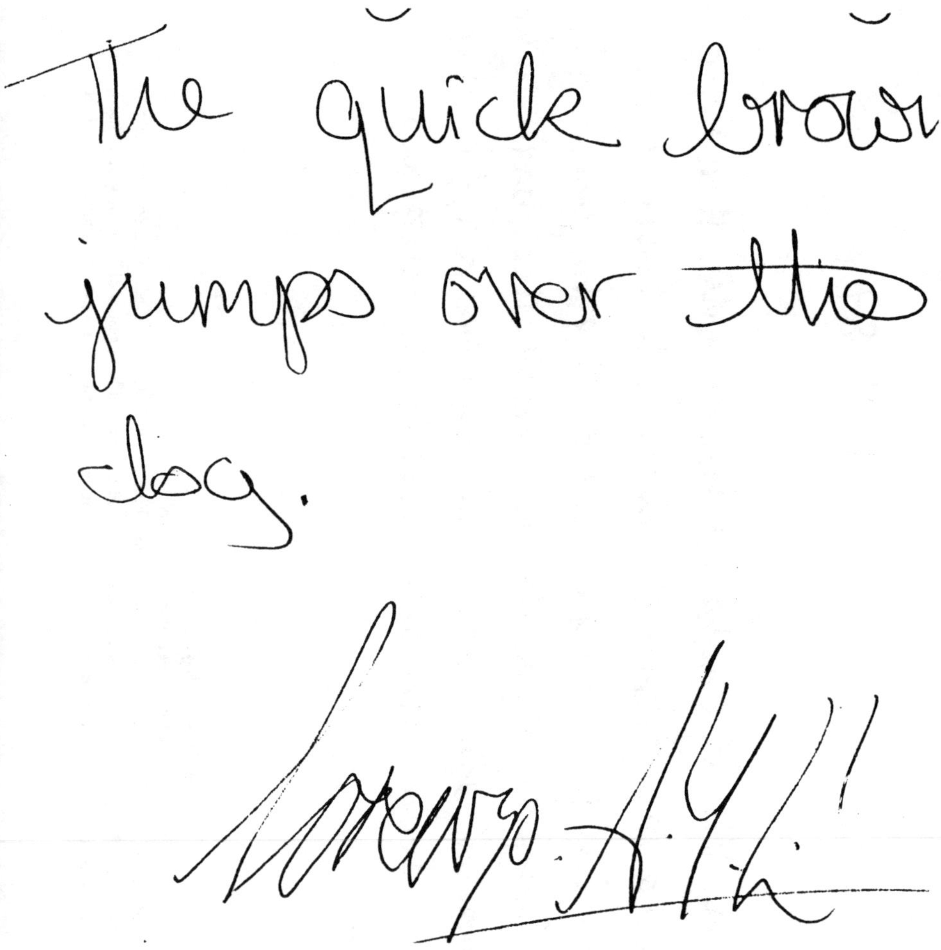

Fig. V.3

Boy, 14 years. Lefthanded.

Black biro on white paper. Pressure: firm.

Stroke: precise, mixed-straight/curved and rapid. Effervescent movement with exuberant dimension and convoluted forms. There are reverse forms, full ovals, angles and arcades with flamboyant regressive movements. The text is evenly and clearly covering the whole page .The signature is larger, narrower, right-slanted and underlined. Not much fear in this young boy's heart. No hesitation or inhibition in affirming himself.

He is "very extrovert. He goes around", say his friends, "everything he tries is superb". He speaks many languages, he is a good salesman, he is a computer genius and he already earns thousands from big companies. "He can do just about anything except sports! " they conclude.

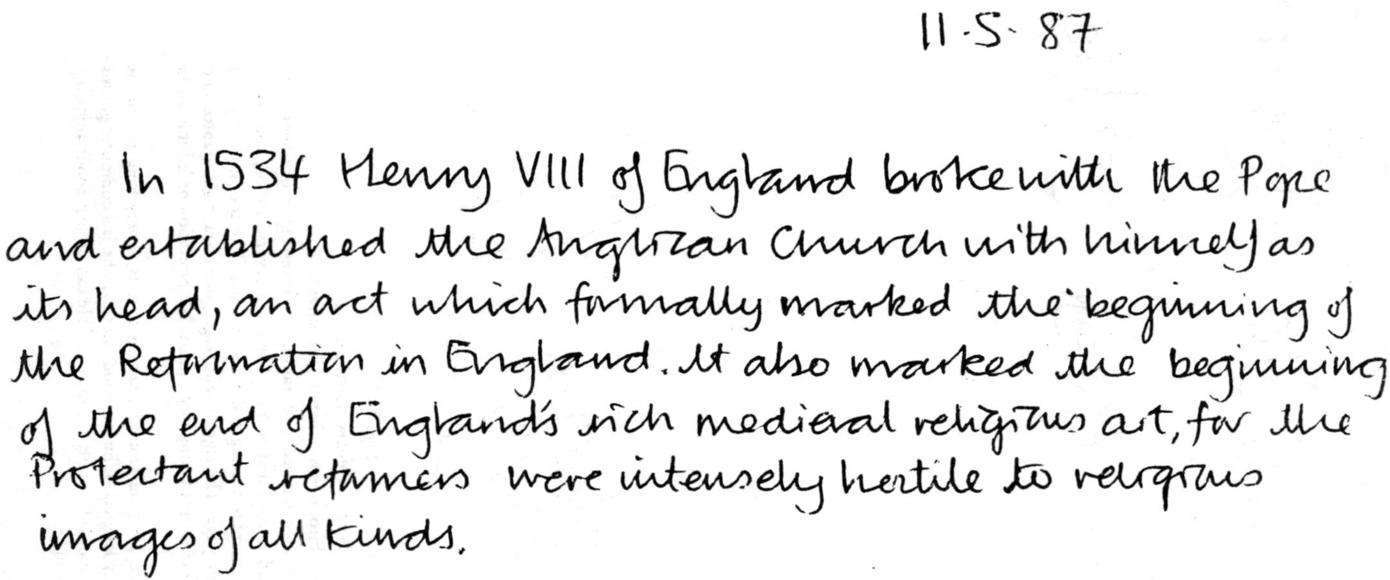

11.5.87

In 1534 Henry VIII of England broke with the Pope and established the Anglican Church with himself as its head, an act which formally marked the beginning of the Reformation in England. It also marked the beginning of the end of England's rich medieval religious art, for the Protestant reformers were intensely hostile to religious images of all kinds.

Fig. V.4 - Boy, 17 years

Black biro on white paper. Pressure: heavy.

Stroke: more or less precise, straight and rather slow, without variation and rather blunt, but well nourished. The compact text is aesthetically situated near the top of an A4 paper. It has a 2.5cm left margin and a 1cm right margin. The script is of italic origin, stylised, neat and moderate. Here the stylisation indicates strong artistic inclination. This boy is not very academic. He went on to art school where he is currently studying.

LECTURE VI

VOCATIONAL GUIDANCE - PROFESSIONAL ORIENTATION

Of all those who consult graphologists, parents and businessmen make up the largest number. The first in order to understand their children, to guide them through the difficult years of youth and to advise them in the choice of a career best suited to their character, talents and vocations. The second seek the advice of graphologists in order to choose the candidate best suited for a specific post.

Vocational choice is of prime importance to both these groups. Graphology treads on delicate ground when entering the area of vocational guidance. It is necessary to get as much information about the writer as possible; both his tastes and his deepest desires. We must not hesitate to ask questions in order to be able to throw light on those corners of the writer's personality which have been covered up or neglected over the years of learning.

When faced with the writing of a young person, we must remember that the interpretations given through conventional graphology apply to adults. Adolescents have not yet found their own personal social identity and may react to the one probably imposed on them by society or by the family.

It is particularly important to play down the Jaminian concept of harmony in young people's writings. The lower the cultural level, the more favourable are the signs of ***homogeneity***, ***simplicity*** and ***sobriety***, since the writing, in the vast majority of cases has not yet acquired fluency. The signature often is not clear and may be constricted, conjured, illegible, complicated, unfinished, uncertain and/or messy. In most cases, where the standard of education and culture of the individual is not high, if the signature is large and stands out, in one way or another, it shows ambition and self-motivation. If the writing is still ***unorganised*** and is also small, modest and unassuming, it may indicate fear, difficulty in self-affirmation, dependency and immaturity.

A young person, whose interest lies in selling, for instance, will sometimes have an "important" signature; by which means he attempts to show that he is 'good with people', thus presenting not only a favourable picture of himself but also of the product he hopes to sell.

On the other hand, when a signature is large, clear and very legible, the candidate may be overly proud of his origins and it is possible that he may be selling himself rather than the product in hand, for which he may even have some contempt. In this case, we should be doubly careful when analysing the handwriting, because, being proud of one's origins does not necessarily mean that one cannot sell well.

Although the concepts of suppleness and rigidity do not allow us to make a valued judgement on the adaptability and degree of evolution of the young writer, they are important in that they allow us to assess the different kinds and ways of adaptation, quick or slow, selective or general. As always in graphology, it is important to take into consideration, the whole writing.

Often, writings of people in their late teens show signs of disintegration, which are natural for that age and indicate uncertainty, self-questioning and apprehension at the thought of responsibility. These are the problems of maturing emotionally. It is extremely difficult to tell how they will be resolved, or, how long it will take and what influence and effect they will have upon the personality of the individual. Yet these teenagers, often intelligent and even fairly well educated, will have to be integrated into society in one role or another. Will they be ready? What choices will they be able to make? As yet, we do not have sufficient knowledge to answer these questions. We cannot tell how these personalities will evolve, or what direction their writing may take. What we do know is obviously based on observations valid in the past. Will these observations still be valid tomorrow? Who can tell? Societies change and so do values. Only the future holds the answers. We, as graphologists, must be careful, conscientious, prudent and vigilant, in order to avoid hasty conclusions which might prejudice graphology.

Let us first examine ***adaptation***.

ADAPTATION

To adapt is not only to submit to the needs and expectations of a group, it is also the ability to have a rapport, a mutual and active collaboration which is beneficial for both parties. Furthermore, adaptation is the objective acceptance of reality.

In the study of adaptability, according to the Swiss graphologist Marcel Meyer, we must consider the following four factors:

(a) the Kretschmerian constitutional typology (pycnic, athletic, leptosome)
(b) the le Sennian characterology
(c) the various types of intelligence
(d) the degree of rigidity of the Ego and of the Superego.

(a) Kretschmer *(see Part 5, Lecture XVII)*

We know that Kretschmerian typology divides people into two main categories: the *cyclothymics* (Jung's extroverts), who are the *pycnics*; and the *schizothymics* (Jung's introverts), who are the *athletics* and the *leptosomes*.

The first are more easily integrated into society, are more realistic and practical and can more easily establish contact. Müller and Enskat's graphic signs of this type are as follows :

> Connected writing, rather large, full, often lightly velvety, garlanded, right slanted, with a rightward direction, often compact, accelerated or rapid and with long finals.

The second (the schizothymics) have difficulty in integrating. They do not establish contact easily, are often stiff, tense, distant, isolated, impractical and their tastes usually run to the theoretical or even metaphysical. The graphic signs are as follows:

> More grouped, with lapses of continuity, thin, neat, regular with abrupt irregularities, angular to filiform, left slanted and aerated or spaced out.

(b) Le Senne

According to Le Sennian characterology(1), it is the *Active Primary* people (*Cholerics* and *Sanguines*) who adapt more easily, and the *non-Active Secondaries* (*Sentimentals* and *Apathetics*) who have the greatest difficulty.

The *Cholerics* and *Sanguines* are ingenious, inclined to be good humoured and, therefore, can more easily solve unexpected situations. They adapt to circumstances with suppleness, grace and willingness. They manage to overcome, or bypass obstacles with practical sense, agility, ingenuity and inventiveness.

The *Sentimentals*, on the contrary, dislike the unexpected, are not very practical and often are full of categorical statements. *Apathetics* can be too anchored in their habits to be able to adapt to new situations very well.

---

(1) R. Nezos, *Graphology, Volume I*, Scriptor Books, London 1992

The supplementary factors of Allocentricity and Egocentricity are also important.

Allocentrism, as we know, is a tendency towards others, an interest in and a need to share in other people's pains and joys. The highest level of Allocentrism is "agape" (love) which was of particular interest to Roda Wieser and is discussed in her book *Persönlichkeit und Handschrift.*

Egocentrism, is essentially, the conservation of the 'beloved Self' and is manifested by irritability, defensiveness against the world, negative attitudes and frequent pangs of jealousy. Any adaptation is only momentary. Egocentric attitudes constantly reassert themselves, making it very difficult for the personality to adapt. Egocentricity has been studied in depth by Emanuel Mounier in his book *Traité du Caractère* (ed. Le Seuil, Paris 1947). (This book has been translated in English by Cynthia Rowland and published by Rockliff of London in 1956 under the title *The Character of Man).*

According to Meyer, the polarity between Mars-Venus is equally important. Mars is a fighter who adapts without weakness, whereas Venus, in an effort to avoid fights, may adapt at any cost. Here, Pulver's interpretation of filiform writing finds all its justification.

(c) Intelligence

We cannot deny, neither can we ignore, the influence of intelligence on the character. According to Piaget: "Intelligence constitutes the state of balance towards which tend all successive adaptations, cognitive and motorsensory, as well as the assimilating and accommodating exchanges between the organism and the environment".

R. Maistriaux[1] distinguishes four different types of intelligence (when it comes to adaptability):

---

(1) Article by Marcel Meyer in *La Graphologie*, No.124, p.25

(1) The ***Verbo-conceptual*** (factor V) which goes beyond the concrete, (connected, homogeneous writing).

(2) The ***Concrete*** intelligence (factor C) which sticks with objective reality, (Signs of Earth).

(3) The ***Generalising*** intelligence (G) which is often abstract, theoretical, speculative and is found mainly in the Emotive Secondary type.

(4) The ***Particularising*** intelligence (P) which sticks to facts, but may be banal, conventional, routine and repetitive of other people's opinions. This kind of intelligence is found mainly in Sanguines (nEAP) or the Amorphous (nEnAP). *(see also Lecture VII)*

(d) The degree of rigidity of the Ego and the role of the Superego

A rigid Self is always an obstacle to adaptability. The Swiss graphologists H. Müller and A. Enskat based their study of adaptability on the degree of rigidity in the writing. This theory was first put forward by R. Pophal.

Pophal's degrees of tension range from 1 to 5, 1 being the predominance of instincts and a lack of inhibition, and 5 being the total inability to adapt. Excessive rigidity in the 4th and 5th degrees comes from extreme tension which is the result of a state of constant alertness. This tension is called "Stress" by the psychiatrists, and is what happens when the organism has to mobilise its defences to face up to threatening situations (Delay).

In these situations the Superego plays an important part. It is intolerant, authoritative and categorical and suffocates the Ego which expresses the concept of reality, resulting in lack of adaptability.

The study of vocational guidance is a branch of personnel selection. In the first, we have the subject (the writer) and we try to match a post (a profession or a skill) to his aptitudes, to discover *where* he (or she) will be most productive, creative, fulfilled and consequently, happy. In the second we have the post and we try to find the subject, to discover *who* will serve it best, having been given the qualities required to fit the post. If we reverse the process, therefore, we can acquire knowledge of the skills necessary for a specific job, and apply it to vocational guidance.

Before we do this, let us look at some additional points which will guide us towards a better solution.

We have discussed ***adaptability, orientation of the Self*** (egocentrism, allocentrism), and ***intelligence*** which are the most commonly required qualities for any job. There are four more which should not be ignored. These are:

(1) Dynamism or lack of it - consisting of:

- Physical and psychic vitality, ability to make an effort; or not.
- Stamina and resistance to tiredness, or lack of energy, fragility.
- Capacity for work; or not.
- Initiative; or not.
- Impulsiveness, regularity and speed; or control, fluctuation of energy, slowness.
- Aptitude to fight; or submission, inertia.

(2) Sociability or lack of it;

- Benevolence or aggression.
- Warmth of personality, co-operativeness, or domineering, critical attitudes, fault finding in people and situations.

- Tendency to seek social contacts and to appreciate other people's company; rather than timidity, isolation, or independence.
- Objectivity or subjectivity.
- Tact, delicacy and diplomacy or social clumsiness.

(3) Will power

- Efficiency and tenacity - or not.
- Leadership qualities, autonomy - or dependence.
- Taste for competition, persistence and decisiveness - or erratic attitudes, versatility, need to be stimulated, indecisiveness.

(4) Morality

- Scale of values
- Ethical or aesthetic values - or not.

Janine Monnot classifies people in two groups: (1) the "*seekers of satisfaction*" which are those who are mainly motivated by factors of efficiency, responsibility, advancement, associated with work; and (2) the "*seekers of status*" which are those who put more importance on environment, discipline, conditions at work and security.

She also stresses that: "Neither the neurotic state of an individual, nor the psychological problems, the conflicts, or the ambivalences, can predetermine professional failure", and further "Some people, in their work, find an equilibrium that they don't find elsewhere; others disturb the group with their behaviour, or they create their own handicaps, when they haven't got enough psychic suppleness or structure".

*

Let us now look at more specific qualities necessary for specific jobs.

SPECIFIC QUALITIES FOR SPECIFIC JOBS

Accountant
Business sense. Common sense. Concentration. Discipline. Discretion. Integrity. Numerical ability. Patience. Planning. Precision. Method.

Art
If a person is talented in any art, the parents, the teachers and/or the subject himself (or herself) will be aware of this. The problem of whether to follow an artistic career or not is a conscious and practical consideration and the best person to advise on this is not a graphologist or a psychologist, so much, as a competent and unprejudiced art critic who will be better able to advise whether the talent is sufficient for the person to take it up as a career or not.

Consultant engineer
Ability to innovate. Activity. Adaptability. Ambition. Authority. Creativity. Independence of thoughts. Ingenuity. Method. Originality of concepts. Perseverance. Sense of organisation. Sense of risk. Strong personality. Team spirit.

Information Technology (computers)
Ability to work alone. Calmness. Concentration. Discipline. Mental agility. Patience. Precision. Reliability.

Journalist
Ability to describe clearly. Courage. Critical mind. Curiosity. Discipline. Good contact. Honesty. Ingenuity. Intelligence. Methodical mind. Perseverance. Scrupulousness. Speed. Synthetic mind. Team spirit.

Legal profession
Authority. Competence. Clarity of mind. Critical ability. Devotion to duty. Diplomacy. Discipline. Good contact at all levels. Integrity. Objectivity.

Personnel management
Ability to listen. Ability to take decisions. Activity. Allocentrism. Authority. Confidence. Diplomacy. Emotional balance. Emotional maturity. Firmness. Impartiality. Logical mind. Memory. Methodical. Practical intelligence. Psychological sense. Sense of organisation. Spirit of enterprise. Talent of observation.

Public relations
Activity. Adaptability. Ambition. Clarity of thinking. Common sense. Competence. Diplomacy. Extroversion. Flexibility. Fluency of communication. Intelligence. Mobility. Practical sense. Sociability. Stamina. Suppleness of behaviour. Tenacity. Width of the field of consciousness.

Sales
Ability to take quick decisions. Ability to synthesize. Audacity. Autonomy. Commercial sense. Curiosity of mind. Enthusiasm. Diplomacy. Imagination. Initiative. Foresight. Methodical mind. Mobility. Morality. Natural activity. Observation. Psychological talents. Sense of organisation. Spirit of competition. Sociability. Taste for responsibilities.

Secretary
Activity. Amiability. Calm. Competence. Conscientiousness. Discipline. Discretion. Efficiency. Energy. Foresight. Initiative. Lack of excessive touchiness to criticism. Lack of excessive inhibitions. Logic. Orderliness. Practical sense. Sense of respect. Sociability. Team spirit. Tolerance. Vivacity of mind. Zeal.

University studies
Academic inclination. Avidity for knowledge. Broadness of the field of consciousness (particularly in the humanities). Curiosity of mind. Intellectual passion. Perseverance. Tenacity.

When we are asked to assess a writing for the purpose of vocational guidance, it is advisable to ask to see the writer himself (or herself) and talk with him. There is nothing wrong with this. It is important to know what he likes or dislikes and his reasons for this, rather than the parents' wishes.

It is better if we assess the writing first, and meet the person afterwards. In this way we avoid any prejudice in our assessments.

GENERAL ADVICE

- Advise parents, and the candidate, to consult a careers centre.

- Propose a range of orientations applicable to the writer, according to his (or her) kind of intelligence, his ability of reflection, his agility, and his general personality (character, temperament, attitudes, etc.). A timid, introvert and inhibited person, for example, would not be happy as an hotel receptionist, or someone very imaginative with a strong sense of fun might be unsuitable as an accountant, etc.
- Finally, always be informed as to the writer's studies and interests.

* * *

SOURCES

BRESARD, S. — *Comment choisir son métier?* Scarabée et Compagnie, Paris, 1983.

CAILLE, Emile — *Intelligences et Ecritures,* Mont-Blanc, Geneva, Switzerland, 1974.

COBBAERT, A.M. — *Graphologie,* Guide Marabout. Bruxelles, 1975.

DESUVIRE, M. — *Étude de l'intelligence,* GGCF 1972-1973.

le GALL, A. — *Caractérologie des enfants et des adolescents,* ed. PUF, Paris, 1973.

La Revue Nos. 123, 124, 164, 165.

PIAGET, J. — *La Psychologie de l'intelligence,* ed. Armaud Cohir, Paris, 1967.

* * *

HANDWRITING SAMPLES of LECTURE VI

Fig. VI.1
Woman, 20 years
Black biro on white paper. Pressure: heavy pasty +/-.

Aerated, disconnected to grouped, rapid with a certain flair, vertical irregular.

Well developed aestheticism - independence, taste, originality. Vocation towards the arts.

☛ Fig. V.1 - see opposite page

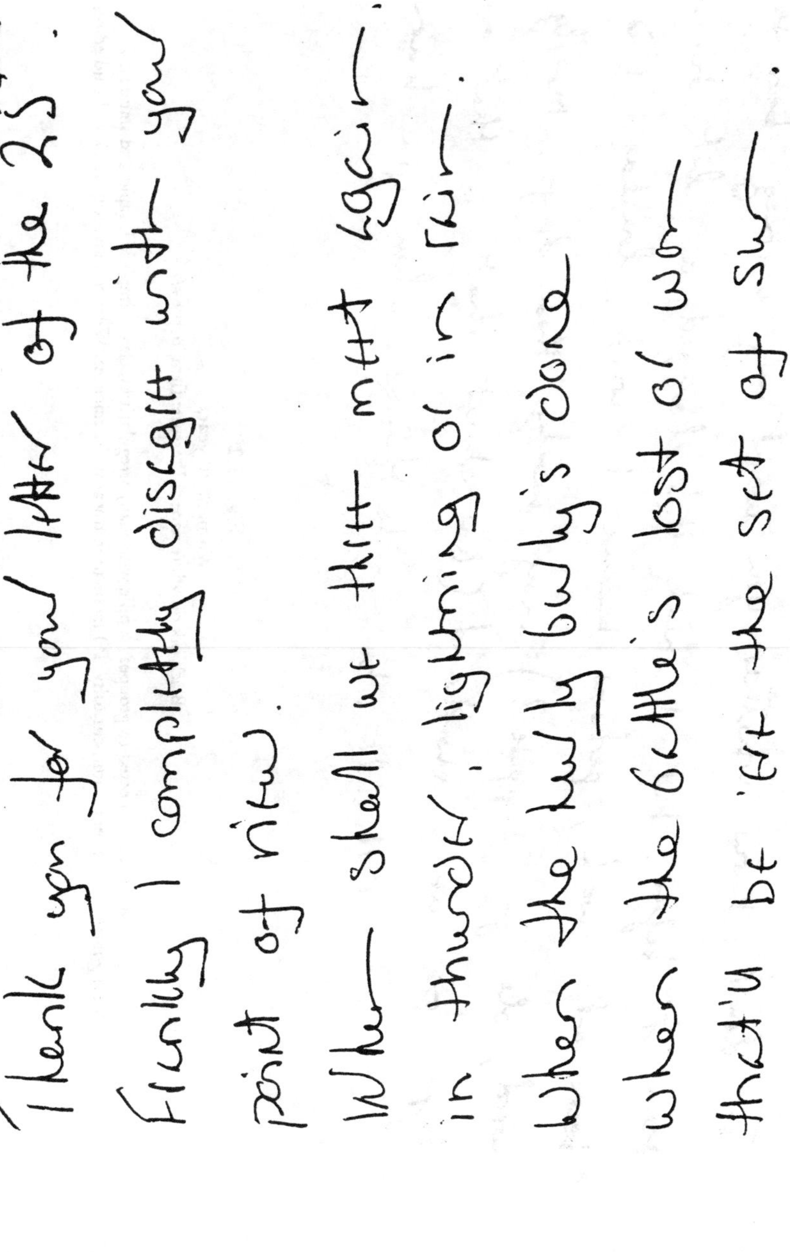
Thank you for your letter of the 25th.
Frankly I completely disagree with your
point of view.
When shall we meet again
in thunder, lightning or in rain.
When the hurly burly's done
when the battle's lost or won
that'll be ere the set of sun.

Fig. VI.1

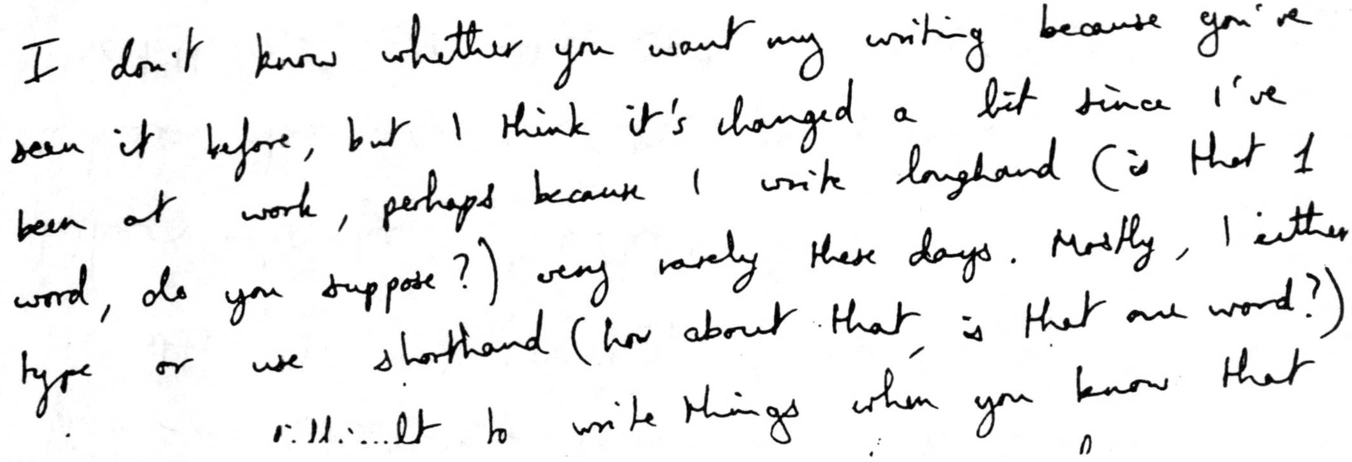

Fig. VI.2
Woman, 20 years
Black ink on white paper. Pressure: firm, pasty +/-

Aerated, connected to grouped, supple with many irregularities, clear, simplified, rapid and sinuous.
Strong intellect, concentration, curiosity (Pi) inclination towards the sciences. Went to university at 17 and studied physics.

LECTURE VII

PERSONNEL SELECTION

Personnel selection is closely linked with vocational guidance. The role of the graphologist is to find, through the writing, the basic direction or inclination of the writer; whether it be to advise in the choice of a career or for a post.

In both cases the diagnosis is oriented towards the fundamental disposition of the personality.

In vocational guidance we are not able to advise for one specific career, among the thousands that exist, but merely to indicate the sort of activity which will give the best chance to the writer to achieve his potential, to be happy and feel fulfilled throughout his working years.

The situation is the same with Personnel Selection. We can only advise whether the candidate's disposition befits the requirements of the specific job (which of course, should be thoroughly explained to the graphologist), or, which one of the possibly many applicants would best fit the post.

The only difference between the two situations is the angle from which they are viewed. In the first case we ask, which job suits the writer, in the second, which writer suits the job? The graphologist's work is similar only the wording of the report differs.

TYPES OF VOCATION

There are classifications of groups of activities or groups of job specifications which help in the assessment of suitability of a person to a job and vice versa.

G. Beauchataud, in her book *Learn Graphologie*[1]. refers to the classification of human vocations made by Dougalls and Watts, as deriving from the three primordial 'instincts' :

(1) The hunter
(2) The shepherd
(3) The farmer (cultivator)

and Fontague's classification which distinguishes between the three "handlers"

(1) The handler of ideas
(2) The handler of men
(3) The handler of things

"because each one of the three main groups of these classifications corresponds to one category of intelligence and to preferential interests that the graphologist has to recognise in the handwriting".

There is an overlap between the categories in the two classifications.

The hunter is today's man of ideas. As prehistoric man was neither fast enough nor strong enough to overpower animals, he had to develop skill and cunning in order to feed himself and his family. Hunting, from the beginning, has been the strongest stimulus to intellectual development.

The skills of the *shepherd* are seen today in all professions of a social character; medicine, commerce, antique dealing,

(1) *Learn Graphology in fiften lessons*, Scriptor Books, London 1988.

education, personnel management, marketing, politics, the armed forces, etc.

The farmer who cultivated the earth, is the ancestor of today's industrial technician and also of today's artist, whose mind is less inclined towards theorising and risk taking and is more at home with the "matter" of any form.

These 'preferential affinities' are guided by the various forms of intelligence.

We know that the concept of intelligence is extremely complex and difficult to define. We also know that there are many kinds of intelligence which can be measured by various modern tests.

TYPES OF INTELLIGENCE

1. Conceptual, abstract, or speculative intelligence

This deals with abstract thought, mostly with concepts which are made of symbols, numbers, words, signs. The use of abstract concepts and reasoning gives a person the ability to face complex situations, and is generally considered a factor of high intelligence. The danger here is that this form of intelligence can sometimes set into a rigid pattern of thinking, becoming pedantic and thereby running the risk of losing contact with the nuances of reality. The person of such intelligence cannot easily synthesize ideas or make deductions from new or unfamiliar concepts.

2. Practical intelligence

This is expressed in action through spontaneity and the ability to find ways to make up or compensate for the deficiencies of reality. This intelligence accumulates images and retains the memory of forms and objects. It is therefore a concrete intelligence, with mechanical comprehension, deductive reasoning, ingenuity in manual work and good co-ordination.

3. Social intelligence

This involves :

- a sensitivity towards affective nuances
- an understanding of people's motivations
- the capacity to put oneself in the position of others and to understand their feelings, emotions and possible reactions
- adequate self-control to contain impulsive behaviour in order to avoid brutal or painful reactions from others
- tact which allows word control in order not to offend and which attracts sympathy
- self-assurance, for easier communication with others, as opposed to inhibition which hinders communication
- suppleness
- altruism, which is "a feeling of human solidarity" and active compassion.

This last intelligence can take two forms :

a) *The diplomat's*, which is manifested by a courteous attitude, with apparent understanding of and respect for others, without however making any concessions or jeopardising the interests he represents and must defend

b) *The leader's* where will power must be evident without, however, reaching hardness or ruthlessness, thus provoking scorn among his subordinates. A truly good leader of men knows how to make himself liked and respected at the same time.

DIMENSIONS OF INTELLIGENCE

Intelligence has also three dimensions (Thorndike), as follows :

1) *Speed* -
   there is rapid intelligence - and there is slow intelligence

2) *Depth* -
   the capacity to solve difficult problems when most people fail

3) *Extension* -
   the capacity to solve the largest number of varied problems.

However, there are many aspects of intelligence, some of which have developed through education, others through talent, or the capacity for reflection, etc. which often will fail dramatically in the face of trivial problems.

For graphology, the concept of "depth of intelligence" equates generally with Le Senne's "narrow field of consciousness", and extension with a "broad field of consciousness".

THE INTELLECTUAL PROCESS

This is comprised of various stages :

1) *Comprehension* - which is the ability to connect 'something' to an idea and to its cause and effect.

2) *Reasoning* - which is the thought process; the logical chain of all relevant thoughts and judgements leading to a correct conclusion.

3) *Imagination* - which is the ability to "see" images; to make new combinations and hence to create.

WILL POWER

But intelligence alone, whatever its kind, will not be of much use and will achieve little unless it is allied to will power, which, as we know, is the ability to realise one's concepts or intentions.

A voluntary action, preceded by a determining idea, presupposes reflection (intelligence) and commitment (responsibility). Behaviour which does not refer to these criteria (impulsive behaviour) is not connected to will power.

We have learned that 'will' has four stages :

1) The conception of an action
2) The deliberation
3) The decision
4) The execution

The fulfilled action is the only proof of 'will'.

For the psychoanalyst, the majority of our actions are determined unconsciously and 'will' is the expression of the whole personality, the unconscious motivations as well as education.

Will for power/self-control

The graphologist need not worry about the origins of 'will', but needs to know that it is dependent on two forces of which one is 'exciting' and the other 'inhibiting'. The first is the 'will' for power which aims at satisfaction and domination, the second is self control which helps in resisting the primitive impulse in order to achieve the set goal better.

The interaction of these two forces is expressed in the writing by the tension of the stroke.

Categories of people

There are 3 broad categories of people :

1) *The passive* : who are the vast majority, and live by adapting to the circumstances.
2) *The dynamic* : who want authority or efficiency. The first are motivated by the ambition for power and the second by the desire to achieve or to make wealth.
3) *The idealists* : who aim high in the field of morality, whether social or religious, and who manage to lift themselves above the social conventions.

MORAL IMPERATIVES

Morality is another important factor to consider in the professional life.

The most important moral imperatives are :

1) Respect for property,
2) Respect for truth, and
3) Respect for honour (responsibility and professional conscience).

These involve intelligence and will power.

Signs of insincerity

There is no one special sign indicating honesty or dishonesty. The following lists of Pulver's "signs of insincerity" are a group of signs which will point towards possible deviations from good behaviour.

1. ***In a slow writing*** (not caused by mechanical or pathological influences) :

   - Artificial or fabricated or drawn (designed) writing
   - Covering strokes
   - Supported connections
   - Arcades; either within words or as a final stroke returning leftwards
   - Spirals, complications, double-joined ovals, bows
   - Fragmented letters in 2 or more parts, disconnected lower extensions
   - Missing letters
   - Reversed movements, ovals open or closed underneath, accentuated leftward tendency in capitals and final strokes
   - Ambiguous forms of letters, one letter for another

2. ***In a writing which is more or less free flowing*** :

   - Threadiness in the middle of words
   - Strong diminishing tendency
   - Undulating lines
   - Confused writing, imprecise, ambiguous forms
   - Different styles of letters for the same letter (mixing of alphabets)
   - Difference between text and signature
   - All exaggerations - Discordances of pressure
   - General discordances (Crépieux-Jamin)

At least four of the above signs in either group should be simultaneously present in the writing before we can deduce that the writer may be insincere, or likely to commit an immoral action.

When a writing shows signs of clarity of thinking, will power and sociability we can generally deduce good morality. If, on the other hand, a writing shows signs of *faulty judgement* (confusion, tangling, lack of rhythm), *lack of will* (weak, disorderly, formless), *lack of truthfulness* (spirals, double-joined ovals, ambiguous forms), and/or *social inadaptability* (aggressive, impulsive movements, discordances, exaggerations), we must be extremely careful before we call the writer "honest" or "dishonest", or likely to commit an immoral action.

MAIN PROFESSIONAL ORIENTATIONS

In industry today, there are many professional groups and orientations. We could probably divide them into 3 main categories :

1) Administrative orientation
2) Technical dominance
3) Relational or commercial dominance.

In a small business, one person will often be required to have a more general ability, probably incorporating all three of the above activities.

In big business, the activities are more clearly allocated. Each activity becomes a specialisation.

The "big chief", or head of a large organisation - be it technical, administrative, political or commercial, should be able to 'govern'. To do this he must have the relevant qualities, such as :

on a general level:

- good vitality
- will power
- mental energy
- nervous resistance
- combativity
- initiative
- intuition

in the intellectual sphere:

- understanding
- good reasoning
- good organisational ability
- logic
- method
- broadness of the field of consciousness

- prudence
- emotional maturity
- experience of life
- ability to command, which involves:
  - self confidence
  - clarity of mind
  - good elocution
  - self control
  - influence
- speed of thought and of decision
- a sense of relativity, which is the ability to distinguish the essential or the urgent without disregarding the details.

on a moral level:

- sense of responsibility
- professional conscience
- spirit of justice
- frankness
- humanitarian feeling
- sense of the general interest.

in the social sphere:

- sufficient extroversion
- emotional equilibrium
- sociability
- diplomacy
- firmness

Very few people possess all of these qualities. The majority of people at the head of big organisations, politics, etc., do lack some of these qualities.

The graphologist must try to distinguish the person who has the greatest number of these qualities and advise the client on the best possible way of handling the newcomer according to his, or her, shortcomings and strengths.

Every job has different requirements and it is only through close collaboration with the employer that the graphologist can appreciate the exact nature of each particular post.

For recruitment in jobs with a technical slant, except for the human qualities which are desirable in any domain of employment, each speciality has its particular need.

For instance, ***a civil engineer*** would need, according to the speciality of the post, to have :

- abstract intelligence
- practical intelligence
- imagination
- inventiveness
- curiosity of mind and a taste for experimentation
- co-operative spirit, since he will need to have to adapt to the client's requirements, modifying plans or blueprints accordingly, and make constructive suggestions.

The construction and maintenance engineer, over and above his specialised knowledge, will need :

- concrete intelligence
- practical sense
- will power
- sense of observation
- ability to command
- orderliness
- initiative
- firmness of attitude
- honesty

The director of commerce needs not only to boost production but also to sell profitably. He needs to constantly update the production programme according to the current economic situation, to foresee the fluctuations of the market, to succeed in the face of competition, to organise distribution, as well as to inspire confidence in clients. He would need :

- ability to assimilate quickly
- good stamina for work
- good nervous equilibrium to overcome difficulties and disappointments
- easy contact
ability to negotiate
- readiness to be available when needed

- dynamism
- combativity
- authority
- sense of responsibility
- and the desire to win

The marketing manager whose job involves collecting information on the market for a new product, studying the chances of development, improving an existing product, or introducing a new one, and who, generally, leading a group of marketing researchers, needs to have :

- initiative
- dynamism
- a sense for seeing opportunities
- a taste for contact
- detachment and availability
- and a good ability for team work

The advertising manager must be able to organise and conduct publicity campaigns, to put together and process all the information from the marketing department, to create all the necessary documentation for the promotion of sales, to deal with the negotiations with various agents and to decide on the budget. For this he needs :

- imagination
- dynamism
- realism
- sense of organisation
- occasionally, also aesthetic sense
- drive
- vigour

The salesman's foremost quality should be persuasiveness. He should be convinced of the superiority of the product he sells in order to be able to convince others. Too critical a mind is a handicap for a salesman. His best qualities are :

- patience
- tolerance
- intuition
- unargumentativeness
- tenacity
- verbal imagination
- verbal fluency
- even-temperedness
- self confidence
- psychological sense

In the field of administration, which is as large as the commercial field, the manager who does not look after the clients directly, but who needs to keep the stock in order and always up to date, needs to have :

- order
- method
- sense of organisation
- sense of service
- sociability
- and the ability to estimate in anticipation

The agent should have a stronger personality than the salesman, he should be able to push doors open. He does not receive the client, he is received, and should know how to make himself presentable and agreeable. He is an active 'achiever' and therefore should be :

- dynamic
- observant
- cordial
- enthusiastic
- convincing

- not touchy
- mobile
- articulate
- and resistant to tiredness

There is, of course, a distinction in the level of general education and 'worldliness' (tact and social agility) between the representative of a small business and one of a large organisation or conglomerate.

The tourist industry involves many skills; from the travel agent to the staff of a hotel (from receptionist to manager), from the marketing manager to the salesman. Requirements vary accordingly. In general, the qualities they need are:

- to be
  - obliging
  - always available
  - enthusiastic
  - dynamic
  - devoted
  - imaginative
- to have
  - psychological sense
  - excellent contact with people
  - the ability to motivate others
  - the ability to sell.

The accountant who needs to register meticulously financial operations according to the precise requirements of the company, to prepare budget forecasts, to analyse the results, and to advise on all the financial matters of the organisation, on top of his special professional skills, needs to have:

- attention to detail
- order
- precision
- method

- care
- concrete intelligence
- speculative intelligence
- analytical and synthetic mind
- ability for abstraction
- ability to anticipate
- a sense of opportunity
- creativity
- adaptability
- patience
- and above all: discretion, tact and diplomacy

In the secretarial world what is needed most is efficiency, order, punctuality, neatness, sedentariness, good social behaviour, lack of excessive dynamism and lack of intrigue.

Ideally, their writing should show :

- a clear mind
- rapid thinking
- sense of organisation
- some dynamism
- initiative
- sense of justice
- even temper
- and good professional conscience

In the social services (including ***nursing***), where the applicants will need to have a lot of altruism as well as routine administrative skills, the writing should show :

- devotion
- amiability
- patience
- clarity of mind
- perseverance
- professional conscience

- calm
- regularity in their work
- efficiency
- and adaptability.

The analyst, whose job is to untangle complicated problems into their simpler elements, to establish their hierarchic value and the relation between them and then to report in a simple and clear way, needs to have :

- abstract intelligence
- analytical mind
- reasoning
- understanding
- sense of simplification
- creativity
- method
- anticipation
- capacity for contact

The computer programmer, who will need to translate the machine's jargon into a comprehensible language and vice versa will need, on top of his/her special relevant skills, to have :

- the ability to concentrate
- order
- method
- a logical mind
- precision
- a sense of continuity
- and great patience.

We have covered most - the more common - orientations of work. But we should remember that in modern business what counts most is the human factor since man is not only the one who creates the product, but also the one who consumes it.

CONDITIONS PROMOTING HARMONY AT WORK

All ways of studying man are good provided they aim to help him find pleasure, harmony and fulfilment in his work.

Research done recently among 5,000 workers showed that, in order to be happy in his work, man needs 8 conditions : -

1) Good health
2) To do a job he likes
3) To feel he is more productive than others
4) To consider his work well rewarded
5) To feel surrounded by a friendly atmosphere
6) To feel appreciated and respected by his superiors
7) Not to have family problems occupying his mind during working hours
8) To have enough recreation and distraction, or hobbies, to recharge his energy.

As a result of these we are likely to see higher productivity, better quality, higher returns, more success and more smiles all round. It makes sense; look after the morale of your employees and you are well on the way to success.

THE REPORT

On compiling a report for personnel recruitment, the first and most important rule is that we make no judgements. We simply point out the relevant qualities or faults we believe we see in the writing, and no more. The fact that we are graphologists does not qualify us to judge. Nothing gives us the right to judge people from their handwriting. Judging is subjective. As in every judgement there is a prejudice involved. For example, if we take the Formlevel, - which is one of the biggest pitfalls for most graphologists - we can go horribly wrong in the case of a computer analyst. The writing may be gross, slow, inhibited, without dynamism, originality or spontaneity, but none of these are relevant to his job. We are trying to keep graphology scientific and therefore objective. Others may, and will, and do, judge us. We shall not, because we have the obligation to use our knowledge responsibly. We analyse *only* and *try* to understand.

In the case of more than one qualifying applicant we must leave the final choice to the employer. He should be able to choose if the portrait is explicit and simple enough. Only if specifically asked, may we try to grade the applications according to certain very specific requirements of the post, as explained to us by our client.

Another rule is to avoid comparisons between applicants, unless asked to do so. The interviewer himself can do this better than we can with the help of the curriculum vitae, the physical presence of the candidate, the better knowledge of his office requirements and environment, and with the help of our report - in that order.

HONESTY

Honesty is one of the first personality traits employers ask about when they send a candidate's writing for analysis and 95 out of 100 times, it is one of the traits to which we can give no clear-cut answer.

Most of the time, when an employer asks "Is the candidate honest or not?", he doesn't mean "is he a saint or does he belong to the criminal fraternity?". What he is asking is whether the person's standards fall within generally accepted norms and no more.

Plenty of articles and chapters have been written about dishonesty and the many different ways it appears in handwriting. Very little indeed has been written about *honesty*.

It is easy to enumerate, yet again, the signs of insincerity. The danger is that this presupposes that all writings which do not have these signs are honest. This should be wrong (theory of the negative sign). Honesty should have its own signs and should not depend only on the absence of the negative ones. But despite the fact that through progress and civilisation, honesty has become positively a "quality" and is no longer a "natural state", it still remains the natural state of being and therefore not an *element* we can see in the writing.

We have learned that adult honesty is a conscious moral quality. It presupposes respect for self and others. It involves courage (to admit to a mistake), self-assurance and confidence (not to feel unbearably humiliated to admit to a mistake). It also involves pride (the right kind - not arrogance), will power and general strength and firmness of character. It is not easy to keep to one's moral values if everyone else's standards drop.

So when in a writing we see :

- respect for self and others (clarity, sobriety, limpidity)
- self-assurance and self-confidence (spontaneity, tension, rhythm)
- courage (firmness in the direction of the stroke, stability, consistency)
- pride (proportion, simplicity, some aesthetic super-elevations in a high FL)
- and strength of character (firmness, precision, dynamism and high FL)

should we assume the resultant, honesty? No. We should assume though, high moral values and hence, probably, honesty.

It is not always the best writings graphologically which correspond to the best prepared candidates for a specific job. In the case of many people applying for the same job, the first choice is made by the employer himself from the information given by the candidate about his necessary practical skills and experience, and in his C.V.

In some cases it is enough to investigate the intellectual, moral or physical ability of the applicant, particularly when it concerns administrative posts. In other cases, where special skills are necessary, such as manual dexterity or physical strength, graphology cannot help much, especially if the applicant does not have enough graphic agility, as is very often the case.

*

The following is a list - in alphabetical order - of 40 basic personality elements relevant to recruitment with a brief explanation and a simplified guide on how they appear, on average, in the handwriting.

40 PERSONALITY ELEMENTS TO OBSERVE IN THE WRITING (in alphabetical order)

1. Activity

Activity is a constitutional element which is not related to stamina or to professional attitude. A person can have good energy (or stamina) and still be non-active or need outside motivation. Activity motivated by the Superego (conscientiousness, scruples or guilt) is not necessarily constitutional activity, but it is an excellent substitute, which can work as well as the real thing.

Activity can be seen in many ways in a writing depending on the cultural level and temperament of the writer and on the kind of activity (cerebral, physical or sexual). Good contact with the paper, dynamic writing, confidence in the forms and their structure (not necessarily well-structured), firmness or tension of the stroke and a natural, spontaneous outlook, are on average a good indication. Often sharp-pointed endings, long lower and/or upper extensions firmly drawn. A certain strength emanates from the writing (a poised or even a slow writing is not necessarily non-active).

2. Adaptability

Is *adaptability* cerebral, social or emotional? *Social adaptability* is the best, because it often incorporates the other two. Is it superficial or selective?

Garlands represent *adaptability* much more than angles. Supple movements with a stroke which is neither too precise nor too pasty. Not many signs of regressive tendencies, nor very egocentric writing. Very often it will be a Venus or Jupiter writing, sometimes Mercury too.

3. Ambition

If the person is *ambitious*, ask what sort of *ambition* he has. Is it ambition for status, money or social position?

The writing is usually tall, with strong colour, large, taut, has a vertical axis, with a strong signature.

4. Clarity of Mind

Is the writing clear, or muddled which indicates a messy way of thinking?

Neat, limpid writing with good spacing, aerated or well spaced, good organisation, legibility and orderliness, usually show clarity of mind and judgement. It can be stylised or mannered.

5. Communication

Is the *communication* free, relaxed, sophisticated and professional? Is it superficial or spontaneous. Is there no communication at all?

The writing should be velvety, right-slanted, connected or grouped. It may be compact or aerated, round or rounded. In angular or narrow writings communication is not always evident.

6. Conformism

It can be productive or sterile. Does he *conform*? Is he patient? Is he independent? Usually these people are conventional, but can be good communicators and are often courageous, brave souls.

Signs of Venus writing, copybook or other conventional styles indicate conformist attitudes.

7. Conscientiousness (Superego)

Is a person meticulous? Does he care about other people's response? In his work is he scrupulous, respectful?

Look for all the signs of a strong Superego.

8. Consistency in Action

It can be dynamic or passive - such as regularity out of habit or out of conscientiousness.

In a dynamic writing consistency is seen in the firmness of the stroke and the movement all the way through the document A vertical axis is more indicative of consistency in action than a horizontal axis. The writing is connected or grouped with rather regular slant.

Passive consistency is indicated by conventional, often cylindrical writings, with a good stroke, stable baseline, regularity of slant. Hegar's 'straight' rather than 'curved', often often with letters close together, narrow rather than spread out. (Saturn rather than Moon).

9. Diplomacy

Consists in mental agility and self-control rather than evasiveness or lying. It is found more often in higher socio-cultural levels. A good educa-tional background creates clarity and broadness of vision, necessary for diplomacy in business, in politics or simply in everyday life.

In the writing it is seen in agile forms, combina-tions, good continuity (grouped or connected), garlands or supple angles. The size can be medium, large or small, (neither 'very large' nor 'very small') the speed may vary from poised to precipitated and the stroke is velvety at its best, but it can be thin if the writing is small. Gentle filiformity - or tendency towards it - without losing legibility is often attributed to diplomacy. Venus, Jupiter, Moon and Mercury are more diplomatic than the other types.

10. Decision Taking

Is the writer able to take independent decisions quickly and correctly and can he stick to them?

Look for firm strokes, angles and a vertical axis more than curves or a horizontal axis; Sun, Mars, Saturn and Earth signs and sometimes Venus too. The writing will have a progressive tendency, with good tension.

11. Discretion

Is the writer discreet, or secretive?

Usually when the writing is spontaneously sober, poised or controlled, with firm strokes and rather closed ovals (though not necessarily), the writer is more likely to be discreet. Secretivity may be seen more in double-joined ovals (though these may also show indiscretion when present in a bubbly, effervescent writing), filiformity in the middle of words, ambiguity of forms with ovals closed underneath, light pressure and covering strokes in the middle zone only.

In a precipitated, light writing, long, thin *t*-bars may also indicate indiscretion.

12. Dryness

A person with a dry personality can be effective and quite creative, but shows little warmth in human exchange, is inclined to irony or sarcasm, with a '*dry*' sense of humour.

The writing usually has a thin stroke, is narrow or angular, diminishing, sharp-pointed, has a clear and rapid tension with light or medium contact.

13. Emotivity

Is the emotivity crippling? Does it affect the individual's performance at work? Is it productively channelled? Does it create perception or retrospection?

All small irregularities in any category indicate emotivity. If it is crippling the stroke loses its vivacity, it becomes dull or "blind" and a monotonous picture may be created. If the emotivity is vibrant and enriching then the rhythm is enhanced and small irregularities are more evident.

Writings with pronounced irregularities may indicate less strong emotivity, such as nEnAS, nEnAP writings.

14. Energy (Stamina, Vitality) (Jung's Libido)

This is the general energy of the individual, but is it usefully and productively channelled?

Energy is seen through the pressure and the stroke, good contact with the paper, solid, consistent and strong, with progressive forms. Speed must also be considered.

15. Extroversion

"Bubbly" writing. Signs of the Sanguine temperament, full curves, large, animated, often with a pasty stroke, fairly open.

16. Flair

Social confidence and a relaxed exchange. It shows imagination.

The writing has spontaneous movements, good continuity, flow, freedom, rhythm and panache (flair). If the movements are mannered, there may still be flair, but it may be acquired.

17. Imagination

Whenever there are curves there is imagination. Relief, fullness, loops, balloons, a good inky stroke on the curves. Spindles and all those forms that have a 'curvy', hopping movement as well as/or rhythm.

18. Impatience

Spontaneous, aggressive final strokes, sharp-pointed, taut writing, with angles and precipitations.

19. Independence

Is the writer mature enough to be independent?

Sun, Mars and Saturn writings with a wide left margin, aerated or spread-out, vertical slant and axis, show more independence. On the other hand the writer may lack independence and feel quite comfortable in the state of dependence. Venus and Moon signs will indicate more dependence or attachments, (to family, the organisation the person works for, the Establishment or past values and traditions). Narrow left margin, strong right slant, curves, light pressure and weak tension.

20. Initiative

Is the writer able to take initiative of his own free will and act on it?

Look for a writing with a rather progressive tendency (any slant), firmness and good ventilation. It may be obstructed or reared, propulsive or effervescent, static or flowing (seldom floating). Supple, firm, taut or rigid tension may all indicate good initiative; slack tension more rarely.

21. Intellectuality

By intellectuality is meant that the writer has pronounced intellectual proclivities, which does not always mean high I.Q. but rather that he/she is more given to mental or intellectual pursuits than the average person.

Usually a small, angular or mixed writing with a precise stroke, often prolonged upwards, but not necessarily, combined and aerated, rapid, often diminishing and agile. It may also be compact and anal, or fine and distinguished.

22. Intelligence

IQ cannot be seen in a writing. There are no set signs for intelligence.

It is only the quality of intelligence than one should point out. Does the writer have: ***particularising, generalising, analytical*** or ***synthetical*** intelligence? Does he have deductive ability and/or ability to concentrate? Is his mind agile and/or penetrating?

Practical and *generalising* intelligence is the analytical intelligence, seen in combined, sober writings, spontaneous, progressive and simpli-fied. Often Susan Bresard's "instinctive organised" writings show a supple, clear and orderly mind.

Particularising intelligence is concrete thinking which deals more in depth with a specific subject. The writing is smaller, usually with a dry stroke and connected. It can be compact, slower and more regular than the previous one.

Agility of mind is seen in the spontaneous and agile change of direction of stroke from clockwise to anticlockwise, combinations and general suppleness of forms in a flowing movement. *A penetrating, curious, inquisitive and critical mind* is seen in rather small, agile movements, with angles or narrow garlands, precise stroke or sharp-pointed endings and syllabic groupings.

Receptive, perceptive - a more "socially" agile intelligence is seen in writings with a dominance of horizontal axis, rapid and often filiform, progressive, round or full, with a slightly pasty stroke (Hegar) or velvety.

Of course, one must always remember that there are no special signs in writings of *geniuses.* It often happens that a very strong mind hinders emotional development, in which case the writing is unorganised, with many childish components, in form, pressure, continuity and speed. (see *Fig. IV.5 - p.114* - man 33 years, with a genius for chemistry).

23. Intuition

This should not to be confused with receptivity which does not necessarily help understanding. Openness to learning and empathy with others is not intuition either.

Intuition consists mainly in knowing when something is right or not, without much mental deliberation. This comes from accumulated knowledge and experience long forgotten.

Does the writer allow his intuition to guide him?

It is usually seen in light and irregular writings with rather a thin, often precise stroke, many open forms, simplified upper prolongments (aerials), often hopping, animated and with a lively rhythm. Mercury, Sun, Moon show intuition. Also some Venus writings with sensitive irregularities may often show strong intuition.

24. Judgement

Is the judgement objective or is it influenced by the writer's emotions, therefore partial or biased? Egocentricity and selfishness can make judgement subjective.

Good judgement can be seen in a clear and firm writing, vertical, and often grouped with good proportions, usually small or medium with subtle superelevations, sober and harmonious (see also **Clarity**).

25. Loyalty

Loyalty is usually the Superego. (It is also the lower loops which close up high inside the middle zone or on the baseline). Good continuity, sober writing, without tremendous variations and flippancy. A more stable and consistent writing with a rather strong Superego (conventional writing).

26. Motivation

The writing is energetic, dynamic or vibrant , with a good quality stroke, good contact with the paper, robust, consistent and spontaneous, without many signs of constraint or inhibition.

27. Objectivity - see: Judgement

28. Orderliness or Organisation

Orderliness of thinking and organisation in life. The writer may have a compartmentalising mind or not.

Good level of organisation and layout; margins and inner spacing are correctly and naturally consistently well kept. The writing is clear with good tension of the stroke. The forms are not necessarily always simplified, but they are clear and sober with consistent direction. Usually Earth and Sun signs show order and good organisation. (see also **Practicality**)

29. Originality

Is the person original? Does he have a constructive originality? Is the originality aesthetic as well, or is it just in the ideas?

Spontaneously original forms far removed from copybook styles. Combined and often rhythmic, with irregularities and small aesthetic disproportions.

30. Patience

Patience incorporates tolerance and good sense. It can be placidity, in which case the writing should be Type II of Hegar. Otherwise patience can be seen in rhythmic, supple writings, limpid, nuancée and distinguished. Also in sublimated or taut writings with an introvert stroke (defended), with controlled movement - more S than P of Le Senne, (but P is not excluded). Calm, harmonious and conformist writings can also show patience.

31. Practicality

Good practical sense is mainly seen in signs of Earth: straight baseline, consistent stroke without much variability, a fair size, without exaggerations. It can be diminishing: shows solid contact with the paper, with good legibility without illogical linking.

32. Receptivity

It can be emotional or intellectual; e.g. Venus has emotional receptivity; Mercury more intellectual.

This can be seen in supple writing, with garlands, open 'cups' and a velvety stroke.

33. Reliability

Is comprised of honesty, efficiency and punctuality. Can the person be trusted to perform his/her duty?

The writing will be consistent, without many irregularities. Stable, with a good stroke and pressure, good clarity and ventilation, spontaneity and constancy. Conventional writings usually show reliability.

34. Sensitivity (Emotivity)

Sensitivity starts from receptivity and can reach touchiness and susceptibility.

Sensitivity can be seen in a writing which is light, with nuancée irregularities in the stroke and the forms. The movement is usually vibrant, but it can be calmer as well as dynamic. The stroke is rather more velvety or nourished than pasty or dry, but it can be thin and precise (in introversion). All contained irregularities indicate a responsive sensitivity. Narrowness of letters, angles and inhibitions may show the touchiness of excessive non-active emotivity.

35. Sensuality

Sensuality is seen in the stroke, good contact with the paper and good size. The stroke is rich, with full loops, often aesthetic forms on a good level, but can be vulgar or crude.

36. Stability

Stability presupposes a certain strength which may be passive (strong Superego, conventionality) or active (despite negative circumstances).

In the first instance the writing is conventional, harmonious, cadenced rather than rhythmic, with a firm and consistent stroke with a certain regularity of slant and spacing, and a stable baseline, though it may be supple. The writing may be rigid or stylised and immobile.

In the second instance the writing is taut and rhythmic rather than cadenced, connected to grouped and combined. It may have amendments and corrections. The stroke has a firm contact with the paper. The movement may be obstructed or dynamic and animated, but constant. (see also **Consistency**)

37. Sociability

Sociability is seen mostly in writings with a dominance of the horizontal axis, curves, filiformity and a flowing movement with progressive forms, a right slant and a velvety stroke. The right side of St. Morand's chart (particularly Venus) is more sociable than the vertical or the left side.

38. Tenacity

Does the writer have the ability to follow through? To achieve goals?

A firm stroke, or taut, robust writing, consistent and determined t-bars and movement, as well as good contact with the paper and fair regularity in certain categories such as Form and Layout, will indicate tenacity.

39. Unreliability

It is wise to try to establish the cause of it.

Generally unreliability is seen in a weak or slack writing with imprecise forms, usually light, round or wide; also in very agitated and unstable writings with either a left or vertical slant, negligent, carried away with light, thin and long t-bars, bizarre or sloppy forms, filiform with mingling letters and inadequate spacing.

40. Will Power

Will power can be conformist or not and may also extend to obstinacy.

Will power is seen in firm or taut writings, with good colour, good ventilation, and straight downstrokes. *T*-bars are firm, strong and not too long or short, though they may be sharp-pointed. The t-stem is straight, vertical and affirmed. The stroke has relief, the margins and inner distribution are good. Usually Bilious, Sun, Earth, Saturn writings show strong will power.

Obstinacy is usually seen in strong diagonal starting strokes, sharp-pointed and long finals in a rather regular, rigid or robust writing.

*

In conclusion, it is equally as useful to know what pitfalls to avoid as it is to know what to include, therefore ..... :

- do not refer to memory or health (they can be a minefield for the unwary);
- do not refer to volume (or quantity) of intelligence such as "highly", "very", etc.
- avoid mentioning the writer's name in the portrait;
- avoid superlatives;
- avoid being vague;
- avoid "hedging" statements, (such as: "but", "however").

And finally on a question of style:-

- avoid expressions like "I think the writer ..." or " I believe ..." or "the writing shows .....".
- also avoid using the word *"thing"*, as in "he can only concentrate on one *thing* at a time".

* * *

SOURCES

BEAUCHATAUD, G. *Learn Graphology in fifteen lessons,* Scriptor Books, London, 1988.

BRESARD, S. *Graphologie,* Masson, Paris, 1988.

CAILLE, E. *Intelligences et écritures,* Mont-Blanc, Génève, 1974.

COLO, C. *Types psychologique de Jung et applications graphologiques,* Masson, Paris, 1991.

CRÉPIEUX-JAMIN, J. *L'Écriture et le Caractère,* PUF, Paris, 1960.

CRÉPIEUX-JAMIN, J. *Les éléments de l'écriture des canailles,* Flammarion, Paris, 1976.

DESURVIRE, M. *Feuillet No.5*, Masson, Paris, 1992.

DESURVIRE, M. *Graphologie et Recrutément*, Masson, Paris, 1991.

GILLE-MAISANI, J.-Ch. *The Psychology of Handwriting*, Scriptor Books, London, 1991.

GOBINEAU, H. de
PERRON, R. *Génétique de l'écriture et étude de la personalité*, D&N, Neuchâtel, 1954.

JUNG, C.G. *Types Psychologiques*, Ed. Georg. & Cie., Génève, 1958.

KLAGES, L. *Les principes de la caractérologie.* Delachaux et Niestlé, Paris 1950.

MAUBLANC, H. de *L'écriture par la méthode St. Morand.* Masson, Paris, 1988.

LE SENNE, R. *Traité de caractérologie.* PUF, Paris, 1960.

PEUGEOT, J.
LOMBARD, A.
NOBLENS, M.de *Manuel de Graphologie*, Masson, Paris, 1986.

PIAGET, J. *La psychologie de l'intelligence*, Ed. Armand Colin, Paris, 1967.

PULVER, M. *Le Symbolisme de l'écriture*, Ed. Stock, Paris.

Revues of the SFDG, Nos. 39, 147, 168, 171, 177.

TEILLARD, A. *L'Ame et l'Écriture*, Editions Traditionelles, Paris, 1966.

TAJAN, A.
DELAGE, G. *Écriture et Structure*, Payot, Paris, 1981.

VELS, A. *La sélection du personnel*, Ed. Mont-Blanc, Génève, 1973.

WECHSLER, D. *La Mesure de l'intelligence de l'adult*, PUF, Paris, 1973.

LECTURE VIII

COMPATIBILITY

This chapter of graphology which we call "compatibility", has as its aim to associate partners in a harmonious and constructive relationship.

There are innumerable tests which may guide people to the right choice, be it for business associates or marriage. Graphology is another of these methods.

Very little has been published recently on this particular branch of graphology. The practice is based, one way or another, on the classical system (as explained further on), and has developed experimentally, without a sufficiently defined correct form of procedure, resulting in the use, by some graphologists, of theories unrelated to compatibility, and an inadequate number of documented case histories.

The study of compatibility is a fairly recent development. There are many schools of thought, none of which has managed, as yet, to produce an operative system which helps to study the different stages of interaction which take place between two people.

Clinical psychology and psychoanalysis merely point out the multiple variables which exist in any relationship, such as the psychological/emotional evolution of each individual in time, the strength of parental (or past) ties, the possibility of change, etc.

These variables indicate the fluidity and flexibility in time of any rapport between people. All psycho-affective motivations are continuously changing, being re-modified by situations and personal, natural evolution.

More recently, graphological consultation on compatibility is oriented towards (1) the description of the structure of the relationship of the two subjects and the communication between them, and (2) the investigation of their motivations.

1. The first category is based on
   (a) the *global* study; which is the study of the different facets of the personality of each individual,
   (b) the *dynamic* study; which concerns a more specific study of the dynamics of each personality and of the two together, and
   (c) the *predictive* study; which describes the possible evolutionary direction of both partners.

The aspects examined concern the different levels of the personality and its ways of integrating, such as :

(a) vitality, force and organisation,
(b) the intellectual ability to structure and to act in accordance with the psychological/ affective state,
(c) the ways of relating on a personal level such as sociability, adaptability, flexibility, ability to discuss (to hold an exchange of ideas) etc.,
(d) emotivity and capacity of reaction which indicate receptivity and response to stimuli,
(e) sexuality as a physio-psycho-relational system (in the case of couples),
(f) general organisation of the personality and the strength which results from the resistance to stress.

The rapport is described according to the following criteria:

(a) Similarities; the possibility of rapport
(b) Differences; ability to maintain individuality within the relationship
(c) Integration; creative contribution by each party to the satisfaction of the other's needs

(d) Disunity; tendency to isolation, consequently resulting in damage to the rapport. In this case the graphologist will investigate and describe the more probable levels of conflict, will discover if there are possibilities for resolving the conflicts; and define operational measures for modification of the relationship.

2. The second category concerns the study of motivations of the deeper self.

This is extremely helpful because it depicts the psychological and emotional factors which operate subconsciously, it relates the new experiences to the previous ones already assimilated by the personality, and allows us to get to the causes of certain attitudes or conflicts.

There are, of course, some problems which remain unresolved, mainly because the graphology of motivations is not yet developed enough and is often attached to old fashioned theories and, also, because parental influence on the emotional development has not yet been adequately validated.

The best approach to date, on this subject, is based on Pulver's *"Symbolism of the Graphic Field"* and Moretti's *"Symbolism of Handwriting"*.

Symbolism shows the dynamic structure resulting from past experiences, the rapport between the Id, Ego and SuperEgo and the level of emotional development in connection with the parental figures, the direction of the motivations (Eg - nEg) which will influence the response (acceptance or refusal) towards the stimuli and the probable orientation of the partnership from the combination of the individual motivations.

Motivation is the first chronological element of behaviour. It is the ensemble of dynamic factors which determine the behaviour of an individual. It has been proven (Lashley, Lorenz and Tinbergen) that behaviour depends on:

(a) internal modifications (neuro-endocrinological) and

(b) external stimuli (environment) which act on the brain.

Classical psychology distinguishes between the "motives" which are the intellectual causes of our actions and the "inconsistency of emotions" which are the affective causes. However, this distinction is pointless since there are many factors which affect our behaviour; conscious and unconscious, physiological, intellectual, emotional and social, in constant interaction. Organic conditions influence the psyche, as much as the psyche influences the body.

The psychological structure of an individual depends heavily on cultural, sociological and educational factors.

The motivations of our behaviour therefore are complex and most often unconscious.

For the harmonious survival of any relationship, business or other, the most essential element is the harmony of objectives. An easy, relaxed communication between the partners is invariably the best basis for success. The two parties should be able to develop the ability and know-how to *negotiate* and *compromise.*

There are two ways of achieving such communication. The first is *similarities in the background*; education, intelligence, drives, attitudes and ambitions. The second is *emotional maturity*, in which case the ability and knowhow can be developed.

Maturity is a continuous process which progresses in stages. Not all people reach the same level of maturity at the same age. Many people progress in age but remain emotionally children and the commonest indicators of this are: egoism, insecurities (creating possessiveness, jealousy and envy), unrealistic ideas of power and domination of others.

Altruism (or unselfishness) is one of the most important indicators of maturity. The emotional needs of childhood are selfish but natural and necessary for the healthy development of the individual. These needs should cease gradually as maturity develops and the individual starts taking responsibility for himself (and often also for others) and is able to acknowledge his errors and learn from them. He develops flexibility, adaptability, and compassionate interest in other people's situations, problems and weaknesses.

The following chart is the classical system used to assess compatibility between any two parties. There are, of course, occasional special situations where some of these factors may be irrelevant and others may need to be added.

COMPATIBILITY CHART	Subject 1	Subject 2	Compatibility + or -
1. Emotional maturity - good, fair, poor			
2. Intellectual maturity - good, fair, poor			
3. Combination of functions (intuition, sensation, sentiment, thinking)			
4. Attitude - extrovert, introvert			
5. Intensity of Libido - strong, weak			
6. Direction of the libido - progressive, regressive, blocked			
7. Perceptive sensibility - good, fair, poor			
8. Association of ideas - good, fair, poor			
9. Imagination - vivid, fair, poor			
10. Judgement - good (objective), fair, poor (subjective)			
11. Faculty of assimilation - good, fair, weak			
12. Will power - strong, medium, weak, controlled or uncontrolled			
13. Practical sense - good, fair, poor			
14. Adaptability - good, fair, poor			
15. Initiative - good, fair, poor			
16. Sociability - good, medium, poor			
17. Loyalty - good, medium, poor			
18. Nervous state - good, fair, tense			
19. Personality - virile, feminine (animus - anima)			
20. Orientation of Self - Eg, nEg			
21. Inner Harmony - good, medium, lacking			
22. Ambivalence - none, medium, strong			
23. Character - (Le Senne)			
24. Temperament - (Hippocrates)			

Compatibility, or lack of it, will depend on the nature of the anticipated partnership. The combination of answers which will indicate compatibility in one situation, may warn against it in another.

The possibility of a harmonious coexistence of any two people is not necessarily indicated by the same answers in all the factors. Most are complementary differences and others, which are not complementary, may be overcome with an intelligent and mature approach.

The following are 9 of the most important elements for compatibility as seen through the handwriting.

1. Cultural level

The general level of handwriting, which is indicated by its originality, speed and co-ordination. Small differences between two personalities are not important, but if there are pronounced differences, the relationship may only work if there is great attraction between the couple. This, however, will not exclude thunderstorms.

2. Basic character

Similarities of basic character are shown in the resemblances between the writing styles.

3. Personal experience of space - unconscious

Personal experience of space, which is indicated by the size, the width, the spacing, and organisation on the page, is a very important element of our unconscious personality. A great contrast in any one of these elements will create difficulties. If, however, there are differences in two, this will indicate that their sense of proportions and their personal experiences of space are so dissimilar that life together will be very difficult.

4. Temperament

The general attitude, (here called 'temperament') which is indicated by the stroke, dimension, flow, direction of lines and by the overall irregularity of the writing, may differ slightly; there are combinations of pessimistic, optimistic, rigid, sensitive and well balanced people, where they complement each other as long as the differences are not too pronounced and they each have their own personal clear rhythm. If they do not, then compatibility is unlikely.

5. Primarity v. Secondarity

Speed and animation are very important, as there is no compatibility between a lively person and a slow one. There will be disputes at every step taken. Small differences, however, may be helpful.

6. Introversion v. Extroversion

The slant, width, pressure, dimension, axis and stroke of the writing are the best means of assessing introversion or extroversion. Contrasts create difficulties. The extrovert will always seek an introvert and vice versa, but the extremes are not compatible.

7. Idealism v. Materialism

Extensions are very important, depending on the zone in which they appear, the stroke quality, the pressure (colour), spacing and spontaneity. If one party extends in the upper zone and neglects the lower zone, for example, whereas the other does the opposite, it is an indication of incompatibility, X has no interest in the part of the world where Y lives.

8. Conformity v. Non-Conformity

Conventional writers, (artificial, stylised, copybook, mannered) who like formalities will find it difficult to get on with people who have natural, spontaneous writings with extensive movements and curves.

Angular writings are incompatible with the filiform, indecisive, sinuous writings.

All other combinations of forms of continuity (primary and secondary) have more or less a reasonable chance of compatibility, depending on the rest of the elements.

9. Initiative - Decisiveness

Large capital letters, high placed *t*-bars and firm downstrokes show good ability to take decisions. If both partners have them, however, there is a good chance of conflict and incompatibility.

When we say that a certain cultural style of writing is more likely to be compatible with another style, we mean, of course, if the other elements also indicate compatibility. One combination alone, must never be decisive one way or the other.

There are three main areas in life where compatibility tests are useful: marriage, family relationships and business partnerships.

* * *

SOURCES

CHIESA, A.-M.	*L'entente à deux dans la vie professionelle,* GGCF, 1981.
COBBAERT, A.-M.	*La Graphologie,* ed. Guide Marabout, Bruxelles, 1975.
FRANKEL, Rachel	*Compatibility* , 1981.
FRIEDENHAIN, P.	*Graphology in the Service of Human Relationship - Write and Reveal* ed. Peter Owen, London, 1973.
GIACOMETTI, F.	*La Graphologie,* No. 176, 1984.
SINGER, E	*La Recherche de la Compatibilité - Écriture et Mariage,* ed. Peter Owen, London, 1956.
TEILLARD, A	*L'Ame et l'Écriture,* Ed. Traditionelles, Paris1966.

The following is an example of a compatibility test.

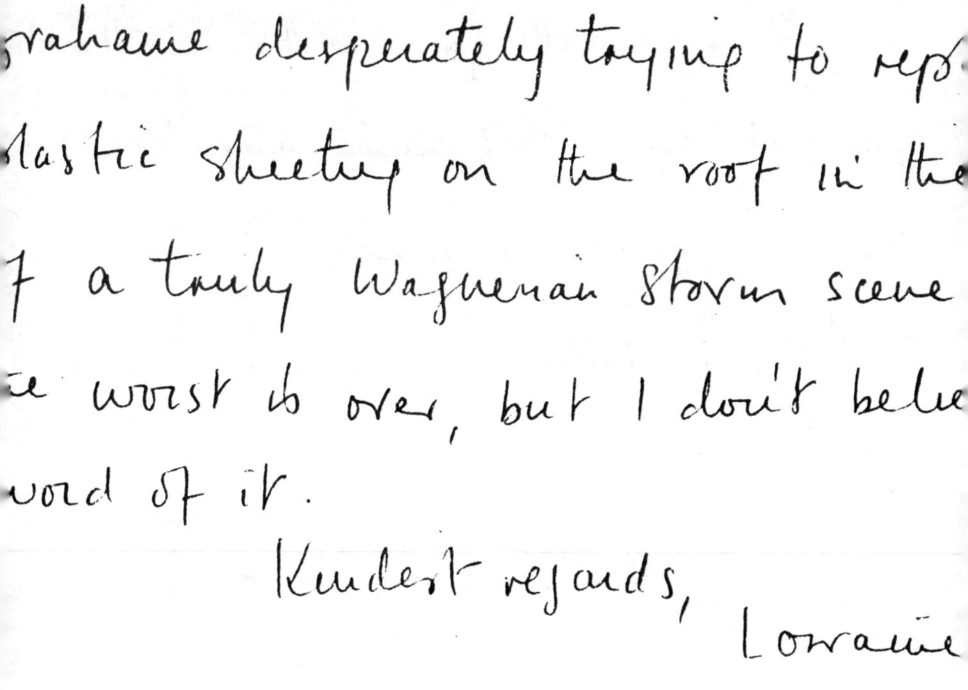
rahame desperately trying to rep
lastic sheeting on the roof in the
f a truly Wagnerian storm scene
e worst is over, but I don't belie
word of it.
Kindest regards,
Lorraine

Fig. VIII.1
Subject 1 is a woman, 50 years.
Blue biro on white paper

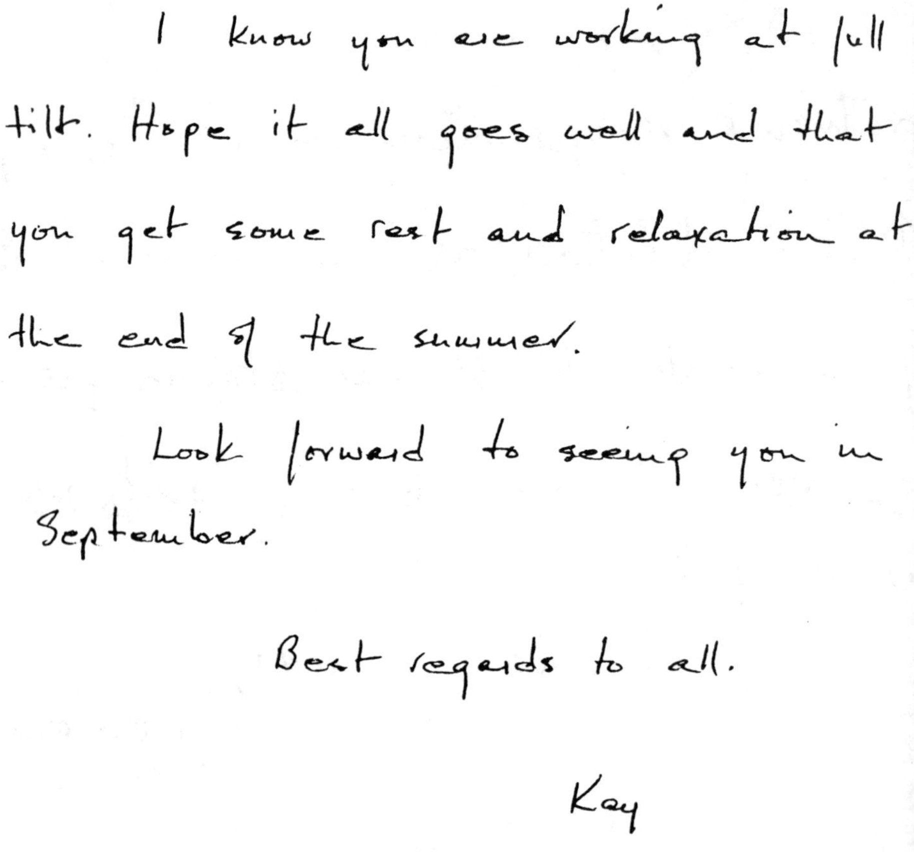

I know you are working at full tilt. Hope it all goes well and that you get some rest and relaxation at the end of the summer.

Look forward to seeing you in September.

Best regards to all.

Kay

Fig. VIII.2

Subject 2 is a woman, 50 years.
Black biro on beige paper

Subject 1

Pressure:	firm
Stroke:	precise
Organisation:	+
Spacing:	aerated
Harmony:	+
Formlevel:	+
Tension:	firm
Rapport:	Form over Movement
Structure:	good
Axis:	vertical
Movement:	controlled

Subject 2

Pressure:	light +/-, irregular
Stroke:	pasty
Organisation:	+
Spacing:	aerated +
Harmony:	+
Formlevel:	+
Tension:	supple to firm
Rapport:	Form over Movement
Structure:	good
Axis:	mixed
Movement:	vibrant, controlled

Both are graphologists and are working together in various academic matters for many years in perfect harmony. Their personalities match in many ways. The maturity levels are good in both their emotional and intellectual spheres.

TABLE 1

	Subject 1	Subject 2	Compat. + or -
1. Emotional maturity - good, fair, poor	good	good	+
2. Intellectual maturity - good, fair, poor	good	good	+
3. Combination of functions (intuition, sensation, sentiment, thinking)	T.I.Ss	T.I.	+
4. Attitude - extrovert, introvert	Ex+/-	Intr.	+
5. Intensity of Libido - strong, weak	med.	med.	+
6. Direction of the libido - progressive, regressive, blocked	progr.	progr.	+
7. Perceptive sensibility - good, fair, poor	fair	good	+
8. Association of ideas - good, fair, poor	good	good	+
9. Imagination - vivid, fair, poor	fair	fair	+
10. Judgement - good (objective), fair, poor (subjective)	obj.	obj.	+
11. Faculty of assimilation - good, fair, weak	good	good	+
12. Will power - strong, medium, weak, controlled or uncontrolled	med. contr.	med. contr.	+
13. Practical sense - good, fair, poor	good	good	+
14. Adaptability - good, fair, poor	fair	fair	+
15. Initiative - good, fair, poor	fair	fair	+
16. Sociability - good, medium, poor	good	fair	+
17. Loyalty - good, medium, poor	good	good	+
18. Nervous state - good, fair, tense	good	fair	+
19. Personality - virile, feminine (animus - anima)	mixed	mixed	+
20. Orientation of Self - Eg, nEg	nEg.	nEg.	+
21. Inner Harmony - good, medium, lacking	good	good	+
22. Ambivalence - none, medium, strong	med.	med.	+
23. Character - (Le Senne)	ES	ES	+
24. Temperament - (Hippocrates)	NB	NL	+

TABLE 2 The following table (ERIC SINGER : *Écriture et Mariage*, Vigot Frères, Paris, 1956) indicates solely the most probable effects of similarities or of differences in the basic behaviour.

WRITING CHARACTERISTIC	SIGNIFICANCE	COMPATIBILITY	MALE	FEMALE	
General type of writing: Axis/ Tension/Structure/Movment	Type of personality	Should be more or less similar	M>F H>V+/- 3-4 Structured obstructed	F>M H>V+/- 3-4 Structured flowing	-, + + +/-
Style of writing	Cultural background	Differences should not be too big	Conventional	Conventional	+
Size, width and spacing	Personal experiences of standard, comfort and style of life	At least two of these species should be similar	Small, similar, similar	Medium, similar, similar	-, +, +
Regularity and direction of lines	Temperament	Small differences help. Pronounced ones could lead to friction	Irregular, horizontal	More regular, horizontal	- +
Speed of writing	Speed of spontaneity, thinking and action	Small differences can be sorted out. Pronounced ones drive to constant friction	Accelerated	Poised	+
Slant of writing	Degree of social inclination (extroversion, indepencence and introversion)	Small differences are useful. Pronounced ones (one rightwards, the other leftwards) indicate no accord	Right	Vertical, slight right	+
Dimension and character of upper and lower extenstions	Intellectual, materialistic or sexual inclinations	If one has exaggerated u/z and no l/z, and the other has the opposite, they will be living in different worlds	u/z simple l/z simple, some △	u/z simple, simple, some full	+ +
Pressure and quality of the stroke	Sensuality and vitality	At least on of these two species should be the same	Heavy, precise	Med - light precise	- +
Forms of connection (copy-book, garlands, arcades, filiform, angles, sinuous lines)	Ways of coping with problems, ways of adapting	The angle and the thread, and the garland and the arcade are incompatible. The rest could work out in different degrees	Angles + arcades mixed	Garlands + arcades, mixed, more curves	- + = +
Style of t-bars, initials and final strokes	Sense of responsibility, demands on the running of the household	Some differences are necessary, but there should not be too much contrast	t-bars strong	t-bars more flying but strong, no start/finish strokes	- + = +

TABLE 3

		Male SUBJECT 1			Female SUBJECT 2			
		Gd.	Av.	Poor	Gd.	Av.	Poor	Conclusion
Mental	Broadness of concepts	●				●		
	Association of ideas	●				●		
	Faculty of assimilation	●			●			
	Judgement	●			●			
	Initiative	●				●		
	Imagination	●				●		
	Intuition	●			●			
Emotional	Sensitivity	●				●		
	Maturity	●			●			
	Self-esteem	●			●			
	Self-control		●		●			
	Nervous state		●		●			
	Loyalty	●			●			
	Inner equilibrium		●		●			
Activity	Energy	●			●			
	Will power	●			●			
	Ambition		●			●		
	Combativity	●			●			
	Decision taking	●				●		
Adaptability (Social exchange)	Attitude: extrovert		●			●		
	Attitude: introvert		●			●		
	Practical sense	●			●			
	Sociability		●		●			probably different fields
	Sense of humour		●			●		
	Adaptability	●			●			

LECTURE IX

GRAPHOTHERAPY

Graphotherapy started with Miss Dreyfus-Hirtz who first published an important article on the subject in the bulletin of the Société Française de Graphologie, in the mid thirties. Since then, many medical doctors, such as Streletski, Carton, Menard and others, have studied and practised this remedial treatment with a great many surprising results. Particularly R. Trillat, who practised graphotherapy for many years at the psychopedagogical 'Centre Claude Bernard', was the first to make it known to the public at large.

Etymologically, graphotherapy means a treatment (therapy) ***through*** the writing (grapho) - just as hydrotherapy means treatment through water or psychotherapy means treatment through the psyche. It is not a treatment ***of*** the writing but only appears so as a consequence.

The treatment *through* the writing, which is also the oldest approach, works in "reverse order" familiar to those who study graphology. Since writing expresses the personality, by changing certain aspects of the writing, we consequently and eventually change certain undesirable aspects of the personality.

This procedure works, because there is total communication between motor functioning and character, as has been indisputably demonstrated by Professor Henri Wallon and Dr. Paul Carton. Every gesture has significance and expresses traits which spring from the deepest reality of the character. Consequently, any amelioration of this expression and any transformation of gestures will modify the behaviour.

On the other hand, the treatment *of* the writing is a treatment of 'dysgraphia', or the re-education of handwriting. This aspect involves the de-conditioning of the unconscious from the acquired writing and the reconditioning of the unconscious movements - and hence the communications through establishing a new psychic motivation by incorporating more relaxed forms and physical movements.

This approach is not - at least not at the beginning - 'psychotherapy through the writing' but is merely a treatment of the handwriting.

Until the mid thirties there was no official orientation of graphology in this direction. It concentrated only on interpretations.

Dysgraphy is a scriptural disability which is not justified by a neurological malfunction or an intellectual deficiency. This disorder affects either the act of writing itself or the stroke.

If we take into consideration that writing involves the use of an instrument, has as its purpose communication, and expresses the personality, we can observe many kinds of dysgraphy, such as the *instrumental* - which affects mainly the stroke in its fluency and speed -, the *relational* which reduces the legibility -, the *reactional*, often due to anger, the *symptomatic*, such as writing in a train, etc.

It goes without saying that we cannot apply the same methods of treatment for the re-eduction of a dysgraphy caused strictly by disorder of the scriptural movement (motor dysgraphy), as for a dysgraphy which is a symptom of a deep emotional difficulty, *relational*.

In this second, more recent approach, we treat the dysgraphic writing itself. The emphasis is on the graphotherapist himself whose profound knowledge of the psychomotor aspects of writing and of psychology is essential, both for amelioration of the writing and to understand the various inner difficulties expressed by graphic signs such as slowness, constraint, confusion, cramp, etc.

From this proper understanding of the writing, the following essential principles emerge. *First*, we must have respect for others and consequently for their handwriting which must on no account be influenced or interfered with; *second*, we must not improvise or impose; and *third*, we must constantly remain aware of the limitations of the treatment and of its curative aspects - which in many cases are uncertain.

All aspects of graphotherapy must be practised only by people of the highest integrity, personal maturity and who have a solid knowledge of psychology It also requires a deep and comprehensive knowledge of graphology.

Graphotherapy has limits. It is helpful in that it plays a certain part in regard to the difficulties which can affect written communication. It can have an even deeper influence on the psychological structure of the subject through the influence which it has on the psycho-kinetic activity but it cannot replace analytical psychotherapy when exercised by competent psychoanalysts, particularly in cases of neuroses. It cannot cure organic illnesses, except, possibly, if they are proven to be of a psychosomatic nature and even then it can only be used as a support to psychoanalysis.

However, graphotherapy will help the child to resolve his scriptural difficulties, which are directly or indirectly related to his writing. It can also help the adolescent towards psychological maturity.

Some psychologists tackle graphotherapy. This is a mistake; we need to know the deeper significance of handwriting before we try to transform it.

For many professional psychologist-graphotherapists, graphotherapy is essentially the treatment of handwriting. They use the term, "graphomotric re-education" which applies to three levels: the motor, the psychic and the mental.

The re-education of movement works as a self-suggestion if the sentences or exercises used evoke ideas which need to be developed in the writer's mind. This will in turn affect the subconscious.

Between the mind and the nervous system exists a two-way communication; centrifugal as well as centripetal, and the movements we execute while writing rebound on our nervous centres modifying our sentiments and our thoughts.

As we have already seen, *one of* the malfunctions of a writing is the *instrumental* which applies to the movement itself; the actual act of writing the stroke and its fluency and speed.

A *second one* is the *communicational* or *relational.* This is examined in two parts:

(a) the horizontal direction which is the one that involves the strictly personal evolution of the handwriting within the family and the social context, and

(b) the vertical direction which discovers hidden messages, the most profound and secret of which are contained in the writing underneath any intentional message.

A *third* malfunction is the *symptomatic* where the writing gives alarm signals or calls for help.

These three functions (instrumental, relational and symptomatic) are interconnected. It is easily conceived that a *relational* dysgraphy affecting mainly the legibility could express itself through the *instrumental* dysgraphy, hence the classic trilogy of dyslexia-disorthography-dysgraphy. As a result, the motor skills are not sufficiently developed to carry out their function of *communication.*

All this shows that the complexity of handwriting needs to be examined very thoroughly if we want to understand the malfunctions and help re-establish normal functioning.

The diagnosis often is as good as therapy itself. To expose a problem dedramatises it through making it objective, and in many cases this alone cures, making therapy unnecessary.

The hand has 27 little bones and 33 muscles (16 short and 17 long ones) which, linked together by the nerves, guarantee perfect mobility.

The graphotherapist must always keep in mind that fine mobility depends on general motor skills which are linked to the subject's level of evolution, which in turn, are linked to his level of emotional maturity. Graphotherapists are familiar with the importance of certain *cramps* - particularly in children when they have done something forbidden.

There is no such thing as a 'healthy writing' without healthy motor functioning, neither is there a healthy writing without proper knowledge of how to draw the letters (ductus) and/or how to link them together.

Fatigue and cramps can, of course, be the result of defective holding of the writing instrument or of an uncomfortable positioning.

The actual shape, form and the fluency of the writing and its simplifications, are the best elements from which to estimate the evolution of the personality and the affectivity.

Graphotherapy, when correctly practised, i.e. taking into consideration the original style of the writing and the personal level of general development of the writer, will lead to a corrective psychological improvement which is a *secondary benefit* (the *primary* benefit being the correction of the actual writing), and will be manifested in many and varied ways such as better academic results, better self-discipline, better memory, improvement in the ability to concentrate, even a happier contact with other people through an improvement of personal conduct, and so on.

The personal relationship which inevitably - and naturally - develops between the therapist and the writer also helps.

The beginning of the therapy consists of rows of garlands. These are associated with the natural rhythm of the writer and while counting during the practice, he (or she) exercises respiratory control. By their nature too, garlands represent a softer mental movement, they also are the basic graphic element: 3 or 4 half loops connected together represent the average length of a word.

Speed, combined with pressure and accuracy are also practised this way. However, the movement must always prevail in importance over the form. Spontaneity and control of the execution of the stroke should be considered over and above the elegance or the accuracy of the shapes.

Garlands made in variable sizes, enable the writer to situate himself in space and to find his own structure which will enable him to restore the proportions of the 3 zones, to follow the baseline, to establish an agility in the continuity of the writing and to develop his personal way of horizontal progression.

After long practice with garlands alone, and only when we have established that they have been totally integrated into the movement, shown by their fluency, speed, pressure and reasonable accuracy, can we proceed with the loops) which really only result in two half-loops put together.

Simultaneously, we add physical exercises to aid movement. These are gymnastic exercises for the fingers and hands, for agility, control and stamina.

After the garlands and the loops come the spirals, the *snails*. The writer should try to make as many turns as possible without moving his forearm.

Before each session, we should do a few relaxing exercises of the parts of the body related to writing, the back, the neck, the shoulder, the writing arm, the elbow, the forearm, the wrist, the hand and the fingers.

These exercises should be rhythmic

(1) *invigorating* - increasing the blood flow - releasing any possible tension in any of the said parts,

(2) *strengthening* - increasing the stamina of - the muscles involved and hence the control over them,

(3) *relaxing.*

Quite often the results of graphotherapy are invisible in the writing even after long periods. The handwriting will remain clumsy, illegible, constrained, cramped, or whatever effects each individual case, long after the therapy is finished. But the effects of it on the personality will start becoming evident much sooner. The writer will show good progress in his academic studies, his overall behaviour will improve and he will start feeling better in him (or her) self.

The handwriting will show these inner transformations, last. It takes between six months to one year, and often longer, for any sign of change to come about in the writing.

Graphotherapy, when practised responsibly, is indisputably among the most valuable and effective of non-analytical treatments, but it could never replace analytical psychotherapy, if this is what is needed, or affect the intellectual quotient.

Paul de Sainte Colombe tells us that in America, graphotherapy is much more advanced than in Europe. He, himself, was a teaching consultant at the Patton Hospital for the Mentally Ill in California. He claimed that he "completely cured-' a 16 year old schizophrenic. He also treated drug addicts in the Department of Psychiatry at San Francisco's Faculty of Medicine where in 1969 he started research on homosexuals, juvenile delinquents and alcoholics. Paul de Sainte Colombe died in 1972.

Doctor Robert Olivaux(1), Doctor of the University of Paris, Doctor in Pedagogy at the Institut Catholique de Paris, and Professor at the École de Psychologues Praticiens, also a psychoanalyst, has been practising this technique for many years with excellent results.

---

(1) For more information about his system, see Robert Olivaux, *Desordres et Reéducation de l'écriture,* E.S.F., Paris, 1971.

SOURCES

COBBAERT, A.-M.	*Graphologie,* Guide Marabout. Bruxelles, 1975.
OLIVAUX, R.	*Désordres et Reéducation de l'écriture,* E.S.F., Paris, 1971.
STRELETSKI, Dr. C.	*Précis de Graphologie Pratique,* Vigot Frères, Paris, 1950.
Revue of the SFDG	Nos.110, 123, 125, 177.
TRILLAT, R.- MASSON, H.	*Experience de Graphotherapie en Psychopédagogie - Méthode de Relaxation Graphique,* Vigot Frères, Paris, 1957.

* * *

PART 3

PSYCHOPATHOLOGY

LECTURE X
Emotional and Mental Problems

LECTURE XI
Clinical Graphology - Graphopathology

LECTURE XII
Problem Writings

LECTURE X

EMOTIONAL AND MENTAL PROBLEMS

It is very difficult to assess accurately the state of equilibrium of an individual. The vast majority of people in the streets are not mad. They are half-mad, such as the mythomaniacs, the mild paranoiacs (one of the largest groups), the erotomaniacs, the nymphomaniacs, the kleptomaniacs, the schizothymics, the depressives, the hysterics, the obsessives, the masochists, the sadists, the perverts, and all those who suffer from all sorts of complexes, neuroses, conflicts and anxieties like guilt, inferiority, persecution, all of which result in lack of clarity of judgement, lack of common sense and lack of appreciation of reality.

The ***Function of reality*** is the only means through which we can appreciate the normal state of the relation between the self and the world. Reality is objective and true for all. Only inner reality may be relative.

This Function of reality is indispensable. Without it, we cannot have a correct appreciation of the world.

The mechanics of a healthy brain produce a successful adaptation to reality. All actions and reactions are precise and in accord. They assure a 'normal', 'balanced' relation of the individual to the world.

When this balance is disturbed, the world appears alien and aggressive. This creates insecurity and dependence, which in turn produce egocentrism and selfishness. In extreme cases there is no longer any dialogue between the individual and the world. It is a constant struggle between possessiveness, domination (physical or intellectual), self-affirmation and depression. Anxieties set in. The individual deviates from reality. He (or she) becomes *neurotic*, and loses touch with reality, living in a delusion.

It is appropriate now to discriminate between *neurosis* and *psychosis* and psychopathy.

Neurosis

Neurosis is a mental disorder which does not affect the essential functions of the personality. The most common manifestations of neurosis are aggression and depression. Others are obsessions, hysteria (*see Chapter on "Freud"*), anxieties and phobias, none of which are certain to affect others or the adaptation of the person. Whatever the manifestation, the common characteristic in all subjects is *lack of emotional maturity*. The sufferer behaves in an adolescent manner and his/her reactions are based on puerile criteria and acute emotions, such as strong emotional attachments and inane subjective judgements. According to the psychoanalytic theory (depth psychology), *neurosis* is an inner conflict opposing the instinctive forces of the Id to the moral conscious (Superego), thus creating anxieties and mobilising inadequate defence mechanisms. The *neurotic* individual (about 1 in 10 in Europe)[1] is anxious and conscious of his uneasiness and morbid state, but ignores the reasons for this.

The writing shows the unconscious symptoms of this illness, but not the degree of the loss of the function of reality. This can only be assessed by supporting signs such as clumsiness of

(1) *Dictionnaire de la psychologie*, Larousse, Paris, 1964.

forms, some bizarre movements, excessive fluctuations of the stroke or agitated and animated writing with irregular pressure, speed and spacing, uncontrolled movements, flying strokes, twisted and/or proteiform. All discordances in the upper and middle zone of the writing, the disturbances of the rhythm and of the concept of space and time, will indicate the severity of the mental or emotional problems of the writer.

In some cases, the more severe the ***neurosis***, the more difficult it is to detect it through the handwriting. The reason being, that for these people, their delirium is much more real than any reality and it is "the others who are not in touch with it".

Psychosis

Psychosis is a grave mental illness characterised by loss of contact with reality and of the ability for human interaction, causing antisocial behaviour and often needing hospitalisation.

The *psychotic* individual is unaware of his illness. He isolates himself from the world and creates his own privileged universe in which he is the master. There are many kinds of psychoses: schizophrenia, paranoia in its delirium state and cyclophrenia (manic depression). Lack of self-observation and of self-criticism, deviated or twisted judgement and unreal perceptions, denote the profound alienation of the individual and constitute the most typical characteristics of psychosis. According to research done during the 7th decade of this century by Pasamanick, 1 in 100 of the urban population suffers from one form of psychosis or another.

Psychosis is often *not obvious through the handwriting.* However, an undifferentiated pressure, stiff regularity, monotony of forms and rigidity, or on the other hand, lack of control of the movements, should alert the graphologist of the possibility.

Obsession

Obsession is a repetitive pre-occupation of the mind (or the emotions) with one certain idea or more. Obsessive ideas may occasionally and temporarily affect normal people after a great fatigue. But if they acquire a permanent and acute state, they constitute the basic symptom called "obsessional psychoneurosis".

A. Adler sees this state as a form of running away from a painful reality, when the individual transfers his battle on another field. Obsessional neurosis is closely linked to the *anal* state and its symptoms are: (a) consistent recurrence of the same idea, (b) compulsive ritualistic actions.

The *obsessional* individual is aware of his condition, which often becomes superstition (or vice-versa) and tries to fight it by hiding it. Outside psychoanalysis there is no other therapeutic cure for the "normal" obsessive individual.

In the writing obsessive tendencies are seen in regularity of form, rigidity of the movement (static), slowness, artificiality, clarity of lay-out and monotony.

Psychopathy

Psychopathy is a pathological mental state. This term is usually applied to characterological deviations of the will and the emotivity, causing antisocial attitudes. The psychopaths should not be classed in the categories of psychotics (who are truly alienated) or of neurotics (who suffer alone of their troubles). Psychopaths are unstable individuals, impulsive and "difficult", whose behaviour disturbs the harmony of the people around them.

Through a research done by W. Sheldon and S. Glueck in the 1950s, psychopaths were found mostly among the *mesomorph* types, otherwise called *athletics.*

There are five main groups in psychopathology in varying degrees. These are:

1. Schizothymia - Schizophrenia
2. Cyclothymia - Cyclophrenia (manic-depression)
3. Paranoia
4. Perversity
5. The Complexes.

SCHIZOTHYMIA - SCHIZOPHRENIA

Schizothymia is the submorbid (pre-illness) state of *schizophrenia* which is, as we know, a disassociation of the personality from the reality of the outside world. The term was first used by the Swiss psychiatrist, Bleuler, and studied by E. Kretschmer. (*see relevant chapter in Part V*).

There are many degrees of intensity of schizothymia. The extreme (schizophrenia) is a pathological state, a 'mental illness'. The patient needs to be looked after by a specialist. He is often totally cut off from the world around him. There is disorganisation of the affective field which is dissociated from the intellectual processes (reasoning). The intellectual acquisitions and perceptions are normal, but the mentality is 'primitive', the thinking follows a 'personal' logic, egocentric and 'magical'.

The *schizothymic* is dominantly characterised by extreme introversion. He might often appear distant, silent, aloof, cold, and unemotive when in reality he is not. His attitude is a defence against hurt. His reactions, often unexpected, are a discharge of accumulated tensions. Intellectually he is mostly an idealist. He is original, systematic and inclined towards abstract concepts and analysis. He is correct, dignified in his behaviour, but also whimsical. In general, the schizothymics are highly intelligent and intensely intellectual; Some famous schizothymics were Metternich, Voltaire, Erasmus, Robespierre, Turner, Kant, Calvin, T.S. Elliott, Savonarola, Jung, and others.

The *writing of the schizothymics* is angular, straight, constrained, sometimes disconnected, with plenty of irregularities, simplified, more or less vertical, with wide margins (*Fig. X.1*).

The *writing of the schizophrenics* is broken, even fragmented, dry, narrow, with brusque changes of direction and slant (ambivalence). It has various discordances, particularly between the vertical and horizontal axes. The upper zone extensions may be reduced; there is dependence of the unconscious and its power and domination (*Fig. X.2*). It can also be automatic; there are cases where the automatism (persona) prevents any abnormality showing through. This is a danger for the graphologist. There has not yet been enough research in the field of automatism in schizophrenic writing.

Another peculiarity of this kind of writing is the tracing over of letters, words, sentences or even whole paragraphs (*Fig. X.3*).

CYCLOTHYMIA - CYCLOPHRENIA

This is the alternating manic-depressive tendency; what is commonly called "moodiness". Cyclothymic people are at one moment excited and 'on top of the world', and the next they can get deeply depressed for some minor reason and wish to stay in bed.

Kretschmer describes the *cyclothymics* as being the best communicators with the world. Their constitution follows the vibrations of their surroundings. They are very reactive to situations, expressing their joy, anger, sadness, etc. They are sociable and realistic. They change ideas very quickly. They are interested in actualities, are practical, cordial and amiable. They can be hyperactive or hyper-lazy.

They go from one extreme to the other without ever finding a happy medium. They are excitable and emotive and plunge into actions with little foresight. Chateaubriand was one good example of such a type.

The *writing of the cyclothymic* can sometimes look inhibited and irregular. Depending on the overall personality, it may be of medium size with garlands and generally curved, or large with various exaggerations. Overall it is consistently unstable hopping, spaced out and may "change" from year to year.

The *cyclophrenic* has more severe symptoms to those above, where the alternating phases are much more pronounced. The manic period produces a febrile agitation and a hyperactivity manifested in working day and night without rest. Then comes the *depressive* stage, where the individual becomes extremely anxious. It is probably necessary to explain some aspects of this state as it does not only affect the cyclophrenics, but almost everybody at some time and at some stage of their existence.

Depression

Depression is characterised by the decrease (diminishing) of psychic energy and vitality. The sufferer takes no initiative, is incapable of facing any difficulties and loses interest in what goes on around him/her. He sees only the negative side of every aspect of life, refuses to participate and cries easily. Occasionally an inferiority feeling may develop which increases his anxiety, isolates him even more and may lead him to suicide.

Depression can be triggered by many causes, some of which are a strict diet, overwork, constant conflict in the home or at work, guilt, grief and solitude. It can also be hereditary and may lead to suicide.

In the writing depression is seen in a usually light pasty stroke with either rising or descending lines, small irregular forms, often jerky, shaky or spasmodic (twisted), slack, angular and congested letters, a floating or inhibited movement, usually slowed down by consequent apathy, and occasionally large white spaces or strict compactness and muddy (smeary) look. The signature occasionally moves towards the left of the page and becomes more gathered.

The *writing of the cyclophrenic* is usually connected, occasionally even overconnected, curved, rather large, easy flowing and mostly fast, frequently slanted either way with narrow or no margins, invading, often with dominance of the lower zone. It will, however, vary in accordance with the periodical mood (*Fig. X.4*).

PARANOIA

This is a state of mind with a somewhat distorted concept of reality. It is an "alienation of thinking" (Jung). An individual suffering from paranoia exhibits :

(a) Social maladjustment

Adaptability is not only obedience and submission to the conditions of life and the environment, it is the ability to accept emotionally and intellectually, the laws and traditions of history, resulting in inner adaptation which is the "adaptation of the different sides of the nature of a person to each other,.... and it is there where the problems of ambivalence start" (Pulver).

Pulver sees three different aspects of adaptation:

i. practical biological adaptation where the individual enters into given circumstances and makes the best use of them for his own interests;

ii. theoretical adaptation, which is the ability to understand logically or scientifically causes and effects, with the purpose of using them to greatest advantage;

iii. moral adaptation, which seeks to bridge the differences created by people through the anarchy of their instincts and their lack of inner adaptation.

Adaptability in a non-copybook writing, is mainly indicated by a 'normal' continuity (harmonious, rhythmic irregularities) if there are no indications to the contrary. Overconnectedness, in a discordant writing with exaggerations for example, will not indicate adaptability, but mania. Suppleness of movement (moderate curves rather than angles) will indicate adaptability while angles, by their constant sharp change of direction, very often seek conflict instead of avoiding it, showing refusal or inability to adapt. Disconnected writing indicates a certain difficulty in adaptation, not an outward battle like the angles, but a conflict between the various aspects of the personality. Therefore, an angular, disconnected writing, indicates inner and social conflicts.

(b) Mistrustfulness

This is usually a result of bad experiences and neurotic anxieties. Many people become mistrustful because they have, or think they have, reasons not to trust themselves.

Mistrustfulness in writing is indicated by the last letters of the line slanting leftwards in an otherwise rightward slanting writing, the signature is illegible, complicated or imprecise (so that it is difficult to forge), or atrophied (an unconscious effort to withdraw from any responsibility), often followed by a full stop, the writing may be spread out and at the same time closed and left-slanted (contradictory signs); a slow speed indicating extreme self-control is no longer due to conscience or correctness but to dissimulation - a necessary distance, to avoid being exposed, a superfluous line drawn between the last letter of a line to the end of the right margin - as in cheques - so that nothing more can be added in that space.

(c) Overestimation of self

This is caused on the one hand by either an exaggeration of the value of one's own personality (imaginary heroism, high aspirations to power, etc.) or by certain traditions embodied in certain social classes such as royalty, the aristocracy, etc., or, on the other hand, by reaction or protestation against pettiness, inferiority, imposed deprivation, or other similar conditions. Such attitudes are naive and show a lack of mature acceptance of reality.

Large spontaneous writings may indicate an exaggerated feeling of value of the self but they may also indicate a reaction to the contrary. Only with the help of supporting signs can we assess whether it is a true feeling or a reactive mask hiding an inferiority. The old concept that "a grand writing indicates the grandness of the feeling of self" is too simplistic.

Superelevations may indicate spiritual will power, or running away from an insufferable situation. They may also indicate an accentuation of the needs of the self. This is biological egoism according to Pulver. A very small writing with long extensions up and down, will show submission as a reaction to oppression from superiors, parents or older brothers or sisters. The self withdraws and exaggerates to the point of arrogance. There is painful timidity and susceptibility and a diminished feeling of self.

Agitations in all levels and directions will show instability, lack of maturity and possible overestimation of self. When the writing does not indicate a mature self-assurance, independent judgement and moderate pride, then the prolongments, the superelevations, the agitations, the disproportions will point towards a lack of equilibrium; for instance if the writing is tall, narrow and possibly squeezed too, with prolongments and superelevations (ambition, inhibition, timidity).

The movement which starts from above and goes down towards the baseline requires a high degree of self-assurance. If there is no such indication in the rest of the writing, then this is a sign of imbalance and unjustified overestimation of self.

When the signature is in the middle of the page it may be that the writer feels he has to occupy this position in life unless there is evidence to the contrary, i.e. avoidance of contact with others and the world, grave inhibitions, etc., then the more the signature moves towards the left, the more serious the writer's inhibitions and discouragement are.

When the address of a letter (Dear ...) is smaller than the text, the writer usually has a higher feeling of himself than he may be admitting to.

All important discordances in dimension and pressure indicate a lack of spatial concept. The concept of proportion is missing. The exaggerated importance of the start of a word through height or pressure will symbolise overestimation of self and subjectivity (often accompanied by touchiness).

(d) Falseness of judgement

Judgement is the ability to appreciate a correspondence between different ideas. It is the conclusion of the process of reasoning and is an essential aspect of cognition concerning the object. It is acquired through distancing oneself from the object and partially sacrificing spontaneity. Correct, impartial judgement illuminates and isolates the object from the subject. "Pure reason guides, the will is free" (Decartes). Rational judgement makes no choice in the acceptance of facts and truths. There is no judgement without a minimum of intelligence and knowledge, although intelligence does not necessarily imply good judgement. A troubled affectivity is enough to cause faulty judgement. Jealousy, hatred, love, for instance, distort the judgement.

The rhythmic and harmonious ventilation of the page is one guide towards the assessment of good judgement. There is rapport between word and silence. The white spaces are creative pauses. If the intervals between the words and the lines become too large, it is an indication of the loss of all spontaneity which may be the result of a 'know-all' attitude (as in adolescence), fear, timidity or mental debility; there is incoherence and gaps in the logic. The writer involuntarily distances himself; the gaps are little deserts between words, abolishing any possibility of contact. If the intervals are too narrow then there is the possibility of confusion and lack of ability to detach the self from the object.

There should be no confusing of the highest degree of mental clarity with the debility of idiocy, even though both may be expressed through wide gaps. Their forms are different, and in the first case the distribution of spacings is harmoniously rhythmic, while in the second it is greatly disturbed.

Proportion - of height and width - is another indicator of judgement. In a squeezed writing with narrow letters, the distance between words and lines should be relative and in proportion with its dimension. Large white spaces will indicate inhibition.

The relief of the stroke also expresses clear and accurate judgement, particularly when it is precise.

To sum up, the paranoiac has excessive pride and is in constant conflict with others and the world. His affectivity is greatly disorganised (a denominator he shares with the schizothymic/schizophrenic). His self is extravagant, his selfishness even greater. He is guilty of constant projection, openly accusing others of his own faults. He is very convincing and difficult to diagnose and can sail happily through life disrupting the existence of everyone around him, and of whole countries.

There are, of course, degrees of paranoia. In extreme, pathological cases, the *writing of the paranoiac* can be impersonal, monotonous, with lots of amendments (*Fig. X.5*). In milder cases (but not less disruptive) it will be spread out, full, with superelevations, ebullient movements, rising, occasionally with reverse slant, irregular, condensed, complicated, often discordant with exaggerations and disorder (*Fig. X.6*). Or it can be bizarre and incoherent, confused, jerky, angular, sharp-pointed and invasive.

PERVERSITY

This is a "distortion of the real end or purpose", a deviation of instincts resulting in a pathological deviation from normal behaviour, particularly in sex habits but also in the direction of sentiments.

Perverts are those who combine egoism, and nastiness with an inability to accept discipline from others or impose it on themselves. They are antisocial, unnatural and unable to sustain hope. They usually end up as delinquents, drug addicts, alcoholics or pyromaniacs, often populating the prisons and psychiatric hospitals.

They are motivated by destructive instincts or indifference towards all living beings (sometimes including themselves), as well as the things around them. Extreme meanness, extreme vanity or passivity (apathy), extreme prodigality, voracity, aggressive excitability, tendency to violence, sadism or masochism and certain sexual or homosexual practices are some of the manifestations of perversion.

This kind of psychopath can be treated and re-educated.

The *writing signs of perversion* are not easily evident either; inharmonious and discordant writings, usually with emphasis in the lower zone; muddy pressure with numerous spindles, particularly in the lower extensions, or with sudden (spasmodic) thickening of the stroke in the middle zone (zone of the sentiments) on the base line, in an otherwise light writing.

THE COMPLEXES

This is a term first applied by Bleuler and later adopted by S. Freud and other psychologists.

A complex is a combination (a collection or a complexity) of subconscious tendencies which determine a person's behaviour, attitudes, dreams, etc.

One group of psychologists sees the complex as an idea, or an associated group of ideas repressed and "strongly tinged with emotion" (Hesnard), in conflict with other ideas which are more or less accepted by the individual. This inner conflict creates opposition between the moral conscience and the aggressive tendencies in any field.

Another group of psychologists (more old-fashioned) believes that complexes are caused by a strong sexual shock; All agree that it is an unhealthy (morbid) phenomenon.

A third school of psychologists/psychoanalysts expresses the opinion that the word "complex" covers a combination of personal traits, desires, emotions, feelings and attitudes, which are contradictory and practically always unconscious, constituting an integral part of the personality.

Complexes are formed during the first years of life in a particular environmental frame. At their root there is always the syndrome "love-hate". Contrary to what is widely believed, they are not always pathological, and can be normally resolved with time. They can, however, assume larger proportions because of various modifications. In such cases, they will create character malfunctions which can turn into nervous disorders in later life. Any important event in childhood can trigger off the formation of a complex. ***For example***, the birth of a little brother or sister in the family, always carries a wealth of contradictory feelings for the older child, mainly towards the mother, which may create a number of frustrations, complexes and neuroses later on, if the mother does not handle the situation intelligently. These feelings are painful and traumatic and even when later on everything comes into perspective, there are traces left in the subconscious which will create a sensitivity towards authority, causing a revolt against any injustices, actual or imaginary. As an adult the personality will be influenced by the memory of these frustrations or traumas. The behaviour will be complex. There will be unconscious protestation and incompatibility with society or with certain people.

There are many complexes, the most common being: inferiority, guilt, mother, father, Oedipus, deprivation (premature weaning), oral, anal, flight, etc.

All people have complexes without necessarily being abnormal. A complex is after all only a "system of ideas (thoughts) over-charged with emotion which animates and provokes certain reactions" (Besnard), (Cobbaert).

As we said earlier, certain complexes created during childhood, will disappear later on. Others, however, may be transformed into any of the above mentioned ones,or may appear as neuroses such as obsessions, anxieties, castration anxiety, phobias (e.g. agoraphobia, claustrophobia, fear of snakes, mice, spiders) even to the extent of terror, sadism, masochism, aggressiveness, etc.

Generally speaking all *sexual complexes* will be *seen in the writing*, mainly in the stroke and the lower extensions. They are often full and bizarre, or in pronounced triangular forms, overdeveloped, with thick, heavy, deviated pressure (on the up-stroke or horizontally), and/or pushed leftwards (introverted eroticism narcissism) (*Fig. X.7*) or stunted and short, almost blending with the middle zone; or formed in simple sticks, firm or flabby.

HOMOSEXUALITY

Homosexuality may have many different signs. In men, a Venus writing with full lower extensions, prolonged and turned towards the left, returning up in a sagging manner may indicate this tendency, particularly if it is manifested *(Fig. X.8).* In women it is extremely difficult to see homosexuality through the handwriting. There are various groups of signs; bizarre forms with discordances usually point towards lesbianism, though not always, since it depends on other elements as well, such as education, social group, other complexes, and general personality *(Fig. X.9).*

All imbalance in the human body, be it mental or physical, becomes evident in the writing sooner or later.

There are two main groups of signs which will indicate imbalance. These are:

1. *the movements of suffering*, and
2. *the movements of defence*

Movements of suffering are mainly "twisted" writing, shakiness, breakages, fragmentations, jerkiness, resting or unnecessary dots, discordances, disorganisation of the writing and disorderliness, usually in a constrained outlook. *(Fig. X.10)*

The *movements of defence* are amendments, missing letters or words, repeated letters or words, suspended letters, and all signs of inhibition.

There is one more state of the soul and of the mind or the body, which should not be overlooked. This is *fatigue.*

FATIGUE

Fatigue is not an illness as such, although it can be a symptom of one.

In the writing, it will be indicated by slightly descending or slightly ascending lines, galloping up or down, less firmness of the stroke than usual, lighter pressure in the evening, diminished size and a general reduction of movements. The greater the tiredness, the more intense the above signs become. The writing loses its orderliness and may become illegible. It may have multiple amendments and mistakes (one word instead of another, less or more strokes than are necessary - for example 'comnunication' instead of 'communication' etc.).

OVERTIREDNESS

Overtiredness is manifested by an intensification of the above signs which will appear, not only in the evening, but at all times.

Where the indications of suffering in a writing are very pronounced, supplementary information is imperative. When this is not possible, the graphologist should never plunge into a medical diagnosis but should advise the writer to consult a qualified specialist.

Handwriting is only one of the many manifestations of cerebral activity and it reflects all the organic variations.

The more graphology becomes recognised as a science useful to humanity, the bigger the responsibility of the graphologist becomes to stick to his skill alone, and that does not include any medical prognosis, diagnosis or advice.

* * *

SOURCES

BASTIN, C. de CASTILLA, D.	*Graphologie - Le Psychisme et ses troubles,* ed. R. Laffourd, Paris, 1990.
COBBAERT, A.-M.	*La Graphologie,* Ariston, Genève, 1977.
DESCARTES, R.	*Discours de la Méthode,* Arman Colin. Paris, 1959.
JUNG, C. G.	*Types Psychologiques,* Georg & Cie. Genève, 1950.
GOUGELMANN, S.	*Écriture dites 'frustes' ou 'primaires',* GGCF, Paris, 1986.
LECERF, A.	*Cours Supérieure de Graphologie,* Dangles. Paris 1947 - (translated into English by E. O'Neill, to be published by Scriptor Books).
PULVER, M.	Le *Symbolisme de l'Écriture,* Stock, Paris, 953.
TEILLARD, A.	*The Soul and Handwriting,* Scriptor Books, London, 1992.
RESTEN, R.	L*e Diagnostic du Caractère,.* L'Arche. Paris, 1953.
Revue de SFDG	No.176
WITKOVSKI, F.	*Psychopathology et écriture,* Masson, Paris 1989.

HANDWRITING SAMPLES of LECTURE X

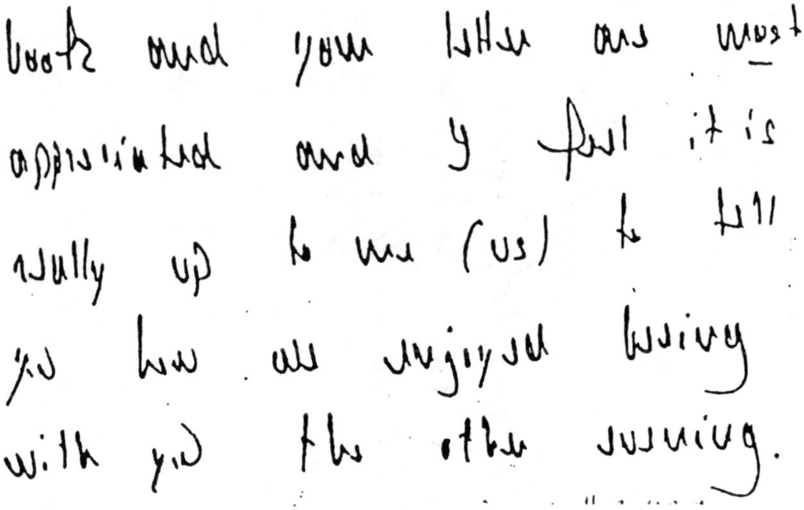

Fig. X.1 - Man, 40 years

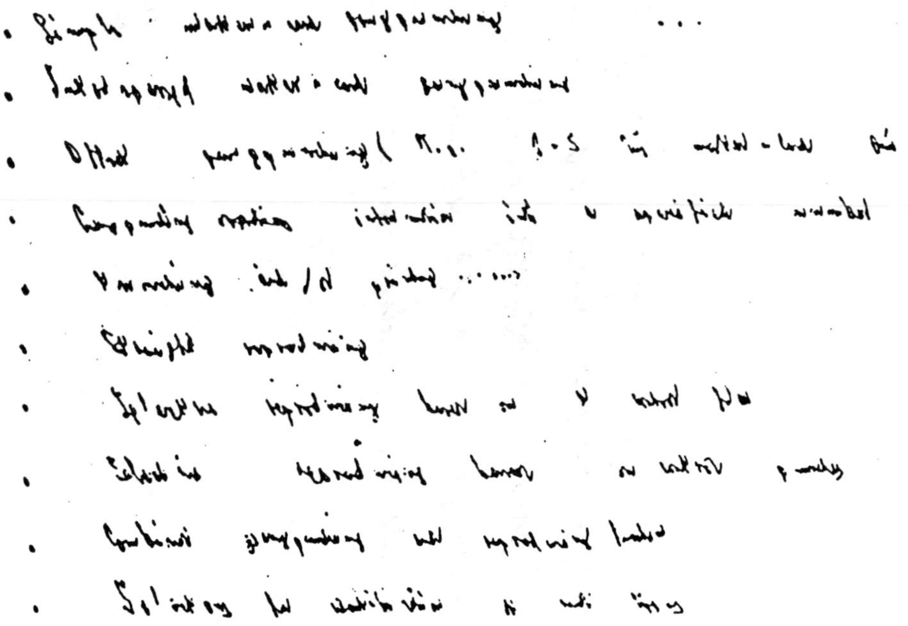

Fig. X.2 - Man, 30 years

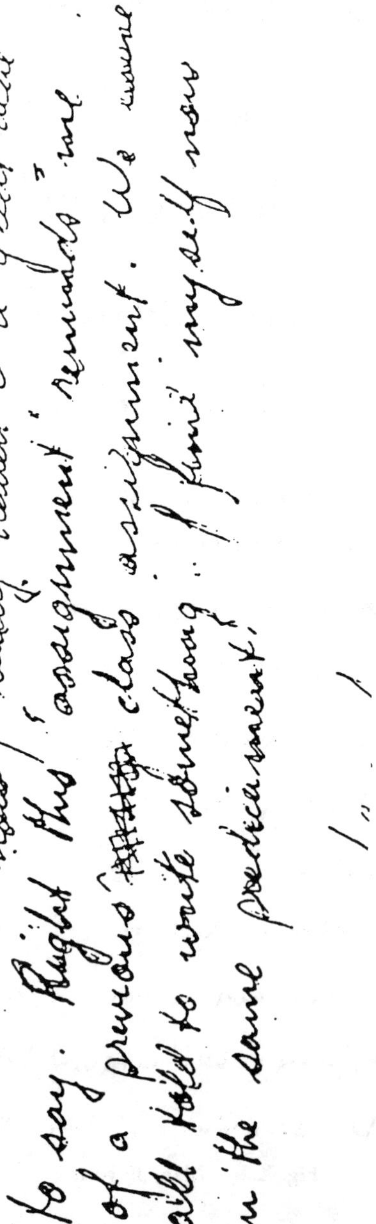

Fig. X.3
Man, 21 years

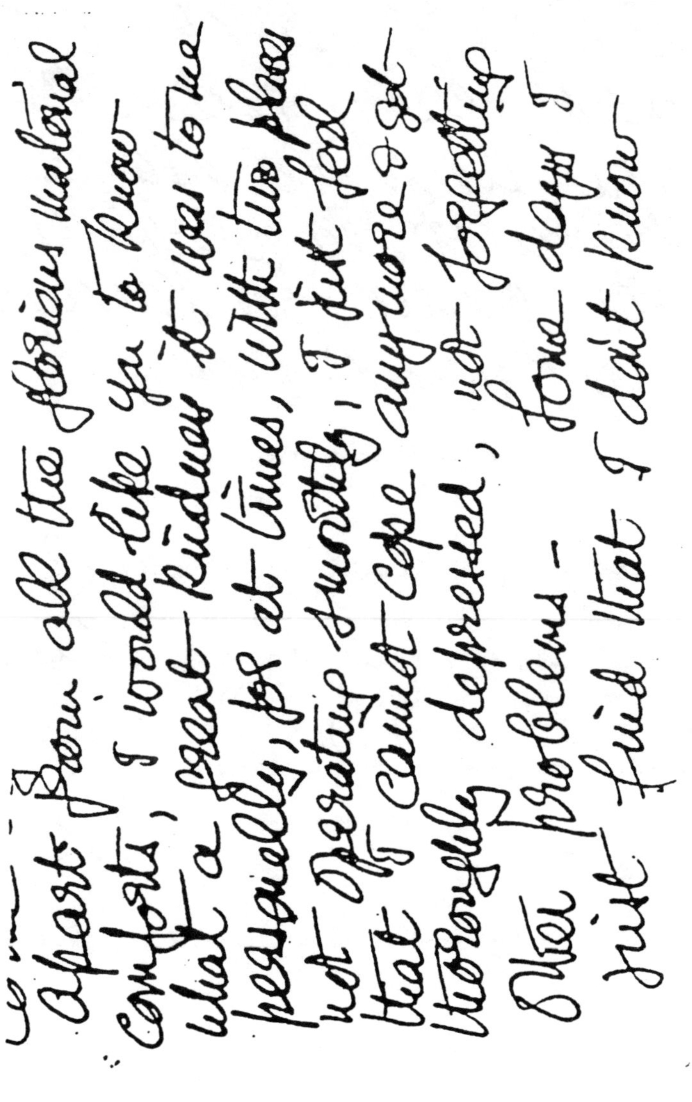

Apart from all the glorious material comforts, I would like you to know what a great kindness it was to me personally, for at times, with two places not operating smoothly, I just feel that I cannot cope anymore & get thoroughly depressed, not forgetting other problems – for a few days I just find that I don't know

Fig. X.4 - Woman, 40 years (cyclophrenic)

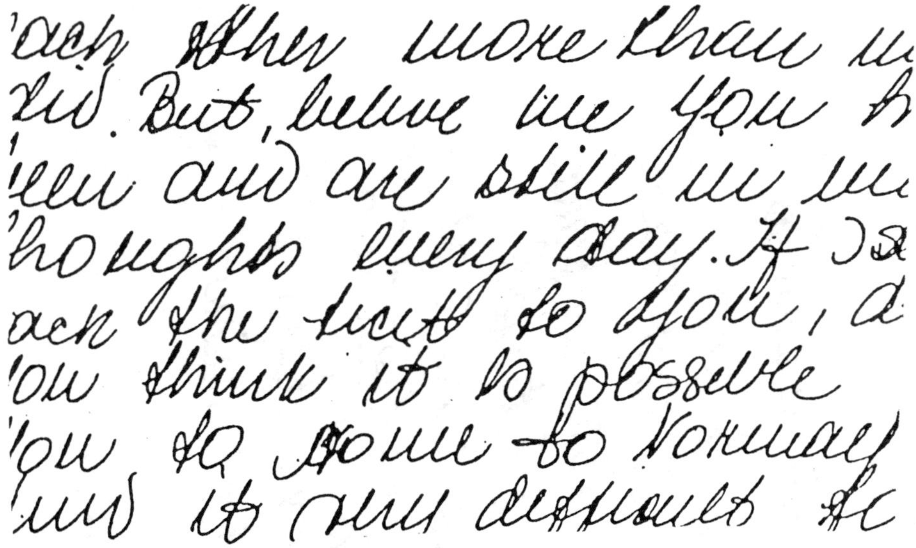

Fig. X.5 - Woman, 35 years

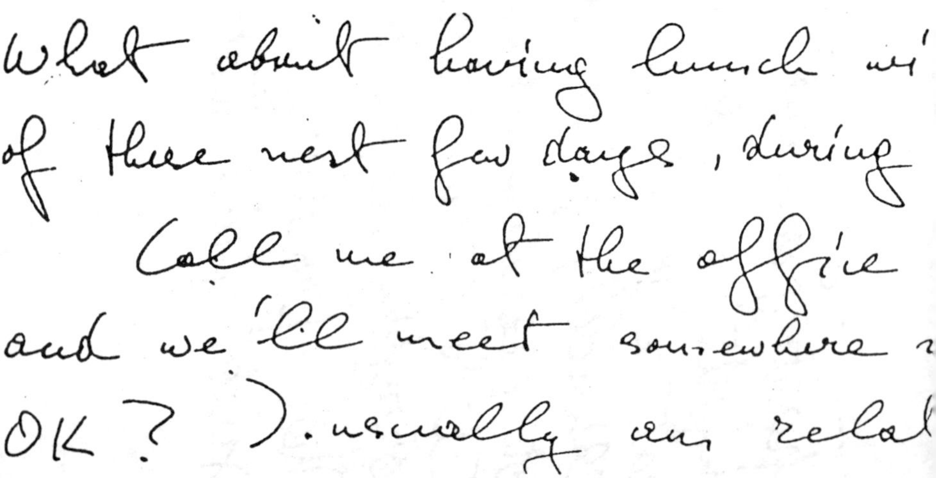

Fig. X.6 - Man, 60 years

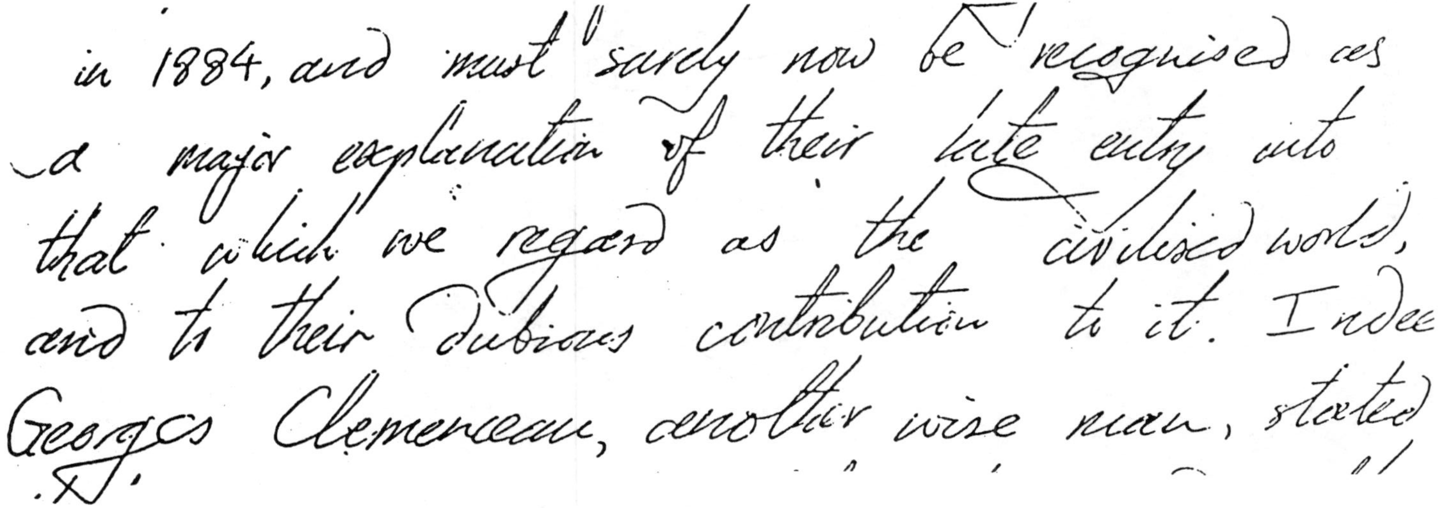

in 1884, and must surely now be recognised as
a major explanation of their late entry into
that which we regard as the civilised world,
and to their dubious contribution to it. Indee
Georges Clemenceau, another wise man, stated

Fig. X.7
Man, 20 years

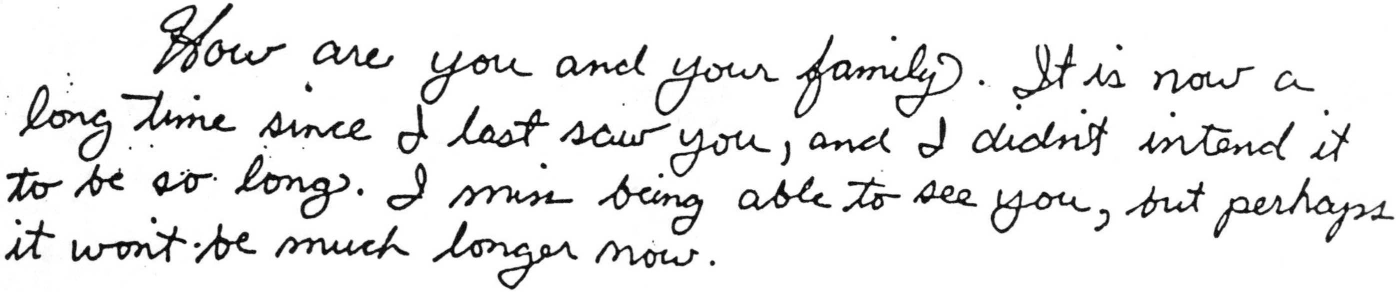

Fig. X.8
Man, 33 years

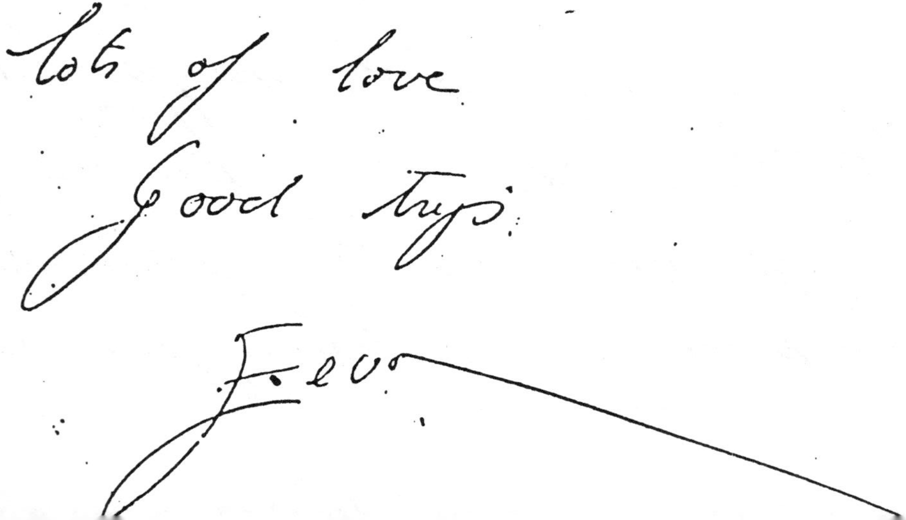

Fig. X.9
Woman, 34 years

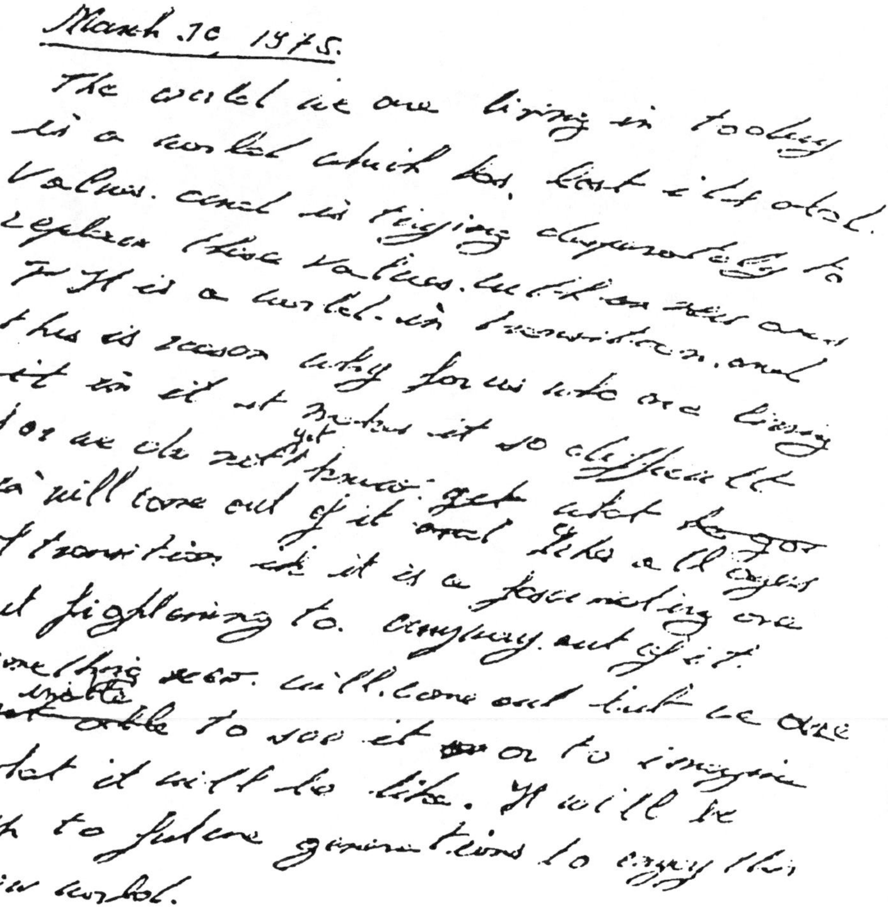

March 30 1975.
The world we are living in today is a world which has lost it's old values. and is trying desperately to replace these values. [illegible] It is a world in transition. and this is reason why for us who are living it [illegible] makes it so difficult for we do not yet know [illegible] will come out of it and what sort of transition [illegible] it is a fascinating one but frightening too. anyway out of it something new will come out but we are unable to see it or to imagine what it will be like. It will be up to future generations to enjoy this new world.

Fig. X.10 (10% reduction)
Man, 40 years

LECTURE XI

CLINICAL GRAPHOLOGY

With *Clinical Graphology*, or *Graphopathology* as it is usually called, we enter into a rather uncertain and quite dangerous branch of graphology.

Uncertain, because there are often many conflicting theories, first about whether specific illnesses are detectable through handwriting and second, whether there is enough scientific evidence for or against it.

It is dangerous, because many irresponsible practitioners of our science plunge into medical diagnoses based solely on speculation and intuition, without taking into account the emotional fragility of most people when it comes to matters of their health. The natural reaction is either: "Rubbish, I feel fine", (which they probably do). Or, if they decide to believe in the alleged illness, they may develop hypochondria, resulting in agonies, loss of sleep or appetite, and in some cases, even lead to relevant physical symptoms appearing to the point of real deterioration of their health.

Are both these dangers for the graphologist and for the client, worth the one possible case where the diagnosis might accidentally, and by mere coincidence, be right? What is the purpose of it all?

We must never forget that, with the exception of very few cases, graphology cannot diagnose specific illnesses - as yet. The reason for this is simple. As with the qualities and faults of each personality, the vast majority of illnesses appear in the writing - when they do early enough - through different combinations of signs in different combinations of temperaments. Every writing has its own particular fragilities and it is these, with very few exceptions, which are first affected by any physical malfunction: for example, pressure. An irregularity in pressure can be caused by 40,000 or so diseases, or morbid conditions, including the common cold, where the pressure during the period of suffering can become either lighter or heavier, according to the temperament of the sufferer.

For example, the Bilious (Choleric temperament) will probably see it as a nuisance, an obstacle to overcome, whereas the Lymphatic (Phlegmatic temperament) might treat it as temporary discomfort to suffer until it passes.

Since 1960, doctors and graphologists in America have been researching the effects of illnesses on handwriting. The Medical Tribune of New York, in the 9th October, 1967 issue, published an article on the diagnosis of Parkinson's disease. It was observed, by Dr. R. Schwab of Massachusetts General Hospital in Boston, and by Dr. J. McLennan of the Minnesota University Hospital, in Minneapolis, that the writing of Parkinson sufferers starts getting smaller, even microscopic, many months before the illness becomes apparent.

The Viennese, Dr. Alfred Kanfer of the Strang Clinic in New York, announced in 1964 that in 80% of cases, cancer can be detected up to 3 years before any symptoms appear, through examining the stroke with a 1000/1 microscope. He based his theory on the fact that the development of cancerous cells coincides with a neuromuscular deterioration which is reflected in the stroke and is detectable under microscopic examination.

But, how many and which other diseases affect the neuromuscular system? Can it only be cancer?

As yet, we do not have all the answers (at least, not to my knowledge), therefore great care must be taken when dealing with medical diagnoses through the handwriting, particularly if we are not medical doctors as well as graphologists.

There can be no doubt that this is a very delicate branch of graphology. Writing does manifest certain anomalies of neuro impulses as well as of a troubled spirit.

Let us see how.

Psychomotor impulses travel from the Cortex, which is the centre of psychic 'build up' (elaboration), to the Thalamus, which is the centre for co-ordination of mimic expressions, through to the Bulb, where incoming and outgoing neural information is gathered (the Bulbic keyboard), to reach the Medulla where it takes a purely motor aspect.

There is no unhealthy (morbid) syndrome, whether momentary or of lengthy duration, which does not affect the stroke and the writing generally.

The *dysgraphic* written document is easily obtained, objective, and has the added advantage that it can be examined without the physical presence of the patient. Dysgraphy may refer- to *calligraphic dysgraphy*, i.e. difficulty in the physical execution of the stroke, or *psychographic dysgraphy*, i.e. difficulty in writing caused by psychological factors. *(see Lecture IV)*

With regard to mental conditions, excesses (manic elation), inefficiencies (depression) and disturbances (various perturbations of the mind) are manifested in what is called 'cacography' (meaning defective or bad writing) - voluntary (intentional) or involuntary (reflex). These writings allow the evaluation of a problem, the determination of possible reactions and the possible frequency of more attacks. But we must not fall into the same temptation as many graphologists do, of saying that a certain sign indicates a certain illness. This is simplistic, insincere and, to say the least, runs the risk of turning graphology back into a party game.

The role of the graphologist is not meant to be daring, spectacular or flamboyant. It is precise, modest, prudent, careful and most of all restricted.

Dysgraphies, relevant to a large number of functional anomalies, can be grouped in 7 families:

1. Dyspnoic (difficulty in breathing)
2. Cardiovascular malfunctions
3. Intoxications
4. Nervous illnesses
5. Mental illnesses
6. Visual malfunctions
7. Psychopathological constitutions

The first 6 are self-explanatory. The most common and at the same time the least easily detectable, is the last one. Let us see them in order.

As a general rule, all functional anomalies produce *inhibited writings*. ***Inhibited*** is a very rich group. It includes in it the largest number of signs in the Jaminian dictionary, such as: suspended, broken, unfinished, amended, constrained, cramped, shaky, false connections, hesitant, faltering, etc., certain groups of signs such as: 'descending + weak + disconnected + poised' also indicate *inhibited*, or 'unvarying + slow + monotonous' will yield *inhibited* and so on.

Inhibitions are not only moral or emotional (psychic) as such, they can also be caused by a physical malfunction or discomfort, momentary or of lengthy duration.

It is natural therefore that *inhibited* is usually the first sign to be noticed in the writing of any of the above 7 categories.

DYSPNOIA

This usually causes suspended and constrained writing, slightly descending lines or end of lines, irregular pressure, often also spasmodic or congested (depending on the particular cause), unnecessary dots and occasional discordances. The down strokes of the upper zone are often twisted. The pace becomes slower. Spacing between letters, words and lines becomes wider and letters may be unfinished or fragmented. The stroke may have breakages. (*see Fig. XI.1*).

CARDIOVASCULAR MALFUNCTIONS

Arteriosclerosis, cerebral arteritis, severe hypertension etc. are usually manifested by a typically 'congested' writing. Letters are half formed (unfinished) and look chewed up, movements are inhibited, jerky, shaky, fragmented, broken, connectedness is irregular (if there is any at all),- the pressure is muddy, irregular and spasmodic (particularly in cerebral arteritis) and lines are descending. *(see Fig. XI.2)*

INTOXICATIONS

With intoxications, such as alcohol, tobacco, and all narcotics, the common sign, apart from inhibited, is lack of harmony; numerous amendments, shakiness or (depending on the temperament) discordant and/or monotonous writing, or very light or very heavy and congested writing might also indicate a form of intoxication.

From a research done recently on alcoholics some signs came up which were common to all: angular arcades and angles, lack of structure and total lack of curves (despite the fact that alcoholism is generally considered to be of oral origin). The writings were arrhythmic and their continuity, depending on the socio-cultural level of each writer, presented a dominance of juxtaposition. When grouped, the groupings of letters were irregular, following no logical (syllabic) sequence and the connected writings were mainly soldered (false connections). There were many lapses of continuity (disorientation). The majority of these writings were spaced out (lack of ability to connect naturally with one's past and future, isolation, emotional dependence, egocentrism). Lack of scriptural control, together with large spacings and sinuous lines showed lack of maturity and inability to adapt to reality. The firmness of the downstroke was affected, which indicated feebleness, lack of virility and inner assurance. The pressure was irregular, pastose and light, indicating immature sensuality, susceptibility to being influenced, difficulty in decision taking and weak will. Most of the writings were right slanted, few were left slanted and very few vertical, but in all of them direction was very irregular. Almost all had sinuous lines. The dimension was also mostly irregular, particularly in the middle zone, with the majority of the writings small and narrow. Those which were large, were also narrow with many gaps, indicating inferiority feeling, inhibitions, distrustfulness, suspicion, and selfishness. The layout was discordant and undisciplined. *(Fig. XI.3)*

To recapitulate, the most specific elements of these writings were:

- irregular pressure - light - pastose - muddy impression
- irregularity of dimension and a generally *confused* aspect
- lack of rhythm - inharmonious - sinuous - spaced out
- jerkiness - narrowness - right slanted - angular - angular arcades.

NERVOUS ILLNESSES

Neurological illnesses like Parkinsonism (which can be caused by anything from encephalitis, arteriosclerosis, or certain poisons, like carbon monoxide - or can be *idiopathic*), are numerous and fairly common. They are, also, probably the easiest (by comparison) to detect through the writing, mainly because of their more direct link with the motor centres. The movement becomes disorganised, the delicate control of the scriptural organ (usually the hand and the fingers) is lost. Predictive signs are extremely difficult to see with any certainty. It is less difficult after the disease has manifested itself, though still not at the beginning. *For example*, all very small writings do not point towards Parkinsonism. There are other signs which support this diagnosis, like slight tremor, jerkiness, uncertainty in the progress of the stroke and slowness.

MENTAL ILLNESSES

These are many and varied. They range from mild kleptomania and go through many kinds of *manias*, to excitations, melancholia, anxieties, obsessions, confusions, persecutions and psychoses of all degrees and orientations. Obviously, therefore, no specific sign, or set of signs, can express each single one of the above and its degree. As a general guide; regressive tendencies, (manifested in kleptomania, persecution, etc. which are centripetal as opposed to outward oriented tendencies seen in excitation, manias, obsessions, etc.) will produce a regressive and closed writing, usually small or medium, often double joined and, of course, discordant, inharmonious, inhibited (suspended, spasmodic, etc.) and all the classical signs of lack of balance and harmony. At the other extreme, almost completely mechanised movement, impersonal, rigid and totally 'silent' will show any mental illness but not its specific orientation (aggression or lack of it, for instance). Excitations, like megalomania, confusion, etc., generally cause an invading writing with disproportions, discordances, confusions, very large size, diving direction of lines, or very ascending, or even circular. Great anxieties are expressed with discordances and by horizontal movements being long and thrown as in t-bars and in volutes, angularity alternating with filiformity, confused writing, excessive superelevations and irregularities. *(see Lecture IX)*

VISUAL MALFUNCTIONS

Depending on their severity, these produce generally disorientated, inhibited writings; the concept of the paper - its size and positioning and of spacing, seem to be non-existent. The stroke is usually broken on the upward movement and uncertain, the irregularities of spacing are excessive, the pressure wavers between very light and very heavy and the size may be very large or very small. Great differences of strength in the vision between the 2 eyes is usually indicated either by a wider margin on the side corresponding to the weaker eye (the text tends to concentrate under the direct visual field of the healthier eye), or by chimneys. (*see VOLUME I, page 39*)

PSYCHOPATHOLOGICAL CONSTITUTIONS

A psychopathological constitution is a mixture of congenital tendencies which is manifested early in life and persist throughout its course. It is a permanent *psychic infirmity* from which many psychoses may develop. The symptoms are often relatively discreet and are apt to appear at critical moments in life, such as physical illness, an emotional shock, and of course at puberty and menopause. These symptoms are spontaneous and, more often than not, affect the movement (kinaesthesia) and the affectivity (emotions). Intelligence is not affected; the individual remains conscious and lucid. The people most likely to be of a psychopathic constitution are the Emotive Primary or *sympathico-tonics* and the Emotive Secondary or *vago-tonics.* The first will have quick and impulsive reactions which will be 'exterior reactions', lively, immediate and generally short-lived. These people are suggestible, mobile, changeable and always effervescent. They get hot flushes and palpitations. The second (ES) are not so exteriorised. They refrain from expressing their emotions, which are deeper and more long-lived. These people do not speak easily of their experiences, but they are painfully impressionable, excessively receptive and the echo of all shocks stays with them for a very long time.

The main signs of the 'emotive constitution' are: irregularities, disconnected or grouped, twisted, jerky, many amendments (corrections) and occasional shakiness.

The EP (*sympathico-tonics*) very often have an open writing with many flying strokes.

The ES (*vago-tonics*) have a closed and inhibited writing; hesitant, often regular, suspended, with unnecessary dots.

It goes without saying, of course, that one, two, or even three isolated signs of the above do not indicate an 'emotive constitution'. For instance, a jerky, or shaky, or irregular writing may indicate strong emotivity, but this does not allow us to conclude that the writer is of 'morbid' disposition.

The pathological state differs from that of the so-called normal, not by nature, but by degree, which would be expressed by the intensity of the above group of signs.

All normal people have ups and downs. We are all subjected to the rhythm of excitation and depression, to the periodic and repeated changes of our 'humour' (mood) and of our activity but between the so-called/'normal' state and the 'cyclothymic constitution' in its most intense phase (*cyclophrenia*), there is a long passage of transition.

The *cyclothymic* oscillates between *enthusiasm* (mania) and *depression*. The excitation of enthusiasm is more productive, relatively controlled and more conscious. The individual doesn't experience tiredness or sleepiness. He, or she, is talkative, active, productive, works hard, has great lucidity and fluency of words and writings, is 'awake', curious, gregarious, optimistic, communicative, enthusiastic, generous and seductive towards the opposite sex. Then slowly, and for no apparent reason, all the excitement disappears and is replaced by sadness, melancholia, depression, disenchantment, timidity, discouragement, slowness, fatigue, sleepiness, laziness. The individual seeks solitude, is fearful, lacks confidence and security, is doubtful and apprehensive of tomorrow and resents his past. He (or she) is full of remorse, lacks energy and spontaneity. He gets easily tired, physically and intellectually, finds verbal communication difficult and does not even desire to talk. He is humble and painfully reproaches himself for everything. *(see also Lecture IX)*

In their circular movement, excitation and depression succeed each other without interruption. In the alternating movement (which is much rarer), each state is followed by an interval of psychic health and more or less normality.

We know that the *neuroses*, which are mental attitudes and cause symptoms and therefore behavioural troubles, are conscious. The patient knows that he is not normal, and often seeks help. We also know that the lack of sense of reality and hence the defence mechanisms, augment as we climb up the ladder of abnormality.

In the *psychoses* the sense of reality is lost. The writing will show a certain fear of reality and a refusal to accept it, and it is repressed into the unconscious along with the instincts. This loss of the *reality function* has serious consequences for the conduct of everyday life. It is manifested in the writing through imbalances in the upper and middle zone, in the rhythm and formlevel, and in the adaptability of the movement in space (dimension, direction) and time (speed).

It has been noticed that the *writing of psychotic* people gives very little information about the state of their mind and their psyche *(Fig. XI.4)*. It shows, most of the time, very little difference, if any, from the writing of neurotics. This is because the reality function is not everything. The writer also has an inner life, most intense and personal. His 'delirium' is a stronger reality for him and he does not think that he stands outside 'normal' reality, but that it is the others who are outside reality. So his writing, in the majority of cases, will show a fair concept of and adaptation to reality; his own personal reality. For instance, if a writing shows strong, overpowering imagination, we must seek other signs which will indicate a relatively conscious behaviour, in order to support our supposition of a psychotic tendency. *(For Examples of this category see LECTURE IX).*

OTHER MALFUNCTIONS

In addition, one must not confuse signs which may indicate:

Arthritis which makes writing heavy, rather rigid and sober, often monotonous and horizontal.

Hyperthyroidic people, whose writing is irregular, 'thrown', jerky, shaky, often also twisted.

Hypothyroidic people, whose writing is slow, mostly round, hesitant, often discordant and twisted.

Liver malfunctions which usually produce a concentrated writing, turned inwards, with 'dry' movement, simple forms without any ornamentations and mostly vertical.

Stomach malfunctions which are indicated by writing that is rather disorganised (mainly in the m/z), descending and amended.

It can never be repeated too often that graphology is not here to judge or to measure the value of each individual. That must never slip out of the mind of anyone who wishes to consider himself or herself as a serious, scientific and conscientious graphologist.

Graphology's task is to investigate, to see and to give help where it is needed, in the form of advice.

In the Western world, 99.5% of the population suffers from one ailment or another, at some stage, or permanently - from simple neurosis to severe mental or physical ailments belonging to any of the seven families we have discussed - **and that includes graphologists.** Let us not forget that.

* * *

SOURCES

COBBAERT, A-M. *Decouvrez la Graphologie,* Tchou, Paris, 1978.

CRÉPIEUX-JAMIN, J. *L'Écriture et le Caractère,* ed. P.U.F., Vendome, 1960.

CRÉPIEUX-JAMIN, J. *Les Élèments de l'écriture des canailles,* Flamarion, 1976.

FRIEDENHAIN, P. *Write and Reveal,* Peter Owen, London, 1973 .

PULVER, M. *Le Symbolisme de l'Écriture,* ed. Stock, Paris, 1953.

Revue of the SFDG Nos. 110, 122, 161, 176, 182.

STRELETSKI, Dr. C. *Précis de Graphologie Pratique,* ed. Vigot Frère, Paris, 1950.

VELS, A. *La Séléction du Personnel,* ed. Mont-Blanc, Genève, 1973.

HANDWRITING SAMPLES of LECTURE XI

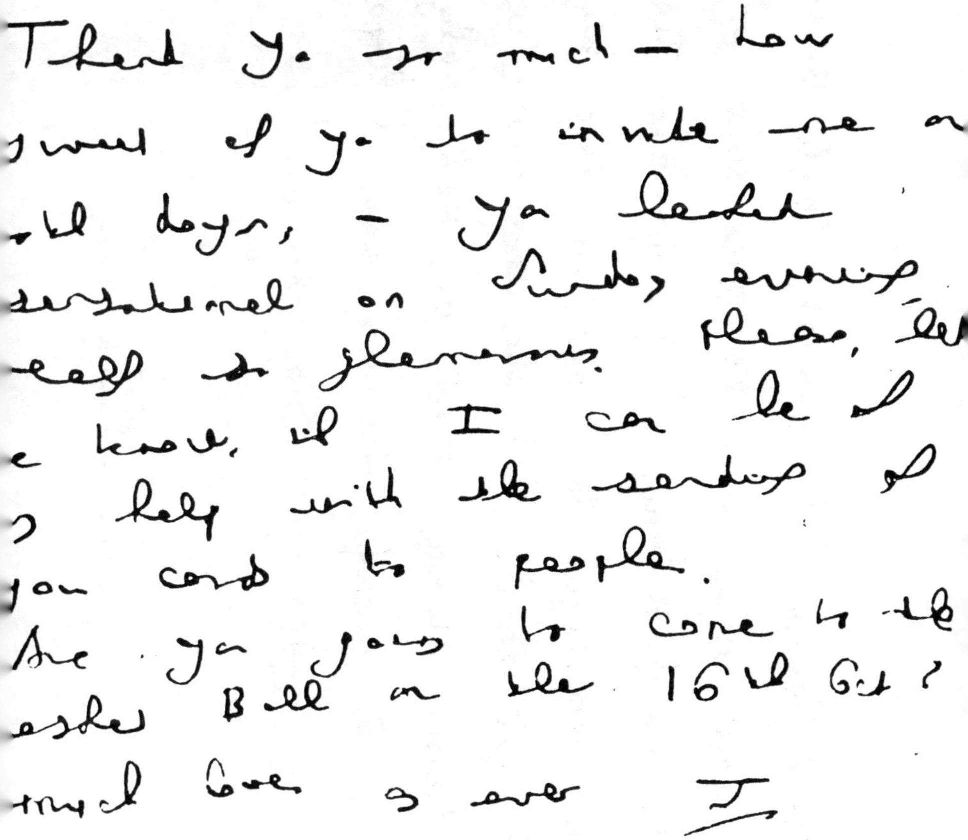

Fig. XI.1

Man, 52 years

An overall slack writing with some bizarre movements. Despite its lack of structure, it maintains dignity and a style of its own. Respiratory difficulties.

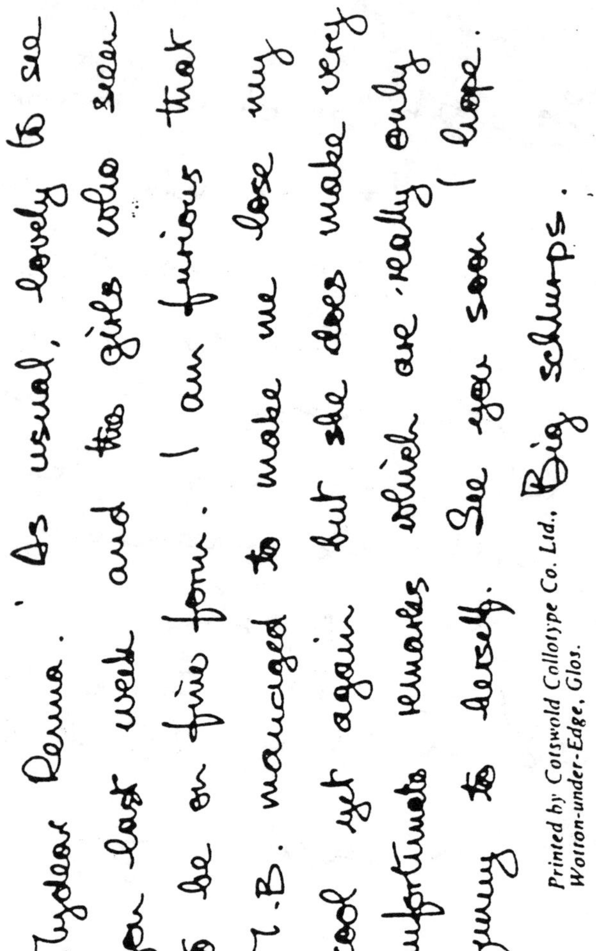
My dear Renna. As usual, lovely to see you last week and the girls who seem to be on fine form. I am furious that M.B. managed to make me lose my cool yet again but she does make very unfortunate remarks which are really only funny to herself. See you soon I hope. Big schlurps.

Printed by Cotswold Collotype Co. Ltd., Wotton-under-Edge, Glos.

Fig. XI.2
Man, 54 years. Cardiovascular malfunction

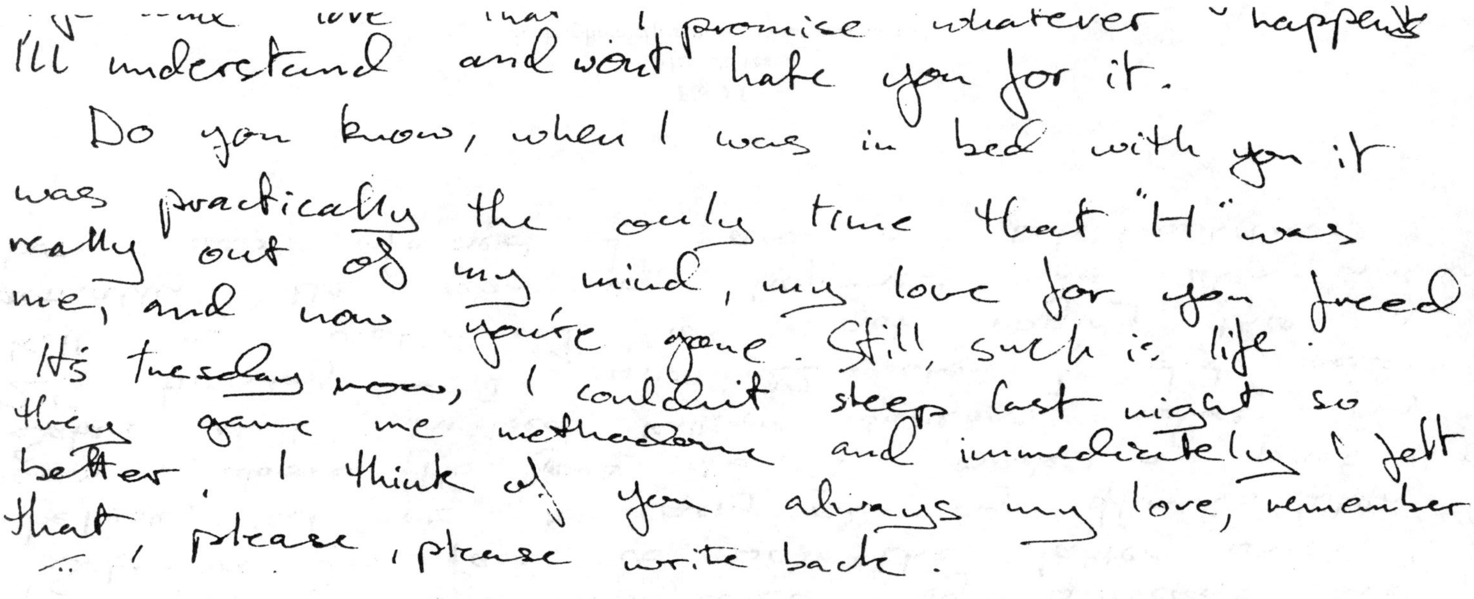

... love that I promise whatever happens I'll understand and won't hate you for it.

Do you know, when I was in bed with you it was practically the only time that "H" was really out of my mind, my love for you freed me, and now you're gone. Still, such is life.
It's tuesday now, I couldn't sleep last night so they gave me methadone and immediately I felt better, I think of you always my love, remember that, please, please write back.

Fig. XI.3
Man, 21 years - Heroine addict.

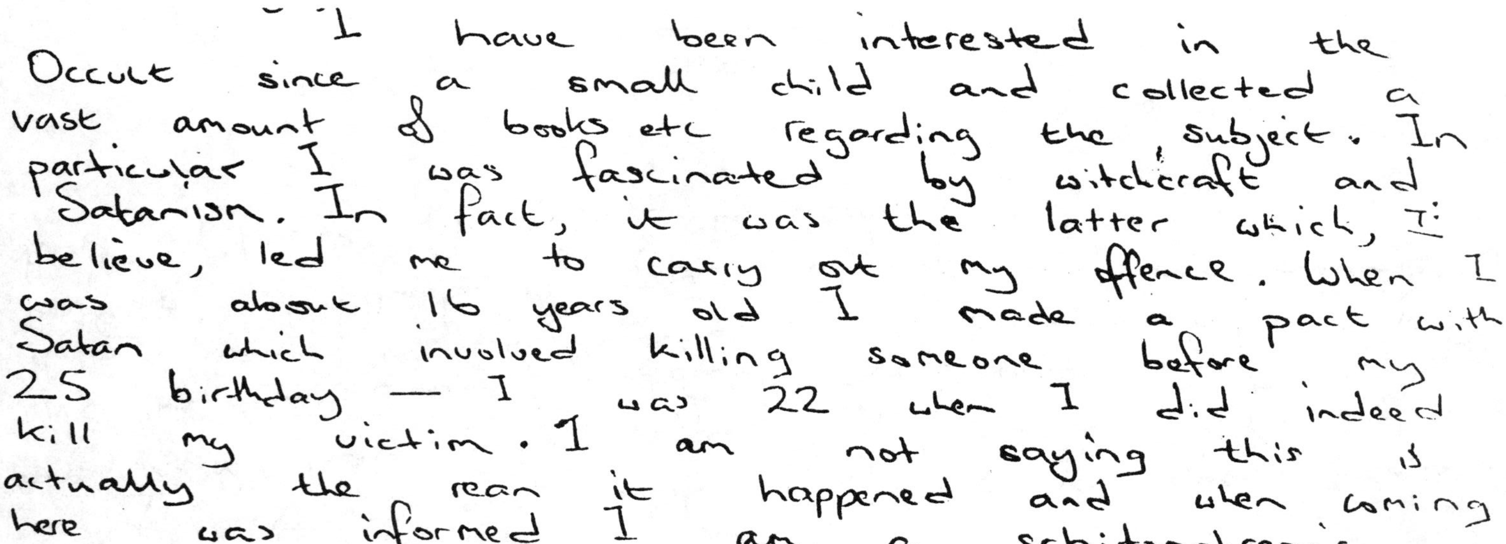

I have been interested in the
Occult since a small child and collected a
vast amount of books etc regarding the subject. In
particular I was fascinated by witchcraft and
Satanism. In fact, it was the latter which, I
believe, led me to carry out my offence. When I
was about 16 years old I made a pact with
Satan which involved killing someone before my
25 birthday — I was 22 when I did indeed
kill my victim. I am not saying this is
actually the rean it happened and when coming
here was informed I am a schitroohrenic.

Fig. XI.4
Man, 26 years
Schizophrenic/paranoïac. *Please read the text.*

LECTURE XII

PROBLEM WRITINGS

People who care to learn graphology and wish to practise it, should first ask the question "What is the purpose of graphology?". Essentially graphology helps us to understand ourselves, which is a necessary precondition to understanding others. We must start with an open mind, admitting the truth about our own psychic structure. We must examine our personality, complexes, ambivalences and neuroses. Both good and bad points must be looked at, as a psychoanalyst would, with rigorous impartiality and without excuses. Only then will one have the right to analyse others, always bearing in mind the necessity for great objectivity and even greater prudence.

The occasions for error are innumerable and ever present. Any writing may be a trap. Simple fatigue can appear as lying; introversion or profound sensitivity as rigidity; dishonesty or silliness as introversion; cunning malice, as adaptability; emotional immaturity, as dishonesty the list is endless.

Bad qualities also have degrees: grossness, envy, disorderliness, aggression, vulgarity, rudeness, trickery and others, on their own, are not necessarily crimes. Paired up with other imperfections, however they *may* be. This will be evident in the writing *only* by the grouping of many different signs.

Three of the most important elements of the personality are :

- Emotivity (depth of receptivity, soul and mind),
- Activity (with all the variations of will), and
- Sincerety (clarity, honesty, simplicity and straightforwardness).

In all writings we must first look for the degree of these qualities.

It is important to assess correctly the degree of intensity of these qualities since they have great impact on all other qualities, good and bad, and will transform them in one way or another.

In the writing:

- Small irregularities are the index for emotivity and its affects,
- Speed and pressure reveal all the varieties of activity,
- Simplicity and clarity show possibly a lack of dishonesty. (Honesty is difficult to see in the writing - *see Lecture VII*).

INSINCERITY

Strong aggression, paired up with amorality, may lead to crime. **Lying** is only one small factor of amorality (others being duplicity, ruse, hypocrisy, dissimulation, secretiveness and dishonesty) but it is one of its most insidious and repugnant aspects. There is, of course, a world of difference between the small social lies which are necessary for any civilised inter-relation (without which the world would be impossible to live in) and the lying of the person who cheats and deceives others.

The more subtle the *signs of lying in a writing* are and the more difficult they are to detect, the graver is the indication. The writer is agile and convincing, and therefore the bigger the risk is that he will be believed, and he may remain undetected and consequently destructive to his fellow men. There are cases when the writing may even appear harmonious or rhythmic at first glance.... .

The signs of lying generally in a writing are multiple and vary from personality to personality.

Never will one sign only indicate lying, no matter how many times it is repeated. Some graphologists tend, for instance, to interpret covering strokes or suspended letters as lying. This is wrong. There are many introverted and inhibited people who dislike close contact and avoid putting themselves forward. They will produce many covering strokes and suspended letters, angles, closed ovals, arcades, and/or light pressure. They are not necessarily liars, they are only timid or too sensitive. Their writing will usually be also constrained or controlled, inhibited overall, the movement may be fragile or uncertain and the letters unfinished. These people may lie in so much as they may answer the question "How are you?" with "Very well thank you" whilst they may not be well at all. The reason is evident.

Real lying is the one exception to the rule which says: "All signs which are not constant or repeated or whose value is not reinforced by others of the same nature should be ignored". For example, in a sober, mature, fluent writing - which indicates an educated person with an agile, well co-ordinated hand - one or two signs out of context, which cannot be attributed to any accident (a push, a sneeze, a fluff on the-tip of the pen, etc.) must put the graphologist on his guard for other indications of insincerity. These might include ambiguous letters (indistinct), reversed movements, unnatural forms, some small ornamentations (in an otherwise simple writing), a signature which differs from the text, a very sinuous baseline and/or undulating words. (see also page 205 of *Graphology, Volume I* and *Lecture VII*).

The Dominants are always the best guide for the interpretation of all the rest of the signs. They are indicative of the general superiority or inferiority of each writing and provide the graphologist with the first deductions.

Insincerity, or ***lying*** can be defensive, pathological or offensive (deliberate).

Defensive lying springs from fear, insecurity, feeling of inferiority or introversion, in which case the root lies in the writer's past, his upbringing, his education or social environment. It is not malign and should not be treated as such.

Pathological lying is an illness. People who suffer from this will lie for the sake of not telling the truth. Paranoiacs often lie for no reason at all, even to themselves. Mythomaniacs and megalomaniacs are two more categories of people who belong to this group.

Offensive lying is the malignant covering of the truth for a distinct and very precise purpose, for example to mislead others in order to gain some profit. Thieves, underworld dealers and all criminals, who are not necessarily unbalanced, practise this sort of lying.

The writing signs of these three groups of people are self-evident. *For instance*, signs of insecurity, introversion and inferiority will guide us towards the *'defensive'* interpretation of lying if such signs are present. *Not all insecure, introverted people with inferiority feelings necessarily lie.*

Signs of lying may differ from one species of writing to another : *for instance*, round writings with bow ties and looped garlands, lassos, etc.; slow, heavy, discordant writings; imprecise and disorderly writings; sinuous, regressive, weak, complicated, constrained writings or writings which are hesitant, formless, having suspended or unfinished letters or very discreetly amended writings with imprecise word endings.

Artificial writings are the commonest indication of insincerity. Crépieux-Jamin calls "artificial" writings those which show an "affected, systematic and simultaneous use" of exaggerations, constraint, complications, and whimsical forms.

Pronounced irregularities of speed will also indicate lying, particularly with filiformity and an undulating baseline.

Great differences of style is another index of insincerity. There are people who claim to have two or more styles of writing. If these are truly different, then this is an unfavourable indication regarding their morality.

The following examples are writings of people with varying degrees of insincerity and morality.

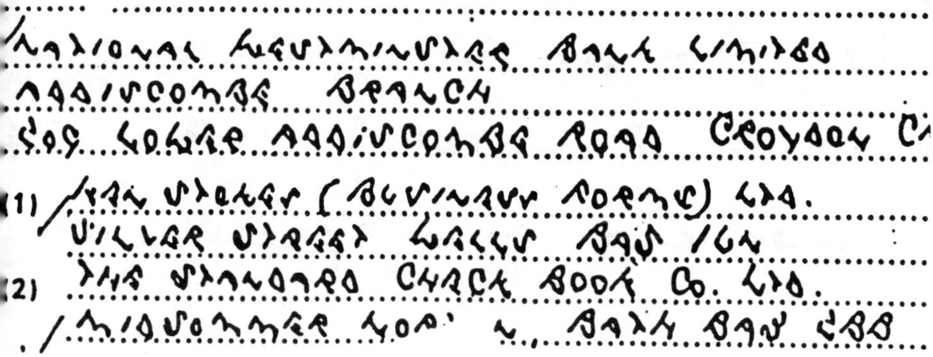

Fig. XII.1
Man, 30 years - defensive

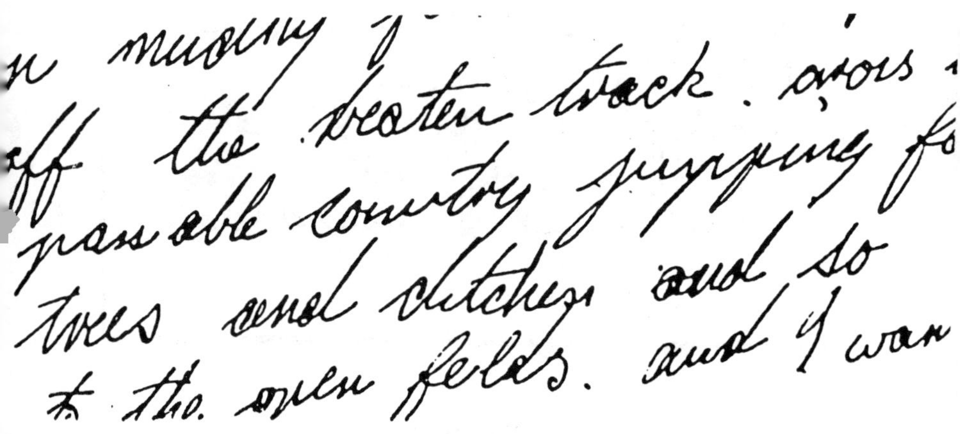

Fig. XII.2
Man, 40 years - defensive

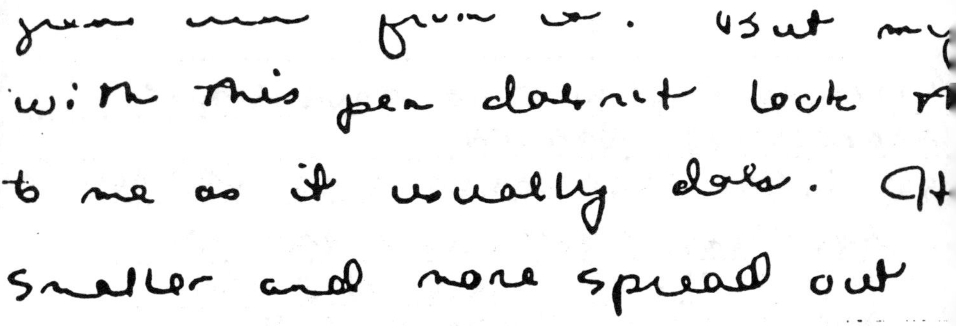

Fig. XII.3a
Woman, 34 years - defensive

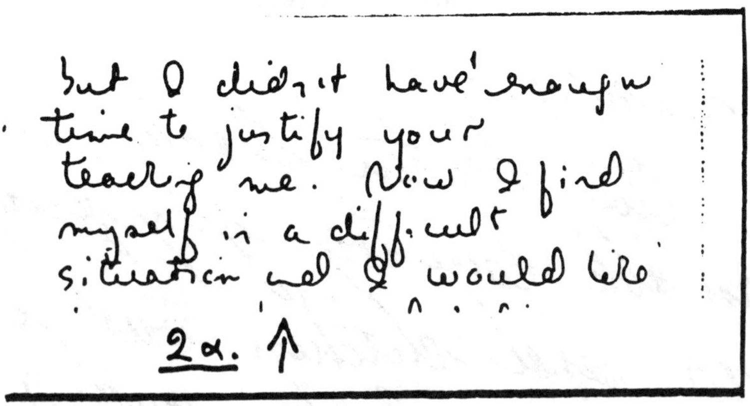

Fig.XII.3b
same as XII.3a

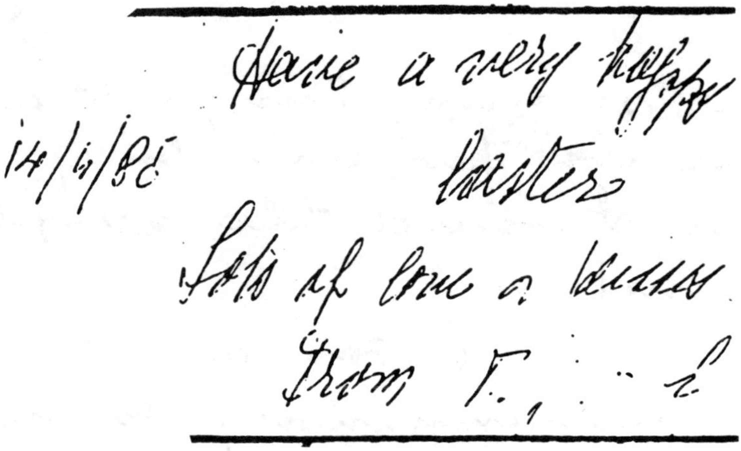

Have a very happy
Easter
Lots of love & kisses
From T. — —
14/4/86

Fig. XII.4
Woman, 77 years - defensive / pathological

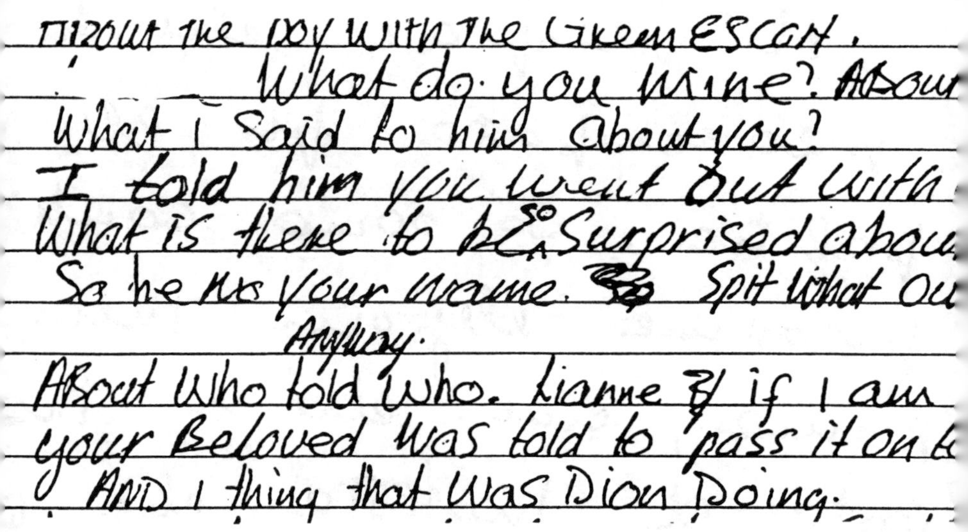

About the boy with the Green Escort.
What do you mean? About
What I said to him about you?
I told him you went out with
What is there to be so surprised about
So he has your name. Spit what out
Anyway.
About who told who. Lianne if I am
your Beloved was told to pass it on
AND I thing that was Dion Doing.

Fig.XII.5
Man, 40 years - pathological

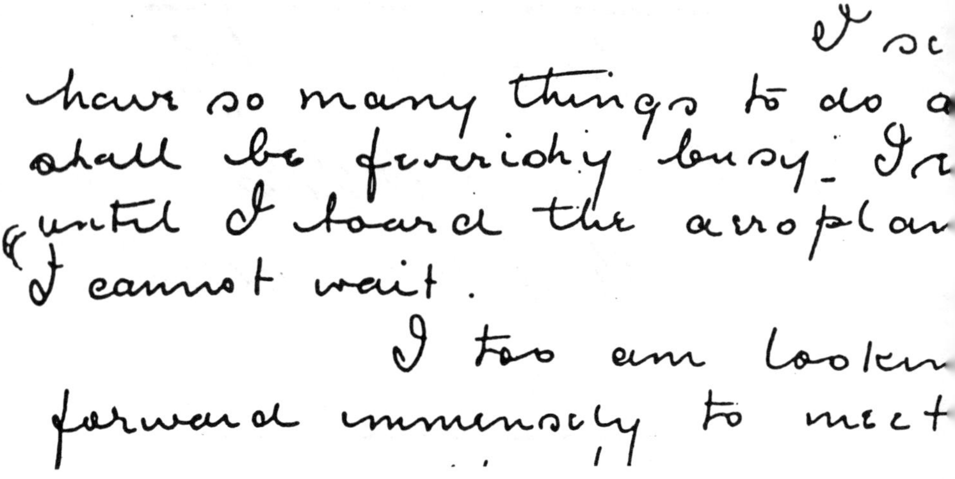

I sc
have so many things to do a
shall be feverishly busy. I r
until I board the aeroplan
I cannot wait.
I too am lookin
forward immensely to meet

Fig. XII.6
Man, years - offensive

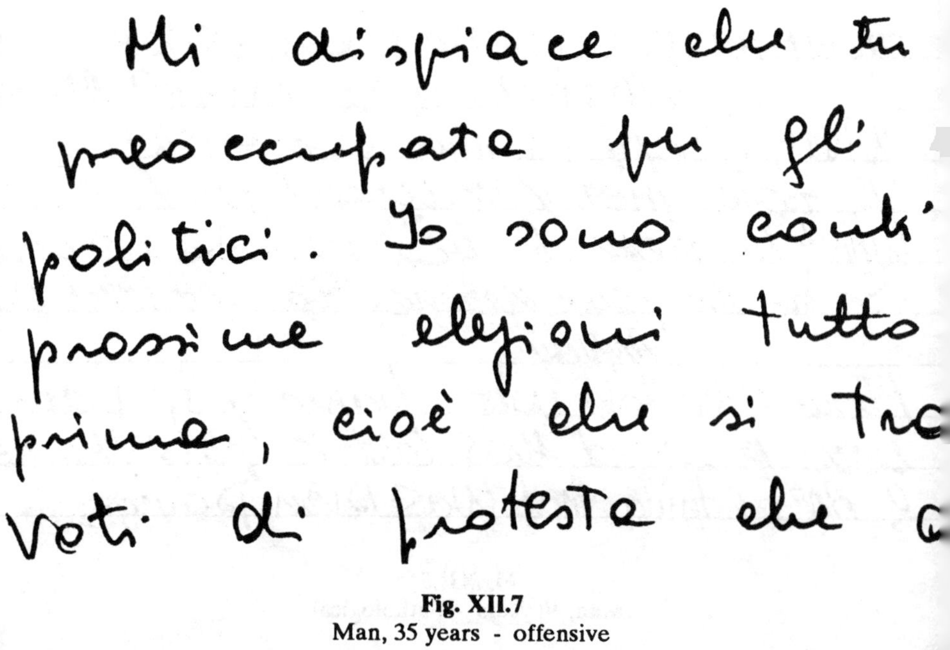

Mi dispiace che tu
preoccupato per gli
politici. Io sono convi
prossime elezioni tutto
prima, cioè che si tro
voti di protesta che a

Fig. XII.7
Man, 35 years - offensive

AGGRESSION

Aggression is as old as man himself. Adler sees aggressivity as a compensation for the worry created by feelings of inferiority and consequently as "will to power over other people". Freud sees it as a projection of the "death impulse".

The multiple meanings of the word *aggressivity*, are due to the *diversity of the situations which cause it.* The most common understanding of it is, 'the tendency to attack with actions or with hostile words, other individuals, in order to gain ground or to eliminate obstacles, or to gain revenge'.

Aggression is more often seen in men than in women. It is probably connected with the male hormone, testosterone, rather than with the 'Y' chromosome, as was thought some years ago.

Out of the four Hippocratic Temperaments, the Bilious (Choleric) and the Nervous (Melancholic) are the most likely to be aggressive. The Bilious is combative, the Nervous is impatient and irritable. The Lymphatic (Phlegmatic) is more passive and therefore aggression, if present, will be manifested more as a passive opposition. The Sanguine is more supple and flexible and any aggression is more likely to be expressed by sarcasm, cynicism or irony.

Aggressive behaviour has many causes such as frustration, dissatisfaction, overpopulation, fear, lack of security, revenge, etc.

Aggression is not necessarily directed outwards, towards other people. It can be inhibited and transformed into indifference or, in other cases, can be turned against the self. This is more or less unconscious. Most suicides and almost all accidents are caused by this psychological mechanism.

Its roots stem mostly from childhood : lack of love (which is the nourishment of the affective life, as much as food is the nourishment of the biological life and education the nourishment of the intellect), lack of compassionate treatment and humiliation are the psychological causes of a non-pathological aggression.

Pathological aggression (and violence) is caused by physical malfunctions, such as alcohol or other drug intoxications, schizophrenia, paranoia, epilepsy, perversion of the instincts (such as sadism), obsessional neuroses, or by some medical conditions such as haemorrhoids, gastro-duodenal ulcers and others.

Aggression can be active, turning outwards or inwards (physical or intellectual) or passive (sulking, omissions, etc.).

Aggression in writing is indicated in many ways. It can appear in writings of any dimension or speed. It can show in a disorderly and confused writing (mental disorder - imbalance), or in a compact writing (anxiety), or in an invading writing (lack of control). The pressure can be heavy to trenchant, muddy, pale, sharp pointed, clubbed, spasmodic and/or precise. The writing may be strongly diminishing or enlarging (brusqueness). Rigid writings very slanted to the right or to the left, or very orderly, or of variable slant with discordances, jerky movements, tangled lines and very connected, also show aggression, as do angular, narrow and thrown movements - particularly in the end strokes or in the *t*-bars. High *t*-bars in the form of a whip or a sword and shark's teeth, when constantly repeated, will also show aggression, *if the pressure is firm.*

In writings indicating anality (Freud) there will be aggressive opposition (if it exists), and in writings indicating orality, there will be aggressive avidity and demand (if they exist).

Finally, it must be stressed that:

(a) the tendency to violence is not necessarily shown, unless it is released or provoked in one way or another (i.e. frustration, alcohol, deprivation, etc.)

(b) one single sign will never indicate aggression in any writing, four or five signs must be present and consistent.

EQUILIBRIUM

Equilibrium is a state of balance between the constitutional factors, resulting in a 'healthy' psychological structure and impartiality of judgement.

This is the ideal target (conscious or unconscious) of every thinking being. In reality, absolute equilibrium is a very rare state indeed. It is also a dynamic state which may appear and disappear, since it is "constantly challenged by exterior influences or by inner vulnerabilities or exceptional talents", (S. Bresard).

Equilibrium presupposes emotional maturity, adaptability, equal balance of the humours, a perfect balance between extroversion - introversion, and an equal development of the Jungian functions. To achieve all this, a good balance of the regional axis, resolved ambivalences and a healthy will are necessary.

Activity and dynamism are the accelerators and inhibitions are the brakes. Harmony between the two will produce equilibrium.

Equilibrium can be achieved in different ways depending on the elan, the defence mechanisms, the quality of intelligence, the depth of emotivity, the ability to adapt and the powers of self-affirmation of every individual. The combinations are innumerable and extremely complex.

There are two main orientations of equilibrium : one which preserves what there is (material, intellectual, or moral) and the other which pushes towards the unknown (pioneering actions, scientific research, or artistic expression). (S. Bresard)

Homogeneity of tendencies, coordinated towards the same target, produces a stable and durable equilibrium, which can be on any level, depending upon the general vitality of the individual and his intellectual quality.

To assess the degree of equilibrium in a writing, a thorough knowledge of the psychology of movement is indispensable, since movement alone explains the significance of forms, pressure, dimension, direction and continuity.

The "Instinctive-organised" - (Susanne Bresard)

"The optimum instinctive equilibrium is between the motivating power of inner forces and the adaptation to outer obstacles. This equilibrium is spontaneous and sustained by vitality". This is how Susanne Bresard (ex-president of the S.F.G.) defines her own observation of 'instinctive-organised' people, as she calls them.

The forms of the letters are inseparable from the movement. They are the result of constant extending and flexing movements rising and returning easily to and from the baseline,"just like the movements of dance, and like the progression of walking". The movement is flowing.

In the *writing of the instinctive-organised*, the stroke, regularly propelled and nourished through pressure, curves in numerous ovoid forms, ("think of the elongated form of the fish and of birds" explains Susanne Bresard).

The movements which produce oviform writing are: clear (flawless), rich but economical in effort and without embellishments, firm and supple, with confident down-movement, precise return to the baseline, and easy (free) re-start.

These movements express a substantial reserve of expansive force, and easy adaptation to the present. They symbolise a "maximum density of vitality with a minimum of gestures for maximum dynamic progress".

"Ovoid forms are the harmonious and perseverant culmination of a continuous adjustment".

This equilibrium presupposes the implicit acceptance of reality, a regular and controlled dynamism and a regular effort constantly renewed against ever-present obstacles.

The more intense the active affirmation is, the more ample is the ovoid movement.

Instinctive-organised people are always efficient. This state is 'normal' and without rigidity. Analytical intelligence does not interfere except in complex situations.

The intelligence of the instinctive-organised evaluates the best means to achieve a result. The individual has a vigilant critical sense without getting sidetracked by intellectual acrobatics, and he is more oriented towards results than towards speculation. He foresees the results of his actions and does not confuse reality with his desires. His judgement is independent, thoughtful, careful, methodical, penetrating and he uses concrete and practical comparisons before reaching an important decision. He adapts his actions to his targets, as well as to his own personal level of understanding. He is an instinctive diplomat and can easily be convincing.

His affectivity is mature and embracing, he has easy contact, spontaneity, and is observant of other people's reactions. He is open to exchange without any kind of effort, is direct and sociable without prejudice or preconceived ideas.

The instinctive-organised has good initiative and a wide range of achieving abilities. His activity is *fluent* and *progressive*, he is practical and adaptable, and is not disturbed by the unexpected. He can control his irritability in the face of slackness and inefficiency (mental or physical) of other people with less vitality.

Excessive sensitivity (which increases vulnerability), an excessive tendency to analyse (which diminishes the reasons for action), a particularly 'gifted' personality, or excessive ambition, disturb the harmony of equilibrium.

Any conscious effort to discipline the above traits will produce difficulties in adaptability, as conflict is experienced in a forced alteration, for instance, a conscious and effortful manifestation of dynamism (or other quality such as ambition, activity, etc.) will inevitably produce anxiety, depression and inadaptability.

All people need renewing, recharging and stimulating, otherwise they may become depressed and cannot perform efficiently.

The instinctive-organised is equipped with self-regulating powers through activity. He needs to be in constant touch with reality. He needs exchange and visible results of his actions. If he is deprived of these he will become deeply depressed. He will seek activities oriented towards the common good as he needs a viable reason for living. He will plunge courageously into a risky venture - although conscious of the dangers - in the search for a new field of action, where he will be able to renew his reasons for action and living.

The instinctive-organised always tries to find how best to use his potential and his abilities for the common good, in order to find the reasons for his existence.

His equilibrium is stable because of the spontaneous co-ordination of his tendencies which results in a good active adaptation to concrete situations.

* * *

SOURCES

BRESARD, S. — *L'écriture empreinte de l'homme,* Privat, 1976.

COLO, C.
GOURSAC, R. de
LIÈVRE, F.
PINON, J. — *L'agressivité dans l'écriture et le comportement.* GGCF, 1991.

FAIDEAU, P. et al — *La Graphologie,* M. A., 1983.

GAILLAT, G. — *La Graphologie,* RETZ, 1973.

PULVER, M. — *Le Symbolisme de l'Écriture,* Stock, 1953, R. 177 - 1985.

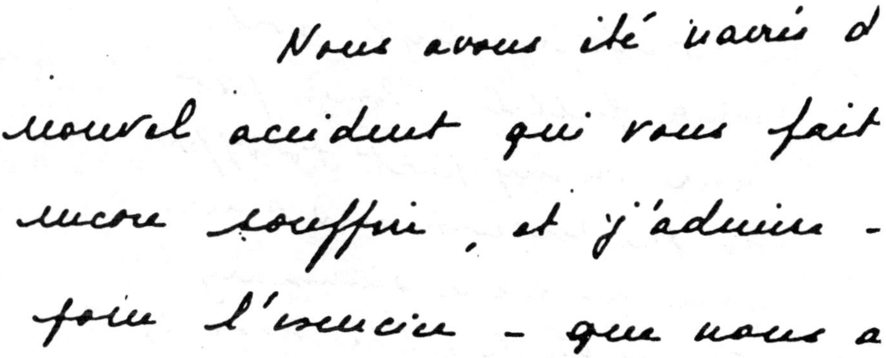

Nous avons été navrés d
nouvel accident qui vous fait
encore souffrir, et j'admire -
faire l'exercice - que vous a

Fig. XII.8
Woman, 53 years - Instinctive-organised

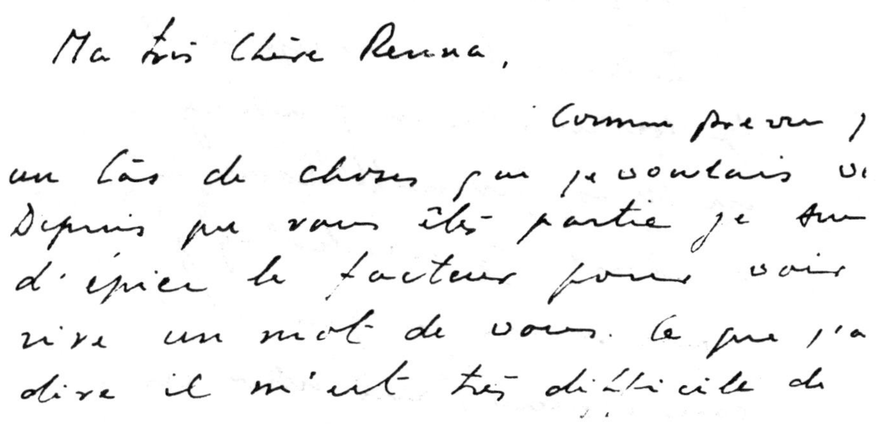

Ma très Chère Renna,
Comme prévu, j
un tas de choses que je voulais vo
Depuis que vous êtes partie je su
d'épier le facteur pour voir
vive un mot de vous. Ce que j'a
dire il m'est très difficile de

Fig. XII.9
Gregorio Garavito - Instinctive-organised

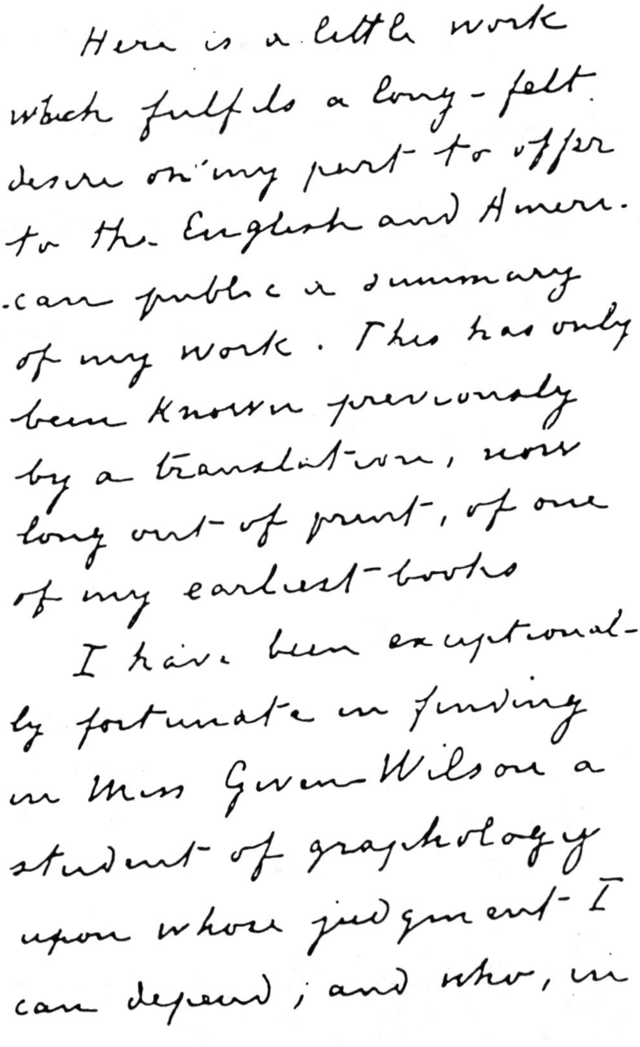

Here is a little work
which fulfils a long-felt
desire on my part to offer
to the English and Ameri-
-can public a summary
of my work. This has only
been known previously
by a translation, now
long out of print, of one
of my earliest books
I have been exceptional-
ly fortunate in finding
in Miss Gwen Wilson a
student of graphology
upon whose judgment I
can depend; and who, in

Fig. XII.10
J. Crépieux-Jamin - Instinctive-organised

PART 4

VARIOUS SYSTEMS

LECTURE XIII
The Psychobiological Approach

LECTURE XIV
Graphometry

LECTURE XIII

THE PSYCHOBIOLOGICAL APPROACH

Graphology is closely linked with psychology, so much so, that there can be no graphology without at least some basic knowledge of psychology. In order to describe an individual in a non-physical way, we have to use psychological terminology, which has to be learned.

There are two ways to teach graphology.

The first is to start from exercising the eye and the mind to observe the handwriting and see all its particularities and to be able to differentiate one species from another and to recognise the various signs and subtle differences between them.

This system however has the drawback that the student would find it difficult to make a correct interpretation with insufficient knowledge of psychology. It is dangerous, whilst ignorant about it, to start giving the various species of writing a psychological significance. Most technical terms have a different meaning when used colloquially than in their original scientific use. Furthermore, it is absurd to use terms whilst ignorant of their accurate meaning. When the student subsequently learns the psychological theories applied to graphology, he will have to reconsider his conception of the various species and the signs, as indicators of such and such an element in the personality of the writer, which apart from being a waste of time, is not always easy for some people and can create confusion and unnecessary work.

The other system is to start from teaching the basic principles of psychology and the typologies applied to graphology. In this way the student acquires the necessary background knowledge and is ready to learn the specific technological information which is necessary for the study and interpretation of the graphic movements.

This system has an advantage in that the student, learning about each sign and species and their indications, forms a clear picture of the writer's whole personality and can describe the structure of his psyche faster and more precisely, confident that he knows exactly what he is talking about when he uses such terms as 'inhibited', 'extrovert', 'ambivalent', 'nervous' etc.

Graphology consists of three main stages:

1. ***The analysis*** (which is two-fold) :
   a. It explores, in order to uncover the mechanisms of a writing;
   b. It searches for the causes which created these mechanisms.

2. ***The consideration*** :
   which is the assessment of the interaction between the various elements discovered through the analysis in every side of the personality.

3. ***The synthesis*** :
   which is where the personality of the writer is pieced together and is presented as a whole, with all its individual particularities.

The first and second stages constitute the Science of Graphology, the third is the Art of Graphology.

Although statistics seem to be an objective and reasonable method to use in analysing a handwriting, the contribution of mathematics in the calculation of most correlations (such as the biological) is of no help. Consequently, graphology cannot rely on numbers to expand its field of searching for the causes which have created the end result.

There are as many writings as there are people. Computers can help in storing information but the final portrait depends for its accuracy on the sensitivity of human intelligence. Computers, somewhere along the line, at this stage of their development, are bound to produce two identical portraits at some time and this would, of course, be erroneous.

GRAPHOLOGICAL METHODS

There are many methods of working out the personality of a writer through the handwriting. The best and most comprehensive is to use a combination of all existing systems, which Gabrielle Beauchataud pioneered in the 1950s. This system has been expanding all the time, incorporating all new developments and discoveries, and it is this which is taught at the London College of Graphology.

PSYCHOBIOLOGICAL TEMPERAMENTS

A later theory was introduced by Leone Bourdel in "The Four Basic Idiosyncrasies" or the "Psychobiological Temperaments" (1907-1966), later developed by Jean-Charles Gille-Maisani in his book, *Types de Jung et Tempéraments Psychobiologiques*, ed. Maloine S.A. Paris 1978.

In the 1930s the French psychologist, Leone Bourdel, devised and used a test involving reaction to music in order to diagnose the deeper tendencies of the individual, as well as his aptitudes, for use in professional orientation.

In the Western world music is based on three principles : harmony, melody and rhythm. Madame L. Bourdel studied her subjects in accordance with their sensitivity to each one of these elements. She distinguished 4 types corresponding to four different visions of the world and four different adaptations of the personality: the ***Harmonic Type***, the ***Melodic Type***, the ***Rhythmic Type*** and the ***Complex Type***. At the same time independently, in America, Raymond B. Cattell researched and created a similar test based on musical preferences, the results of which he published in *The Journal of Applied Psychology*, volume 37, 1953, under the title: "The measurement of personality and behaviour disorders by the IPAT Music Preference Test", and in volume 39, 1954, under the title "Musical preference and personality diagnosis: a factorisation of 120 themes", and in his book, *Personality and Social Psychology*, published by Robert R. Knapp, San Diego, 1964.

The relation between the psychobiological temperament and the blood group has also been studied, first by Dr. Paul Carton, then by Takeji Furukawa who researched in Germany, later by the Swiss Dr. Schaer (based on Kretschmer's blood groups) and more recently by Leone Bourdel who established her theory on the basis of statistics collected in thousands of cases. Since then, many other psychologists have tried to relate the two.

In Britain, May and Stirrup researched the connection between neurosis and the blood group but did not manage to come up with any viable results (at least as far as I know).

Let us examine the Types *Harmonic, Melodic, Rhythmic* and *Complex* one by one.

The Harmonic

These individuals often have creative abilities. They are affective, and sensitive to the environment. Selective in their relationships, their biggest problem is that of expression and their major handicap, inadaptability. Their prototype is the artist. They usually direct themselves towards independent, creative professions. Generally introverted, reserved, or even inhibited, they can be exuberant when they allow themselves to explode. They are emotive and their activity is irregular. Although they appear pessimistic, in reality they are profoundly optimistic. When all those around them lose courage, it is they who will lift the morale.

They like beauty, they are creative and have a deep sense of responsibility. Their need for expression is great, not for communicating their feelings or inner thoughts as they are the greatest introverts, but as an outlet for their creativity.

Their blood type is A.

***Profession* :**

The Harmonic type will mostly choose philosophy, art, literature, research in the sciences or in technology.

***Business* :**

In business they need time to adapt to new situations, are not easy to command, and dislike brusqueness and nagging. They need the confidence of others and authority and will only obey a loyal, courageous boss. The Harmonics like to generalise. They are 'globalists' and love to synthesise.

***Pathology*:**

The Harmonic, particularly of the Rh+ group, is inclined towards schizophrenia (introversion) or paranoia (accusing others of their own inadaptability). They are probably potentially the most criminal type, although not in actuality because of their inhibitions.

An individual born with a Harmonic disposition will develop secondary characteristics of the Melodic or Rhythmic type. If the environment is favourable they will become H.-M., fulfilled, creative and brilliant.

The Melodic

They are a more adaptable group. They receive their inspiration from their environment, like outside contact, are extrovert, optimistic and active. They dislike and avoid solitude and are the people most able to benefit from their circumstances. Their ideal is goodness and philanthropy. While tending to be superficial, counting on the high opinion of others, they are also warm hearted, simple mannered (American type), liberal with strangers, and like what is new and modern. They are generally competitive.

Their blood group is O.

***Profession*:**

The Melodic type is attracted by social professions such as public relations, personnel work, medical practice, teaching, and the commercial field.

***Business*:**

They adapt quickly and easily to a new job but may become easily bored. They need variety in their work as they dislike routine. They are concrete and realistic in organising their business. As managers, they see their duty as a co-ordinator. They will move more readily than any of the others to new countries. Those who leave their country of origin are more apt to be of the O blood type.

***Pathology*:**

The Melodic is the most inclined towards mythomania and manic-depressive psychosis (J.B. Parker, Alberta Theilie, Charles D. Spielberger. *Journal of Mental Science*, Volume 107, U.S.A. 1961). When the psychosis is pronounced this could result in abuse of confidence, stealing, cheating, swindling, etc.

The Rhythmic

These types are active and methodical but at their own pace. They don't waste time, like movement and are perseverant. Their emotivity is not very strong. Objective and critical, their reasoning is deductive and they resent silly expressions of emotions. Being mostly fatalists they rarely have a deep sense of responsibility. They like planning and execution. Among the Rhythmics there are many religious fanatics as well as militant atheists.

Their blood group is B.

Profession **:**

They are attracted mainly by the professions of execution, such as officers in the armed forces, the police, management-production, technical or manual. They prefer to specialise. Disciplined and organised, they will follow instructions to the smallest detail and like to be commanded firmly, even inflexibly, working best when "put on rails".

Business **:**

In business the Rhythmics are specialists. They will organise their business methodically, starting by documenting a project and then analysing it scrupulously before taking any action. They like continuity in action.

Pathology **:**

When pathological the Rhythmic is a pervert/sadist. Mentally they will become schizophrenic. In society they are more prone to murder and rape having weak emotional brakes, and being less inhibited by their milieu. Statistically group B is the most criminally inclined of the four blood groups.

The Complex (HMR)

This type possesses all 3 previous main characteristics with equal intensity. They have the most complex personality and the greatest difficulty in harmonising their tendencies.

After the adolescent years, the HMR is forced to make a choice, consequently their behaviour suffers. Wanting everything, they pass from one type to the other abruptly and cannot stand inactivity. As the inner conflicts worsen so does the complexity. Through the (H) he is avid for contemplation and for beauty, through (M) for drive and worldliness and through (R) for action. Through (H) he does not want to hurt others but through (R) he does not want to give up his rights either, while the influence of (M) makes him agonise that time is passing and he is missing out. *The Complex* is attracted at the same time by ideas and by action, by people and by things, by purity and by pleasure. Never satisfied, wanting everything, they are anxious, tormented and pessimistic. This may worsen during adolescence, but life forces them to make choices which destroys their psychic balance. In a favourable environment, they will achieve an integrated equilibrium and can realise their gifts. In an unfavourable environment they will stay in a state of perpetual ambivalence and dissatisfaction.

Their blood group is AB.

***Profession* :**
Sometimes, depending on the environment, they will choose a profession involving discipline, or one which will be fulfilling, allowing them to function successfully through an orderly synthesis of their complexities and wealth of characteristics.

***Business* :**
At work the HRM types find it difficult to take orders. Their stability is fragile and they dislike routine and monotony and need to use all their potential. They need controlling,

having little sense of responsibility. Adaptability will be helped by the M element which adapts to changes of pace. R will have a favourable influence imposing some stability on the potential anarchy of the Complex type.

***Pathology*:**
The HMR is full of anxieties of all kinds. Sado-masochists are often found amongst this group which also has the highest percentage of suicides. Amongst psychiatrists there is a high percentage of AB blood types. This is because they find mental pathology fascinating as it encompasses the totality of human experiences and allows them, in a way, to live 'by proxy'. The antisocial acts of the Complex type result from their avidity, stealing, dealing in stolen goods, cheating, deceiving, etc.

These are the descriptions of the pure types which, of course, are very rare.

Their handwritings

As we know, no sign out of context ever has any significance and, as we also know, no type is pure. There is always an influence of another para-type.

The Harmonic type's writing is the most difficult to characterise because there is almost always an interference of Melodic or Rhythmic (since the pure type H is very rare; more often than not there are secondary tendencies of adaptation or affirmation).

***The writing is*:**

1. Usually varied, with irregularities in the rhythm of the movement (pressure, speed, continuity, dimension), nuancée, vibrant, with dominance of movement over form (Klages distinguishes the immediate expression - instinctive or 'reflex' (movement), from the representation

(form) connected to a guiding image (Leitbild), producing an impression pleasing to the author and also putting across to people a representation conforming with his desires).
2. Simple and sober; when evolved it is more simplified than enriched.
3. The layout, the personalised strokes, often indicate an instinctive aestheticism. Capitals are sober and at the same time, graceful.
4. The margins are well respected, the letters are often small, ovals are rounded, there are many inhibitions and often short finals.
5. In a personalised writing originalities in the combinations diminish the legibility, as if the writer were writing for himself and not to communicate.
6. In typology, any of the temperaments and any Jungian type can be found in the H type however the Intuitive Introvert is the most common. *(Fig. XIII.1)*

The H - M have a more fluent writing ample, progressive.

The H - R writing is firm, heavy and often angular. The reactionary attitude is expressed by strong firmness with irregularities, by conscious inhibitions (A. Lecerf) and often by the style of compensations (exaggerations in weight, narrowness, soarings).

***The Melodic type's writing is*:**

1. Larger and more ample than the others.
2. The stroke is nourished.
3. The stroke is fluent, spontaneous, round, spread out, curved, in garlands, with centrifugal finals.
4. The rhythm of the movement is fluent, easy, not hindered. The tension is often less than average.
5. The forms are enriched and complicated more than the H or R - particularly the capitals, which are often ornate.

6. The writing is usually right slanted with sinuous or convex lines.
7. Margins are careless, often narrow.
8. In Jung's typology, this writer is usually extroverted and Sentiment will be prominent. There is an important Sanguine influence (Jupiter). *(Fig. XIII.2)*

In the mixture M-R there is more stability of movement (homogeneity, verticality, more rhythm in the downstrokes). There may often be many regressive curved movements, lassos, double joined; Sensation (Jung) is well developed.

The writing of M-H is smaller, nuancée, often light and inhibited. The forms and the layout are aesthetic with some graceful movements.

***The Rhythmic type's writing is*:**

1. Connected, with even speed, width and pressure. It has stability of the motric rhythm, of direction and slant. This 'stability' might reach a stereotyped regularity, for example in the vertical pressure, the t-bars or the m/z letters.
2. It is tense and the connectedness is angular or semi-angular.
3. The stroke is almost always precise.
4. In typology R is more often than not the B/N and Jung's Thinking. *(Fig. XIII.3)*

The writing of the combined R-H type also has aesthetic, sober forms and layout.

The R-M usually has a connected, right slanted writing, decisive, semi-rounded, with some signs of M, such as ornate capitals, curved and ample strokes.

***The Complex (HMR) type's writing*:**

The Complex types are the least common of the four. Only a few basic indications can be given on their handwriting.

1. Often the RM and the MR writings can be confused with the Complex.
2. A tormented writing, with thrown movements and precise stroke (anxiety, internalised pessimism, need for action).
3. Signs of avidity, for example numerous small regressive strokes in a writing with ample ovals.
4. Many mutually contradictory signs, such as graceful movements blending with vulgar ones; sudden interruptions of rhythm, such as thrown movements alternating with stoppages and brakes, i-dots placed forward in an overall vertical and inhibited writing.
5. Finally the HMR writings usually have an un-aesthetic layout and form. *(Fig. XIII.4)*

Recapitulation of Dominant Signs :

H - Sober, nuancée, simplified, movement over form, rounded, good margins and layout, rather small with inhibitions. (Jung: mostly Int. intr.) *Figs. 1, 8, 15, 44, 45* of VOLUME I.

M - More ample, fluent and progressive, nourished, round to rounded, less tension than average, some complications, some enrichment of forms, sinuous, convex, right slant, careless margins, horizontal dominance (wide). (Jung: Sent. ext.) (Jupiter). *(see Figs. 3, 4, 9, 11, 14 of VOLUME I).*

R - Stable in direction and slant, connected, even speed and pressure, tense, precise, angular or semi-angular, regular. (Jung: Th.) (B/N) *(see Figs 18, 25, 49, 61 of VOLUME I).*

HMR - Tormented writing, some thrown and precise strokes, contradictory signs such as small regressive strokes with ample ovals, unaesthetic layout and forms, sudden interruptions of rhythm. *(see Figs 17, 23, 24, 28, 38 of VOLUME I).*

* * *

For more information on the Psychobiological Temperaments, see :

BOURDEL, Leone & GENEVAY, J. — *Sang, tempérament, travail et races,* Maloine, 1946.

BOURDEL, Leone — *Groupes sanguins et tempéraments,* Maloine, 1960.

BOURDEL, Leone — *Les Tempéraments psychobiologiques,* Maloine , 1961.

BOURDEL, Leone — *Sangs et tempéraments,* Fayard, 1962.

CARTON, Dr. Paul — *Diagnostic et conduite des tempéraments,* Libr. Le François, 1961.

DESURVIRE, M. — *Feuillets de Graphologie,* Masson, Paris, 1992.

GILLE-MAISANI, Dr. J.-Ch. — *Psychologie de l'écriture. Études de Graphologie,* Payot, 1969. *Translated into English and published by Scriptor Brooks, London, 1992, under the title: *Psychology of Handwriting.*

GILLE-MAISANI, Dr. J.-Ch. — *Écritures de poètes de Byron à Baudelaire,* Dervy-Livres, 1977.

GILLE-MAISANI, Dr. J.-Ch. *Types de Jung et Tempéraments Psychobiologiques*
Maloine, Paris, 1978.

LECERF, André *Cours supérieur de graphologie,*
Dangles, 1947.

SCHAER, Dr. Phil. K. Fritz *Charakter, Blutgruppe und Konstitution,*
Rascher, Zurich, 1977.

SAINT-MORAND, H. *Les bases de l'analyse de l'écriture,*
Vigot, 1937.

SAINT-MORAND, H. *L'écriture et la typologie planetaire,* 1973.

TEILLARD, Ania *L'Ame et l'Écriture,*
Ed. Traditionelles, 1966.
*Translated into English and published by Scriptor Brooks, London, 1993, under the title: *The Soul and Handwriting.*

VELS, Augusto *L'écriture, reflet de la personalité,*
translated from Spanish into French,
Mont-Blanc, Genève, 1966.

* * *

HANDWRITING SAMPLES of LECTURE XIII

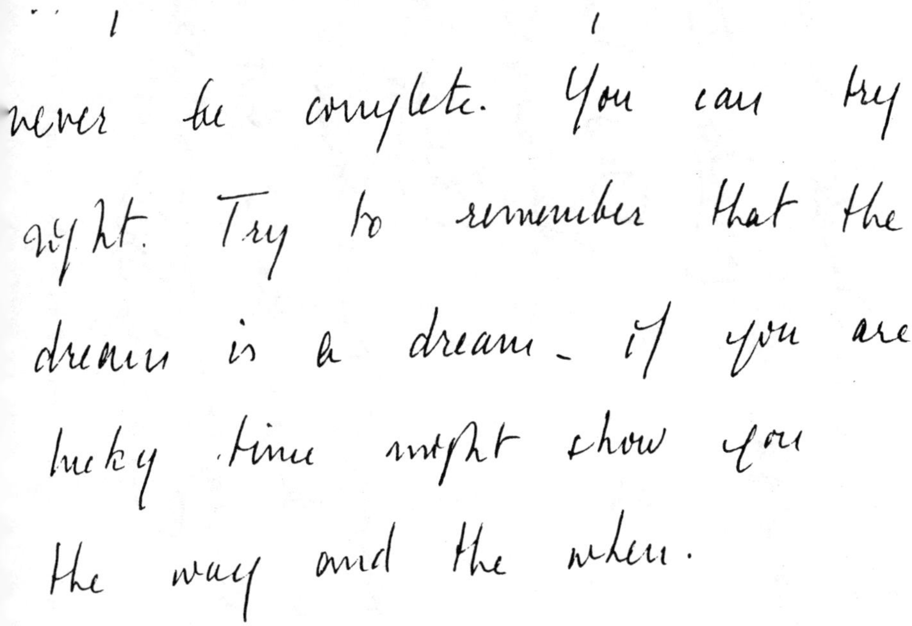

Fig. XIII.1 - Harmonic
Woman, 58 years.
Black biro; Pressure: heavy, precise

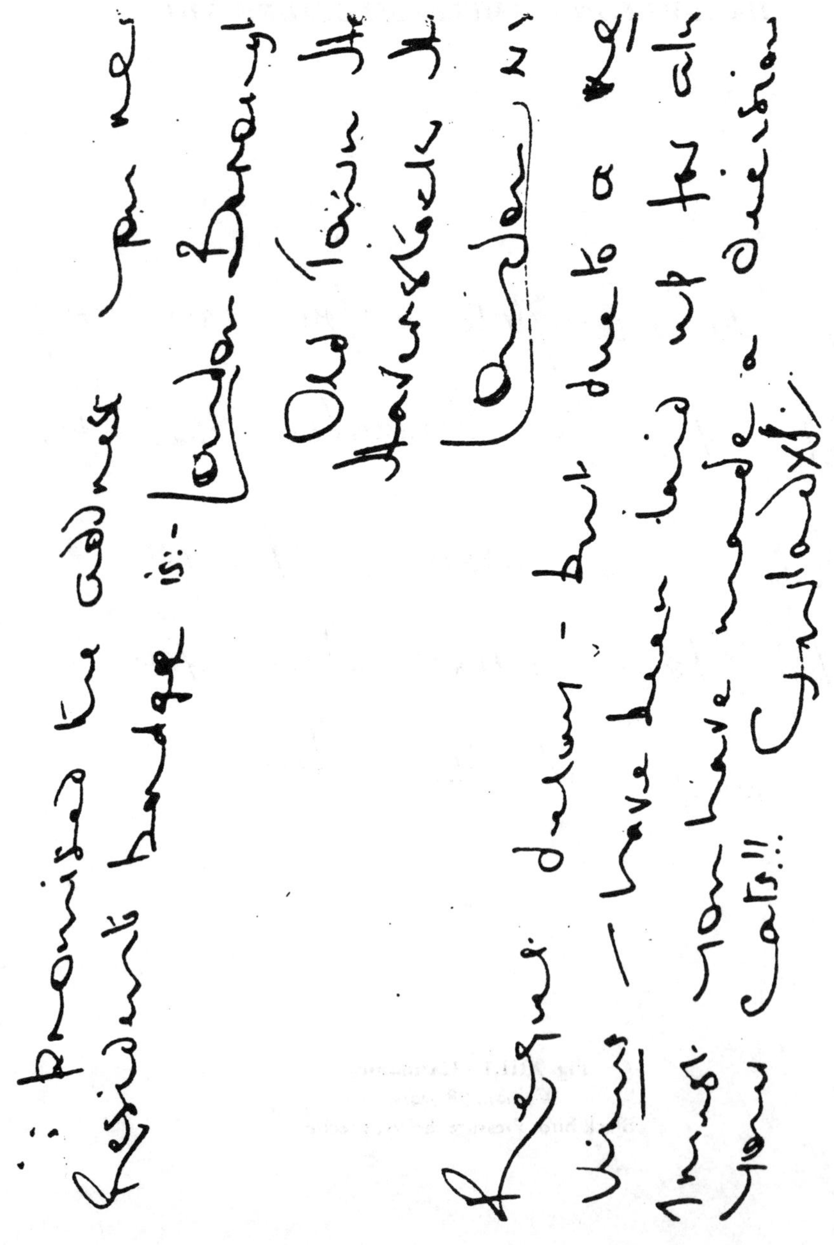

Fig. XIII.2 - Melodic - Woman, 70 years. Black felt; Pressure: light, pasty.

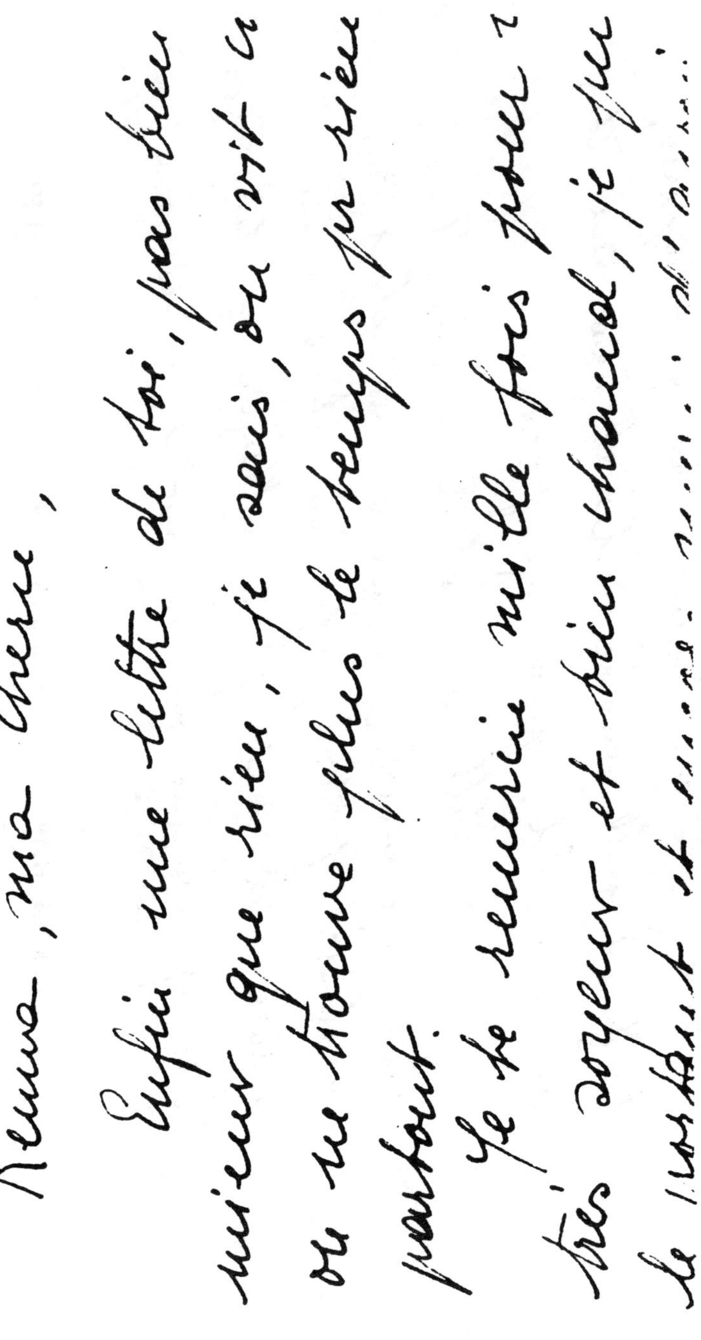

Fig. XIII.3 - Rhythmic - Woman, 74 years. Blue ink on pink paper; Pressure: firm, pasty

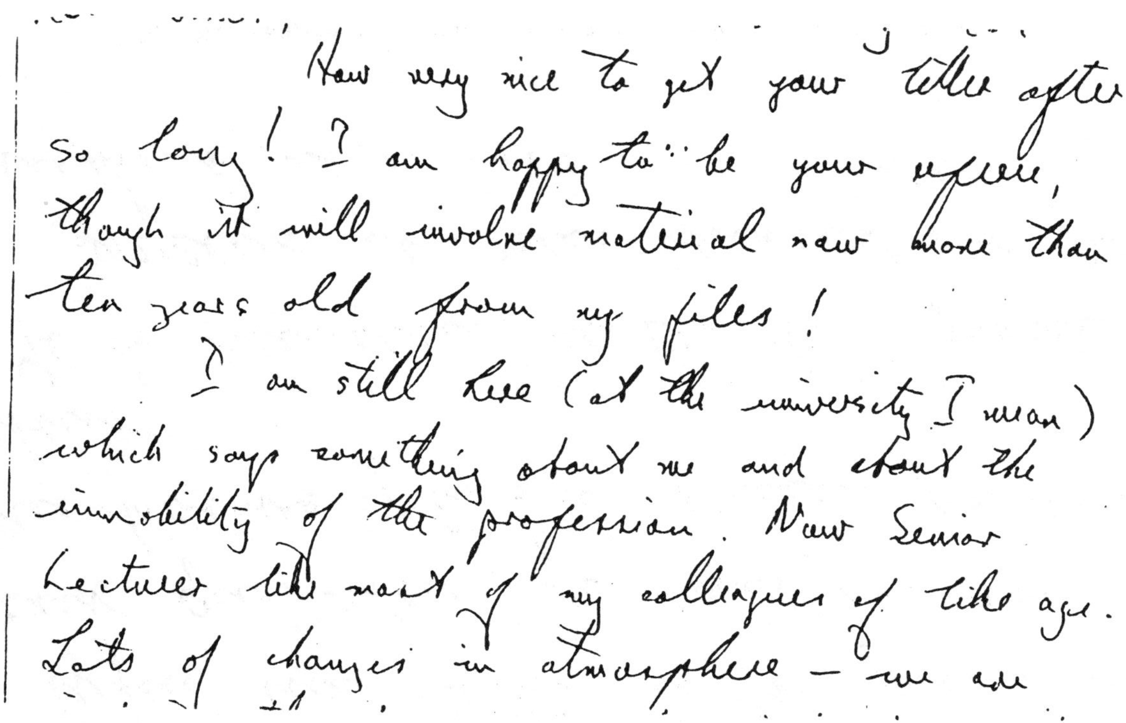

Fig. XIII.4 - HMR - Man, 45 years. Black biro on white paper; Pressure: light, precise

LECTURE XIV

GRAPHOMETRY

"One of the reasons why graphology was not taken seriously for so many years is that graphologists did not scientifically try to control what they 'sensed' intuitively. They did not apply the necessary experimental rigour and systematisation in their work", say H. de Gobineau and R. Perron, the founders of Graphometry.

De Gobineau and Perron devised a system inspired mainly by the scientific methods used by psychologists in the Psychology Laboratory of the Henri Rousselle Hospital, under the guidance of M. Zazzo.

This work is divided into two parts: the *Method of Research* and the *Diagnostic Technique*. These two aspects, although they require different attitudes of mind, are intimately connected.

1. METHOD OF RESEARCH

The *Method of Research* should constitute a sufficiently solid guide despite the complexity and variability of the phenomena it studies. This variability is threefold:

(a) Intra-individual variability

All tests capture only one moment of the individual's existence. Nobody is psychologically the same before a meal as after, or before a row as after and so on. Over a longer period of time; a person is not quite the same at 30 as he is at 50.

Many events in life effect changes, yet, we expect a sufficiently complete picture, despite these passing variations.

This intra-individual variability is a risk, but also an advantage. The advantage being that it allows us to obtain a more exact evaluation of the subject during a specific time and to evaluate his degree of variability. Some people vary less than others while other people's writings vary even in accordance with the context of their text.

The dangers of intra-individual variability are controlled partially by systematically varying the tests.

(b) Inter-individual variability

To study this variability statistically, we take a number of subjects of similar background, education, environment, etc.

There is considerable variability, quantitative as well as qualitative, among individuals, even of the same sex, age, education and profession. The analysis of these variations establishes them and measures them. It does not distinguish the causes.

This is the classic, most commonly used method for adjusting and standardising all aptitude tests.

(c) Inter-group differences

To study these differences, we compare two clearly defined groups. For example, we take a group of men (i) of set age - say between 25 and 40 years of age -, of the same educational level and profession, in the same conditions (office, etc) and study them in comparison with another group (ii) of 40 to 60 year olds of the same educational level, profession, etc. as the previous group (i).

This refers to the differences between groups rather than to variations inside one group.

This is the procedure followed in differential psychology.

2. THE DIAGNOSTIC TECHNIQUE

The above test based on a triple plan, serves as a diagnostic tool. That is, when applied to a new subject it will help to place him in a group of other similar subjects. Therefore the diagnostic technique is metric. This is adequate only when we need a concise outline of an individual's personality and we keep in mind the necessary percentage of error. To reduce to the minimum, the risk of pigeon-holing and if we want to really understand the individual, we must bring into use all sorts of corrective nuances, such as "possibly", "probably", "occasionally", etc. Then, all the complexities and inter-dependences of the psychological phenomena become evident, and it is then that clinical experience and intuition become necessary.

This stage separates the simple technician from the practitioner of skill and art.

In graphology, as with any other psychological method, to produce viable work we must consider quantification without allowing the figures to imprison us. In research, figures produce crude results which need refining by subtle means.

In graphometry, apart from age and sex, we need to have information about family, school and profession.

The writing is influenced considerably by biological and social conditions.

* * *

SOURCES

de GOBINEAU, H. *Génetique de l'écriture et étude de la Personnalité.*
PERRON, R. *Essais de graphometrie.*
Delachaux et Niestlé, Neuchâtel, 1954.

PART 5

FURTHER PSYCHOLOGICAL THEORIES APPLIED TO GRAPHOLOGY

LECTURE XV
Sigmund Freud

LECTURE XVI
Alfred Adler

LECTURE XVII
Ernst Kretschmer & William Sheldon

LECTURE XVIII
Karen Horney

LECTURE XIX
Eric Fromm

LECTURE XX
Abraham Maslow

LECTURE XV

SIGMUND FREUD (1856 - 1939)

Depth psychology and *psychoanalysis* were first mentioned by Sigmund Freud at the beginning of this century. Psychoanalysis is a system of treatment of mental/emotional disorders based on the in-depth psychological investigation of the *dynamic unconscious.* This analysis is geared to bring to the surface the hidden effects of traumatic experiences of the past which affect the actions and motivations of the patient. This investigation was started by Freud using initially hypnosis. Later he abandoned hypnosis and adopted the "free association", the interpretation of dreams and the explanation of apparently accidental, unintentional actions and errors (such as the slip of the tongue or of the pen). Through obsessive observations Freud came to the conclusion that these actions are not at all accidental, but are the result of inner conflicts which greatly influence our lives and affect our sexuality.

In his treatise "The Question of Lay Analysis" (1926), Freud developed his theory of the structure of the mind with its "Ego" and "Id". In it Freud gives his best account of psychoanalysis and its relation to medicine.

Today psychoanalysis is in common use and a part of life in many western countries. The notions of *conscious / unconscious*, *Superego* and *Ego, oralily-anality,* as well as *neuroses, hysteria* etc. are an integral part of our language.

It was natural that these concepts would enter the field of graphology. But there is as yet no comprehensive work published to help graphologists to take a Freudian view more confidently in the study of the personality through handwriting.

The following approach is, however, universally accepted and used where it helps.

THE UNCONSCIOUS

By its nature, the unconscious cannot be embraced directly; it contains all the hidden secrets of our existence which reveal themselves in the manner in which we act, speak, feel, suffer and love. It is a hidden force over which we have no control. It affects our behaviour but escapes our conscious understanding.

According to Freud, this hidden force, which, as he discovered, created so many problems for his patients, was closely linked to sexuality and its attendant problems.

Freud described the unconscious as having three axes (or directions), which he called "Metapsychology".

1. **The regional axis,** which he described as the ID, the EGO and the SUPEREGO.
2. **The dynamic axis**, i.e. the co-operation or conflict between the above three.
3. **The economic axis**, i.e. the quantitative aspect of these forces; the energy.

It is probably easier if we give the psychological expression of the three forces of the psyche separately, although they are very closely interrelated.

1. The ID

The Id is located in the unconscious - *the instincts and their drives* are hereditary and cannot be separated from their physical expression.

Any conscious concepts like order and reason are excluded from the Id. Its needs can only be met through the Ego, which tries to find ways to satisfy its secret desires, but because the latter is conscious, it will use logic and judgement to avoid dangers and great risks. The Ego also has to consider the commands of the Superego in order to avoid anxieties and guilt.

The influence of the Id on the personality can be either enriching or impoverishing.

2. The EGO

The Ego develops from the Id from childhood and progresses with our increased awareness of our exterior world. In the course of its development it becomes an opposition to the Id and the Superego.

It is thus that we form our image of ourselves. It is the manifestation of our interests and it develops in the conscious mind as attentiveness, perception, acquisitiveness, logic, the concept of time and space, judgement and reasoning.

In the unconscious mind the role of the Ego will be either appeasement, compromise or satisfaction. It acts without our being aware and uses a variety of defences which it has acquired during the course of its development.

From the graphological point of view, what is important is to evaluate the strength of the Ego, to assess its limits, its means of defence against the Id and the Superego, or the external world. The Ego is really a mediator.

3. The SUPEREGO

The Superego is really the moral conscience. It is formed from the moral values imposed by the parents and the environment. "This is how traditions and ethical values are carried on through generations", said Freud.

The person in order to preserve his self-respect must conform to the ideal image which he himself has created. The higher this is, the more difficult it becomes.

Parts of the Superego reside in the conscious mind (moral conscience, self-observation, ideals) and parts remain in the unconscious, creating feelings of guilt, unconscious prohibitions, conflicts and misery.

Let us now see how these three forces show up in the handwriting.

Graphic Signs of the Id, the Ego and the Superego

1. The ID (Signs)

As a general rule fantasies reside in the white spaces and in the strength of the impulses in the pressure and movement.

We should examine:

- whether the white spaces are well contained within and defined by the ink trails,
- how they are manipulated,
- whether they are a source of *enrichment* or *impoverishment.*

The Unconscious, because of its association with the imagination and the impulses, shows up mainly in the white spaces - open or enclosed - and signs of suppleness in the handwriting. That is:

(a) in the harmonious ventilation of the layout on the page, i.e. the gaps in the distribution of black and white (spaces between words, lines, etc.);

(b) in the flexibility of the baseline, the curved shapes, the originality and fluency of the movement;

(c) the nourished pressure and/or pastosity

(d) and in the freedom of movement *(Figs. 3, 5, 31, 45 of VOLUME I)*

Enriching influence of the Id leads to imaginary bridges between words, good rhythm of distribution, pleasantly full forms showing integration of the imagination into reality. Traditionally, the letter inflations related to the Id have been associated with the lower zone, the zone of instincts, but inhibited desires show in the middle and upper zone inflations. Loops which return to the middle zone show good integration (enrichment). Firm, nourished pressure and lively, dynamic movement and good rhythm are a sign of vitality and awareness of instinctual desires. *(Figs. 4, 10, 13, 27 of VOLUME I)*

Fantasies stemming from the Id and leading to anxiety, hinder the functioning of the Ego and indicate impoverishing influence of the Id. Arrhythmic, inharmonious breaks, large gaps, open ovals, suspended letters, incomplete forms, over-inflations, congestions, or insufficient spacing all reveal disruptive effects of the Id making itself felt on the conscious mind, and present in illness and anxiety. *(Figs. 19, 20, 26, 32 of VOLUME I)*

This conflict can also be seen in the dryness of the stroke, in the inflexibility of the movement, in the rigidity of the forms, of the stroke, of direction, dimension and of the baseline *(Figs. 30, 38, 50, 53, 63 of VOLUME I)*, or in very wide gaps, very irregular distribution of black and white *(Figs. 7, 41, 56 of VOLUME I)*.

When the Ego defence mechanisms are ineffective, letters can be deformed (onslaught of the Id - disruptive Id). *(Fig. 17 of VOLUME I and Fig. XV.1)*

Weak, light pressure, blurred stroke, suggest lack of vitality which will usually be corroborated by mechanical, or even static writing. *(Fig. 19 of VOLUME I)*

2. The EGO (Signs)

The Conscious mind shows up mainly in the writing itself, in the forms of the letters and movements, and in the control.

General layout (exterior aspect and signature position will show its adaptability, its social commitment and the distance it keeps from the world.

The spacing between black and white (interior aspect) will, in a harmonious layout and clearly formed letters, show well defined limits of the Ego - the writer knows exactly what to show and what not to show. *(Figs. 25, 27, 47 of Vol. I)*

Lapses of continuity will indicate the interference of the unconscious, and whether this produces inhibitions or enrichment of the conscious.

Pressure (indicates the Primary Process - the unconscious)

well-nourished - shows receptivity and a capacity for making good use of irrational concepts. If also firm - good adaptability.
precise & firm - clearly defined limits of the Ego and independence.
pastiness - little resistance to inner or outer influences.
dryness (fine) -negation and repression - the writer is reluctant to accept the unconscious interference and this might cause anxiety.
firmness + vertical slant + nourished - strength and diplomacy.

Direction

Suppleness or rigidity will help us understand the intensity of whatever the slant reveals.

left slant - defensive attitude.
right slant - less independence and difficulty in keeping one's distance.
varying slant - ambivalence, possibly openness of Ego, ability to solve problems in an unconventional manner.

When dealing with slant it is difficult to separate the Ego from the Superego - this is because of interaction between the two.

Signature

Consider similarity or difference from text, position on page, fullness or leanness, gaps (-indicative of the Ego), dimension, tension, fluency, pressure, paraph, etc.

3. The SUPEREGO (Signs)

Layout - This is mainly indicated by the left margin - whether rigid or not, uniform or not, and the general layout.
Unvarying writing with a stable baseline indicates respect for others, a certain hierarchy of moral values or an ethical outlook. *(Figs. 1, 3, 7, 12,15, 19, 32, 41, 42, 44, 47, etc. of VOLUME I)*

Form - is chosen to comply with the writer's ideals.

Clarity - underlines their genuineness.

Signature - when simple, similar to text, on the right and not too close to the text, shows the social involvement and therefore moral conscience (Superego).

Paraphs - (above or under the signature) indicate a need for exterior guidelines and a lesser degree of integration than a simple signature would show.

i small and isolated, *t* in the shape of a cross, heavy accents near the middle zone, compressed loops, congested letters, telescopage, diminishing words and retouchings (amendments) are all signs of guilt and anxiety and one can deduce a dominant Superego in opposition to the Id and preventing the Ego from achieving satisfaction, thus creating neuroses, conflicts, ambivalence and illness.

Some signs indicate all three states of the psyche simultaneously.

THE FOUR STAGES OF DEVELOPMENT

According to Freud all individuals go through four basic stages of development which, at the time, forcibly create conflict. These are: the *oral*, the *anal*, the *phallic* and the *Oedipus*.

Oral and Anal

There are two initial conflicts born of the primary biological tendencies - the *oral* and the *anal*, (which may also become sado-anal).

The Oral Stage

This is the predominance of the nutritive function over any other.

During infancy this is a normal state, as the baby needs to eat in order to grow. Certain people retain this need in adulthood, in which case orality is manifested as:-

(a) *dependence* in personal relationships. The person has difficulty in maintaining emotional distance from others and cannot rely on his own judgement.

(b) *aquisition* of material goods, as well as of knowledge or of people; the person wishes to "own", to suffocate the loved one. He is jealous and irrational.

(c) *flight* from reality, logic and responsibilities. Tendency to fantasize, laziness, often cowardice. Lack of precision in thinking.

Defence Mechanisms

Introjection - allows the person to absorb objects (and their inherent qualities) unconsciously. The individual takes in and adapts other people's qualities as his own. Introjection is connected with the process of identification.

Projection - this is the reverse process of the above. The person attributes to others his own feelings, desires or faults.

Negation - the person denies reality to avoid unpleasantness.

Graphic Signs of Orality *(Figs. 18, 26, 32, 35 of VOLUME I - also Fig. XV.1)*

Layout - Poor spacing, invading, chimneys, showing little Ego definition.

Movement - Static, monotonous, without rhythm. If there is movement, it will be badly controlled and inefficient, more agitation than active determination.

Dimension - Dominance of middle zone, spread out, inflated forms. Filiformity. Poor differentiation of the three zones (lack of differentiation with people).

Pressure - Mostly pasty (vulnerability, indecisiveness), or dry (defensiveness). Lack of relief.

Form - Mainly curved, childish formations of letters (immaturity), often artificial (lack of independence and individualisation).

The Anal Stage

This stems from the first "battle for independence" at potty training. The child discovers his first chance of choice to refuse to obey a given order (sado-anality). He can control or release at will.

From this (later in life) derives aggression and stinginess, possibly physical uncleanliness, or the opposite (over-compensation); mania for cleanliness. This complex usually goes together with sharp thinking and strong mental activity -

"Order, parsimony and stubbornness". (Freud)

(a) *order* - Ability to organise, classify, plan. Administrative aptitude. Punctuality and lawfulness.

(b) *acquisition* - Stinginess, economy, also good managerial ability.

(c) *stubbornness* - A strong sense of reality, foresight, determination. Precision, perfectionism, distrustfulness, good reasoning, tendency to hairsplitting, pettiness. Efficiency and adaptation to reality, but inability to know when to give in.

Defence Mechanisms

Retro-active Annulment - The person tries to avoid the occurrence of his *ideas, words and old actions* through putting on a behaviour which has the opposite significance. Cancelling past actions.

Reactive Formation - Attitude or behaviour opposite to the *repressed desire* (i.e. excessive cleanliness in opposition to pleasure from uncleanliness).

Rationalisation - The person tries to give a rational explanation to an attitude or action, the motive of which he does not quite understand.

Isolation - The person protects himself through isolation.

Graphic Signs of Anality *(Figs. 20, 21, 22 of VOLUME I, and Fig. XV.2)*

Layout - Compact or squeezed. Orderly with good margins.

Movement	-	Lack of fluency, occasional breaks in rhythm, usually connected or disconnected, rarely grouped. Sudden changes in direction. Gaps. Alternations between control and release.
Dimension	-	Often abbreviated, mostly small, with irregularities in the middle zone.
Pressure	-	Either overloaded with ink (cramped, messy), pasty or muddy (concern with dirt), or pale, dry or light, with vertical slant (concern with excessive cleanliness).
Form	-	Generally well structured. Rather angular than curved, with spikes (aggression, ambition, entrepreneurial aptitudes). Often sharp-pointed. Claws. Occasional broken letters, hooks, dashes, dots, final strokes prolonged in the lower zone and amendments. Signs of hesitation, ambivalence, anxiety. End strokes entering the lower zone. Filled-in ovals (congested).

The Phallic Stage

According to Freud the phallic stage is the period of psychosexual development. The child, through the *anal stage,* becomes aware of his/her body and of the sexual differences between male and female.

The awareness of possessing a penis gives the boy the need to affirm his superiority and he demands to impose his authority. It is during this period (between 3 and 4) that the feeling of ... rivalry with the father sets in and creates the Oedipal conflict and the fear and anxiety of castration by his rival - the father! This is of course one of many examples of Freud's projection of adult thought on a child.

In graphology, large capital letters and firmly extended upper and lower projections are some dominant signs which will indicate this phallic need of authority, in both men and women - by compensation. *(Fig. XV.3)*

For more detailed information on this absurd theory see the April 1992 (No 20) issue of *Graphology*, the quarterly journal of the British Academy of Graphology.

The Oedipus Stage

This is also called the ***Oedipus Complex*** and occurs between 4 and 5 years of age, according to Freud. Parents are the first objects of love for children. According to Freud, up to the age of about five, little boys are 'in love' with their mother and want to dispose of their father (the rival) and little girls are in love with their father and are jealous of their mother.

During this period of the child's life, Freud believed, there is great ambivalence; on the one hand the little boy wishes to "kill" his rival, but on the other he realises that he is emotionally and materially dependent on him. This provokes feelings of aggression towards father, conflict and unhappiness. In order to solve his problems the boy will renounce his mother, and, interiorising his conflict, will identify with his father.

The same process occurs with the girl's love for her father. In reverse order, she will eventually identify with her mother.

The intensity of the Oedipus conflict will decrease around the 6th year of life, when the relationship with the parents is desexualised and the "infantile amnesia" sets in, erasing all memories of conflicts of the first three or four years.

Defence Mechanisms

Identification - Incorporation and introjection, i.e. copying and/or adopting new characteristics - an essential process for the formation of the personality.

Repression - Repressing all manifestations related to the impulse into the subconscious (inhibition).
Sublimation - Redirection of impulses towards a non-sexual and more esteemed target.

Freud believed that although the Oedipus conflict of our early years colours all our lives, it will only manifest itself in three instances:

1. During our conflicts with authority.
2. During the formation of, and rapport with, our Superego.
3. In our choice of partner in life.

Graphic Signs of the Oedipus Conflict

- ***In MEN (more orality - anima)***

Layout - Script mainly concentrated on the left of the page, left margin diminishing.
Movement - Centripetal or regressive movements and general left tendencies in the upper and/or lower zone. Signs of ambivalence, little release (irregularities of direction), signature different from text.
Pressure - Well-nourished, velvety (warmth and vulnerability), or dry and light (lack of defences).
Form - Mainly curved forms, round, inflated, signs of orality (often indicating hysterical defences), signs of superficiality (anima writing - dominance of middle zone, etc.). Occasionally lack of harmony, curves replacing angles, triangles, breaks of continuity in the formation of down strokes (separation of the middle zone part of the

letters ***d***, ***g***, ***q***, ***p***, from their extension) indicating inner conflict between masculine and feminine identities. Difficulty in identifying with one or the other. Immaturity. *(Fig. XV.4)*

- ***In WOMEN (more anality - animus)***

Layout	-	Mainly invading.
Movement	-	In preference, masculine forcefulness, not necessarily progressive.
Pressure	-	Strong and rigid writing will show strength, energy, strong will and often aggressive determination to achieve and/or dominate.
Form	-	Independent and individual forms occasionally lacking discipline (indicating the need to establish her independence, refusing the monotony of daily routine). Occasionally the forms may be full but rapid. *(Fig. XV.5)*

In both men and women the writing will be irregular in all the genres, jerky, discordant and more or less homogeneous. Irregularities will often be in large capitals, upper prolongments (discrepancy between aspirations and achievements, dissatisfactions, unachieved ambitions = unresolved Oedipus conflict). The more the Oedipian identities are assimilated into the structure of the personality, and the more the ambivalences and irregularities of the writing become integrated into a homogeneous and well-organised whole, the higher is the degree of maturity and independence.

HYSTERIA

According to Freud, *hysteria* (which occurs in both men and women) is a physical manifestation of the repression of sexual problems of infancy, i.e. the consequent unconscious "conversion" of the anxiety caused by this regression, into physical pains. Apart from physical pains or imaginary disease, it may also cause fear of all forms of sexual impotence in men, or frigidity in women.

Expressions of Hysteria

Over-dramatisation	-	The individual will exaggerate the expression of his/her emotions with irrational emotional behaviour, screams, crying, fainting, etc.
Need for an audience	-	The person needs an audience in order to "perform" the above.
Lying	-	He/she will lie about some physical malaise or other.
Mythomania	-	He/she will invent stories about themselves which they will tell and may even believe.
Hypochondria	-	The person believes he/she suffers from any disease (or physical symptoms) that they hear discussed or read about. In extreme cases this creates genuine physical indications (like paralysis, loss of speech, or other imaginary illness).
Erotisation of relations	-	The person finds it difficult to establish a normal relationship with the opposite sex, without the undercurrence of sexual ideas.

Graphic Signs of Hysteria

Layout - Bad distribution of the text on the page - irregular or no margins, and irregular (either spaced out or little) spacing between words.

Movement - This can be either uncontrolled, with disproportions and exaggerations in all zones, or monotonous, unnatural, with ornamentations with slow speed. Irregular slant, animated.

Pressure - Usually deviated on the lateral movement or on the upstroke, spindles, long sharp-pointed finals, or other spasmodic signs. Occasionally heavy pressure with firm downstrokes.

Form - Big capital letters, spread out forms, mainly in the middle zone. Threadiness, irregularities in dimension, mainly in the middle zone generally full ovals. Prolonged *and* full lower extensions. Tangled lines due either to excessive prolongment or to inadequate spacing, or on the other hand, unnatural, artificial forms, illegible, mannered and monotonous with some triangles and angles. *(Figs. XV.6, XV.7)*

NARCISSISM

The theory of Narcissism first emerged in Freud's work in 1910. Initially it was associated with the exclusive direction of the Freudian libido towards the self, and in 1914 he wrote a paper on it.

"The libido - which we find attached to objects and which is the expression of an effort to obtain satisfaction in connection with those objects - can also leave the objects and set the subject's own ego in their place".[1] This way of allocating the libido, Freud called "narcissism" and he borrowed it from a perversion described by Paul Näcke (1899) in which the person "treats his own body with all the caresses that are usually devoted to an outside sexual object". Later on he modified this concept and in his book *Beyond the Pleasure Principle* (1920) he specifies that narcissism must necessarily be linked to the "self-preservative instincts" and to egocentricity.

Freudian psychoanalysts see this as a character disorder which originates from lack of parental empathy before the individual was able to talk, "and therefore untreatable by psychoanalytical methods, as it is not amenable to verbal analysis".

The Freudian associations of narcissism incorporate self-indulgence, self-involvement, exaggerated sense of self-importance and lack of objective self-assessment, all of which hide a feeling of low self-worth. This, like most of Freud's approaches is an exclusively unhealthy (morbid) aspect of narcissism and can be taken as a "reaction for survival" or as just another defence mechanism against a deeply rooted inferiority complex, which is a destructive state as it results in the exclusion of all exchange with others (the object), in the inability to give, to love, to care, and creates alienation and misery. It is of course consistant with the majority of Freud's views about the nature of man, which often include great lengths of chain-reaction logic in order to explain and prove his theories of hopelessness and incurability of the human condition.

But there is the constructive narcissism too, which consists of the objective and educated understanding of self-worth, from which grows healthy self-esteem, self-love and self-respect.

---

(1) S. Freud, *Introductory lectures on Psychoanalysis*. Penguin, London, 1973. p. 463-465.
B. Engler, *Personality Theories*. Houghton Mifflin Co., U.S.A., 1985.

The person who appreciates his true worth automatically inspires trust. He emanates a feeling of well being and confidence, and by not agonising about his own status or value, he has the time and room to care for others, to give and to love. Lack of adequate self-respect - whether it is covered up with narcissism or not - is a source of constant anxiety, unhappiness and worry, it leaves little room for others and makes the person unattractive and boring.

In graphology the dominant syndrome of strong narcissism is: large + regressive + full forms sprawled in an invasive manner across the page with a mainly horizontal axis and a thick trail.

However, if the forms are not gross and the whole keeps an aesthetic and rhythmic image, this narcissism is not necessarily negative. Many actors, priests and artists (painters, sculptors, architects) have this syndrome in their writing and consequently this strength of narcissism. It does not cover up a lack of self-esteem. (Rhythm does not cover anything up). It simply shows their inner feeling of well being, at least as regards their worth.

In the more run-of-the-mill writings, narcissism in its constructive state, is seen in the elasticity of the stroke, the easy, confident flow of the forms and in the harmony and general disposition of the text.

* * *

SOURCES

AYMARD, J. — *"Freud"* from *Les Bases de la Graphologie,* Pierre Faideau et als, ed. M.A. Paris, 1989.

ENGLER, B. — *Personality Theories,* Houghton Mifflin Co., Boston, 1985.

FREUD, S. *The Ego and the ID*, W.W. Norton & Co., London, 1962.

FREUD, S. *Inhibitions, Symptoms and Anxciety*, W.W. Norton & Co., N.Y., 1959.

STAFFORD-CLARK, D. *What Freud Really Said*, Penguin Books, London, 1969.

* * *

HANDWRITING SAMPLES of LECTURE XV

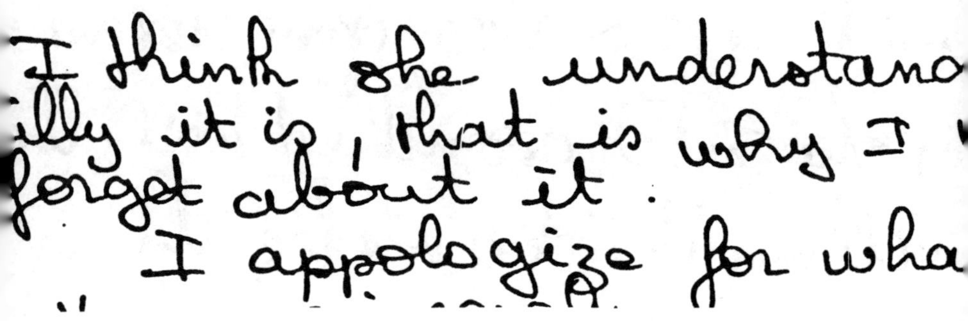

Fig. XV.1
Woman, 26 years. Orality.

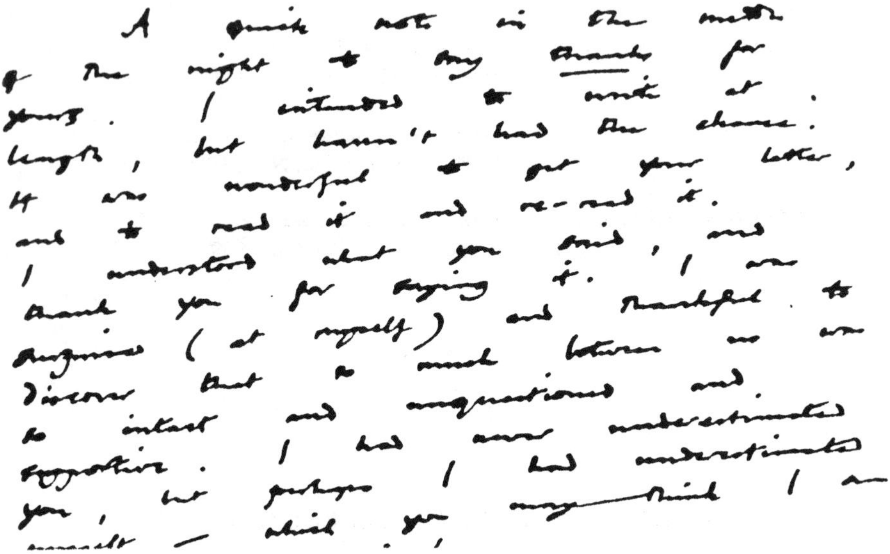
A quick note in the middle of the night to say thanks for yours. I intended to write at length, but haven't had the chance. It was wonderful to get your letter, and to read it and re-read it. I understood what you said, and thank you for saying it. I am surprised (at myself) and thankful to discover that so much between us was so intact and unquestioned and supportive. I had never underestimated you, but perhaps I had underestimated

Fig. XV.2 - Man, 50 years. Anality.

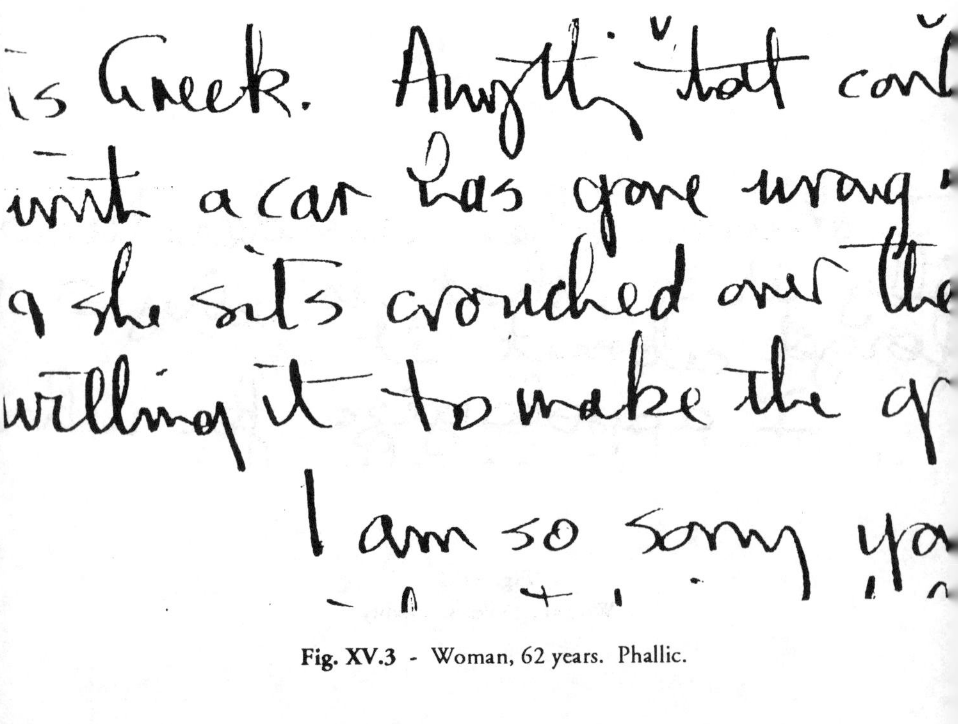
is Greek. Anything that could
with a car has gone wrong
& she sits crouched over the
willing it to make the
I am so sorry you

Fig. XV.3 - Woman, 62 years. Phallic.

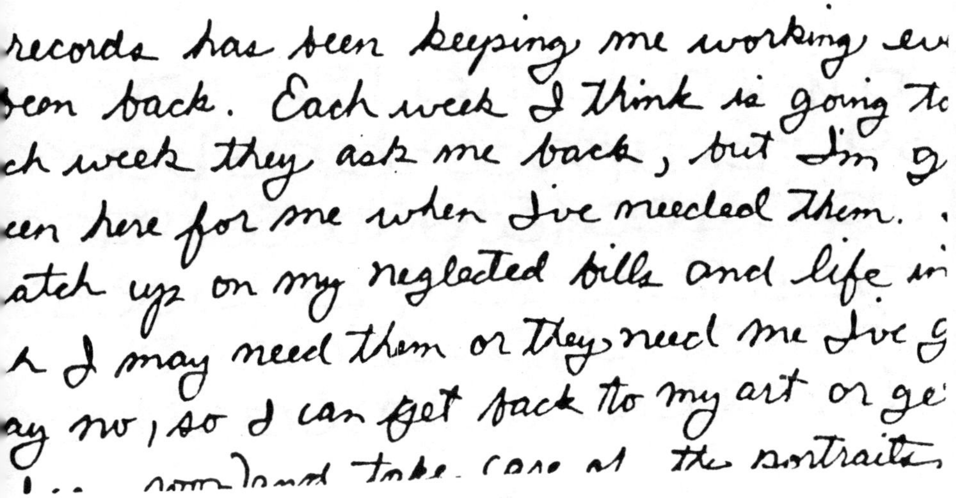

Fig. XV.4

Man, 33 years. Oedipus.

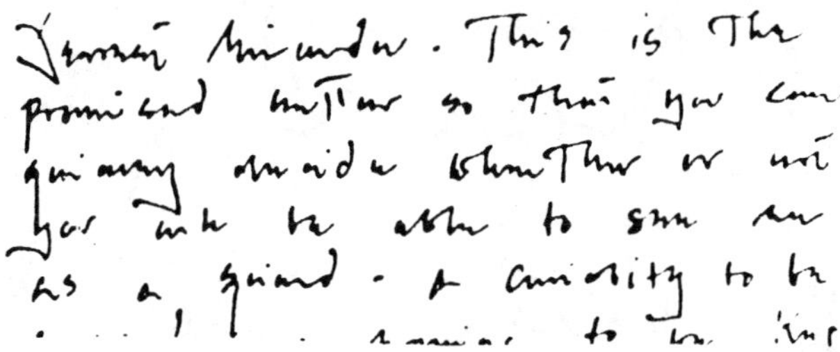

Fig. XV.5

Woman, 38 years. Oedipus.

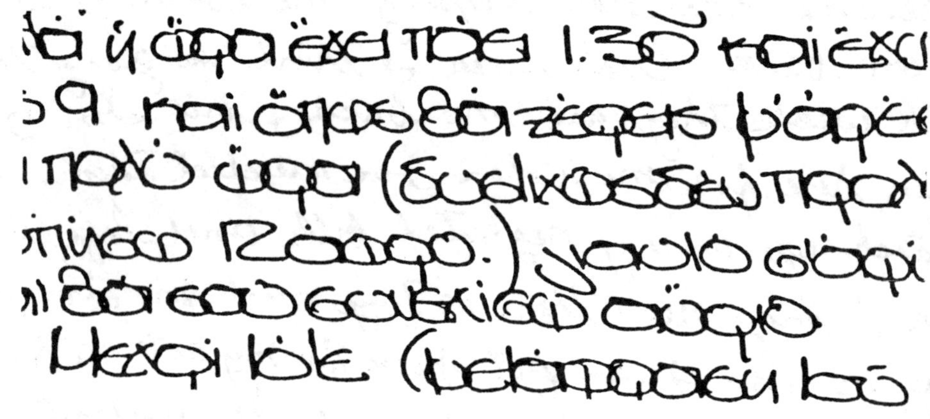

Fig. XV.6
Woman, 17 years. Hysteria.

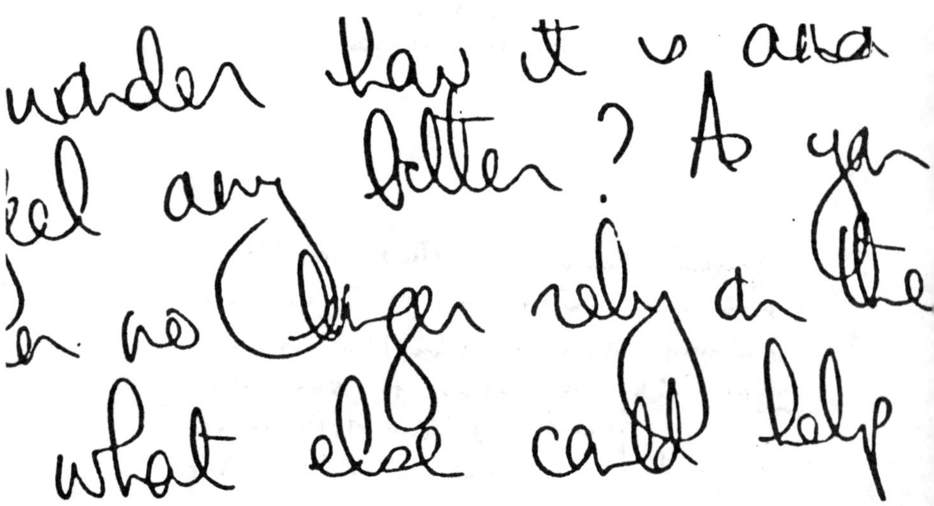

Fig. XV.7
Woman, 18 years. Hysteria.

LECTURE XVI

ALFRED ADLER (1870 - 1937)

A. Adler was a Viennese psychologist, contemporary of Freud, who together with Jung and Freud, was one of the three great names of depth-psychology.

As a child he was of a delicate constitution, often ill and obsessed with the idea of death. The doctor who looked after him became for him an all powerful image of healing and security. It is no surprise therefore that he chose this path for himself.

After he qualified in 1895 he decided to follow general medicine rather than any specialisation, in order to devote himself to a wider social group.

Of humble origins and a devoted socialist (he had a perfect knowledge of Marx's work), he had a fervent interest in the working classes, believing that man's health is directly connected with his work, the conditions under which he works and his financial status. Therefore man is the product of society, but first and foremost he is himself the architect of his own conditions of life, of his own "style of life", as he liked to say.

He believed that the child during his first 5 years forms his own "style of life", his line of orientation based on his youthful experiences and his innate character. This will determine his attitude and behaviour for the rest of his life and will make him uniquely different from other people. However, this uniqueness is part of a personality which belongs to a specific social group, and it is this specific social group which will condition him and determine his physical and psychological (biological) state. This way he tried to transform the (medical) care of the sick body into care of the human being in its totality.

All his work is coloured by this principle. In 1898 he published *The Health and Profession of the Tailor*. In it he tries to prove that illness is caused by the inferiority of organs. By this he means that one organ of the body has not developed normally, either the whole or part of it, and this affects the normal functioning of the individual, physical and psychological, either directly or indirectly, through the double effort needed to adapt in a normal manner with an abnormal organ. This is how he attributes psychological maladies to physical malfunctions.

With his book *Study of the Inferiority of Organs* (1907) Adler puts across the "feeling of inferiority". All people go through this, for instance, the child facing adults and authority.

The normal child, when his Ego starts to build up, will react instinctively with opposition, trying to measure the extent of the adult's superiority, and at the same time establishing the development of his own personality and its satisfaction. However, "all this process is starting from an inferior situation to achieve a superior one". (Adler).

He will try to widen his limits (will and ambition). As he succeeds he gains confidence and satisfaction and little by little he will shed the feeling of inferiority and its inevitable consequence: insecurity.

But the evolution and the reactions of a child are not always as satisfactory. There are children who are unloved or always ill, or deformed and need constant attention and protection. Also the slightly mentally inferior, the hunchback, the asthmatics, etc, will all have to submit to a lesser development of personality (regression). Their idea of their own value will be lower, more modest. This is a feeling of inferiority that they will always carry within themselves. It will never find a healthy outlet; it will create neurotic reactions and attitudes, which are collectively called "inferiority complex".

Whereas the "feeling" of inferiority is conscious, the "complex" is subconscious.

In his principal publication, *The Nervous Temperament* (1912), Adler explains in detail his ideas on the inferiority complex and the neurosis.

Although he knew early on (1904) that he could never give Freud the total obedience that the latter was expecting (he was 14 years his junior), he was convinced nevertheless of the psychic origins of neurosis and of the important role that the unconscious plays in their creation. But he refused to accept the theory that all neuroses stem from sexual causes, or the incestuous desire in the Oedipus syndrome, or for that matter, Freud's interpretation of dreams.

Adler believed that dreams confirm our "life style" and no more. He also refuses to agree with the theory that the (Freudian) libido is the source of the neurotic manifestations.

For Adler the starting point of neurosis is the "menacing feelings of insecurity and of inferiority" which engender the irresistible desire to find a means to make life bearable through establishing a target, a source of calm and security.

These theories were obviously totally opposed to the Freudian notion of "causality".

Adler attributes the causes of psychic troubles to the 3 basic duties of the human being :

1) To fulfil his needs through practising a skill (job)
2) To create a home and fulfil his sexual role
3) To establish relationships with and gain the co-operation of his peers.

The healthy individual will have within him the strength to accomplish these duties.

The neurotic individual turns away from objective reality and cannot face up to problems; neither can he find within himself the necessary strength to accept his deficiency and to try to cope with it. Instead he takes refuge in symptoms (migraine, vertigo, agoraphobia, illness, etc.), which prevent him from fulfilling his obligations, which in turn create in him remorse and guilt. So he goes through life believing he is not intelligent, he is not strong, he is not beautiful and behaves "as if" he really is none of these.

Some people compensate their inferiority complexes in a spectacular way, like Demosthenes, who suffered from a stutter. Determined to overcome his disability, it is said that he placed pebbles in his mouth and practised speaking to the waves at the seashore. Eventually he became famous as one of Greece's best orators.

Some people, however, do not manage so well. It is important to note that human suffering depends not so much on the objective deficiency as on the way they learn to cope with it.

Compensation and Overcompensation

Compensation of an inferiority complex is to learn to live with the inability and develop a side talent or skill.

Overcompensation is to develop vanity, arrogance or will for power, authoritarianism and domination, which is usually based on denigrating others in order to shine oneself.

This last reaction Adler called ***virile protestation.*** He considers it a false solution to life's problems, which can be seen in men as well as in women.

In men it consists of an accentuation of the masculine traits; the individual feels important, strong, arrogant and superior, particularly towards women whom he treats with contempt.

In women it is an opposition which consists mainly of the refusal to accept their femininity. Their attitude and behaviour is virile, their behaviour is aggressive, rebellious and hard.

Both men and women, whatever their circumstances, will

fight for position, superiority, virility and will try hard to keep the position of "master" of the situation. Often also, the neurotic will try to seek more proof of his (or her) superiority, but he lacks the necessary objectivity and realism to achieve it. He cannot face reality, take a decision or a responsibility. He/she lacks courage, he is indecisive and hesitant.

But he is too anxious to keep up the facade of superiority, so in order to evade responsibility he will resort to all sorts of strategies and neurotic manifestations: hysterical pains, paralysis, impotence, etc. These will take the shape of real, autonomous diseases.

Adlerian psychology is centred around the need to give the child the necessary social mind and sense of community, which will help him/her later to cope with and solve the problems of life; to throw light on this neurotic world (which to Adler was similar to a dark room where one cannot find the exit), through making conscious the individual "style of life" and thus correcting the faults and constantly re-educating and making him aware of the obstacles and the responsibilities of life.

The individual's lack of reaction reinforces the inhibitions, the lack of initiative, the pathological timidity, the discouragement and he/she risks being driven towards the passive refuge of alcoholism or drugs.

On the other hand, *reaction* is characterised by certain aggression and the search for compensation : vindictiveness, systematic opposition, destructive criticism, vanity, pride, irritability or evasiveness, running away. The writing will have signs of aggression (angles and sharp points), of systematic opposition (many small, oblique starting strokes), of vindictiveness (*t*-bars oblique - impulsive writing invading the page), of "running away", avoiding (imprecise writing, blurred, slack, with chimneys and irregular word spaces). *(Fig. XVI.1)*

Compensation will show in the vain capitals and the eccentric forms. The timid writer who is likely to react with a brusque, audacious impulse will have violent and sharp-pointed end strokes. An emotive will mask his sensitivity with a small, straight, rigid and mechanised writing. *(Figs. XVI.2)*

The signs of *overcompensation* are much more spectacular. The writing is disproportionate and excessive. The weakness is manifested in the lack of harmony, occasional breaks of the flow and the clumsiness of the forms (vulgar, gross, ungraceful, etc.). The overcompensation shows in the disproportionate upper prolongments in the text, as well as in the signature. *(Fig. XVI.3)*

The *virile protestation* is not easy to see nowadays, when the sexual differentiation is dying away. In Adler's time it was manifested in men with accentuation of masculine superiority, i.e., spasmodic writing, angular, narrow, clubbed and rather regular and resolute. *(Fig. XVI.4)*

In women angles were the sign of masculine aspirations, of her revolt and of her dissatisfaction with everything. Her need to impress and to protect the weak was evident in the long, heavy and high-placed *t*-bars which is also, according to the symbolism of space, the characteristic sign of exaltation and utopia.

* * *

SOURCES

ADLER, A. — *Understanding Human Nature,* George Allen & Unwin, 1942.

ADLER, A. — *What life should mean to you,* George Allen & Unwin, 1942.

FAIDEAU, P. et al. — *Graphologie,* M & A, Paris, 1983

HANDWRITING SAMPLES of LECTURE XVI

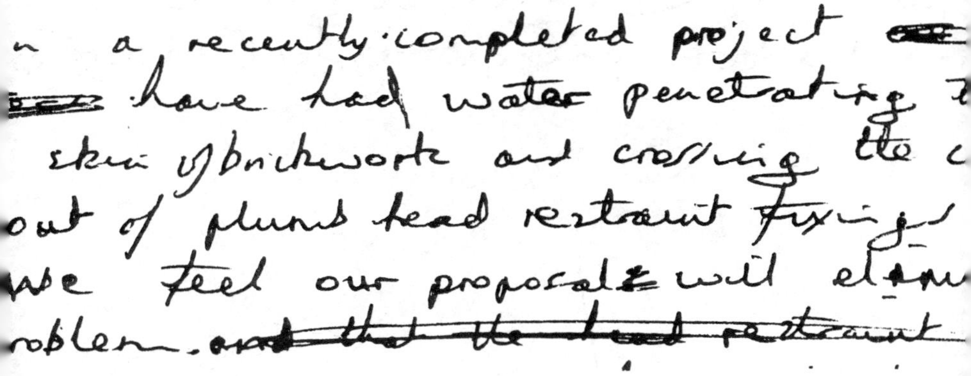

Fig. XVI.1
Man, 30 years. Reaction.

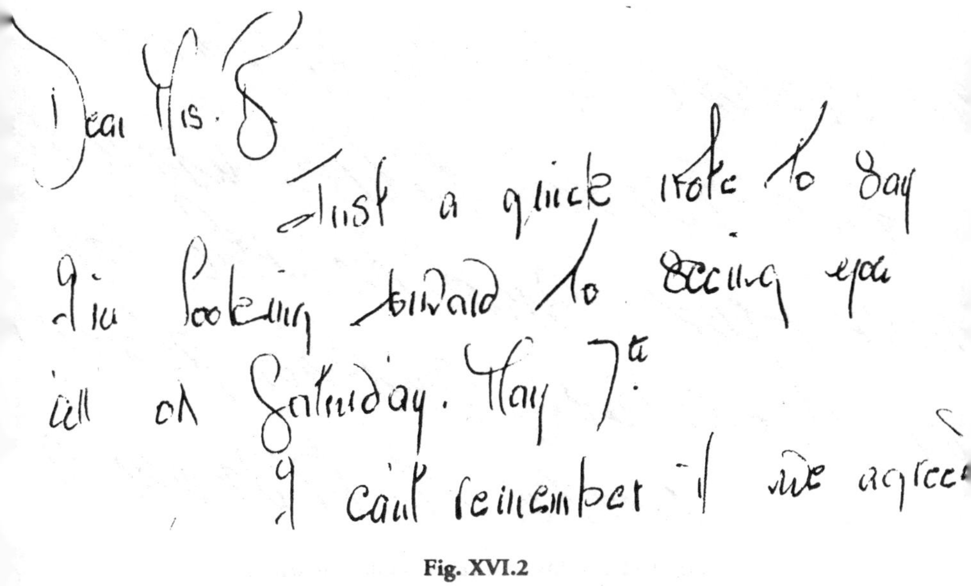

Fig. XVI.2
Woman, 50 years. Compensation.

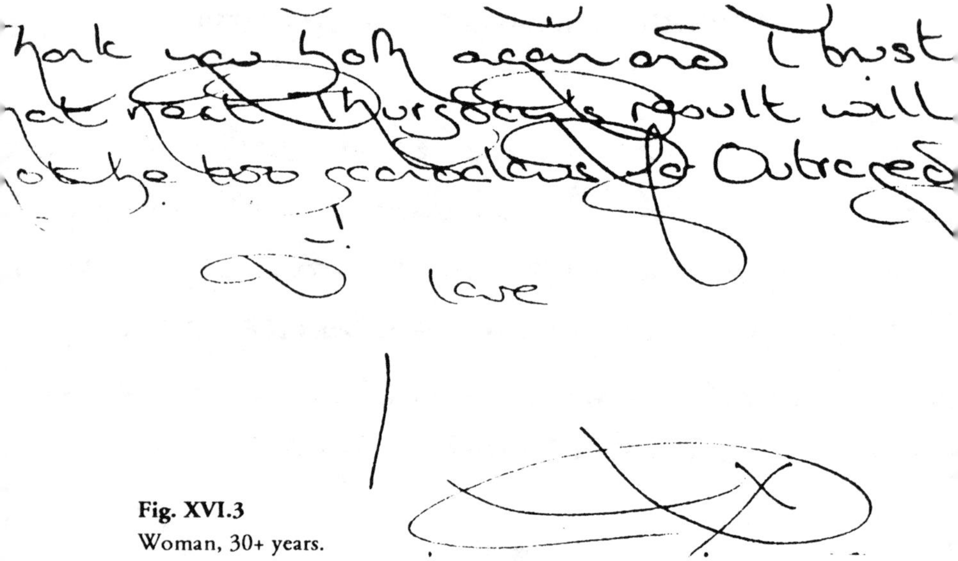

Fig. XVI.3
Woman, 30+ years.
Overcompensation

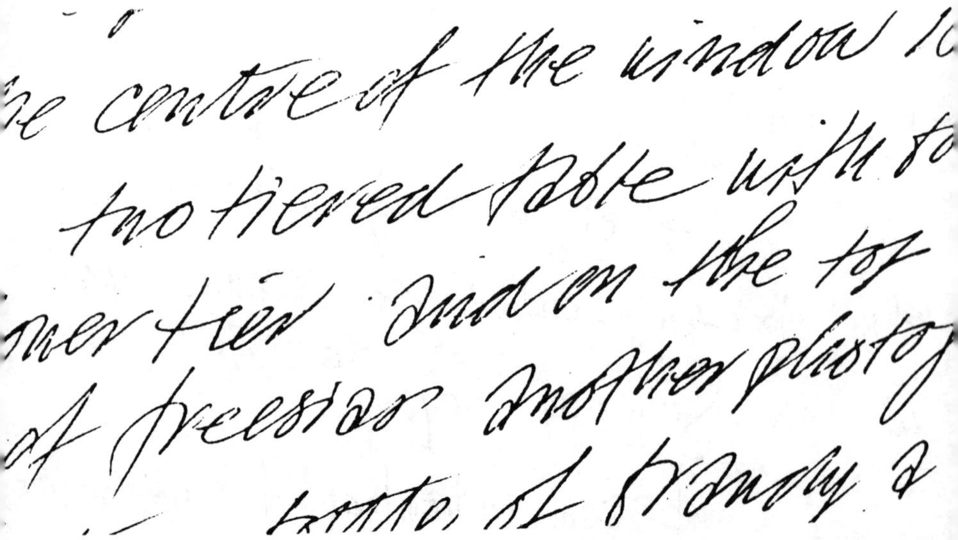

Fig. XVI.4 - Man, 50 years. Virile protestation

LECTURE XVII

ERNST KRETSCHMER

Since Galen (130-200 AD) nothing much happened in the field of Temperaments until Ernst Kretschmer early this century.

Kretschmer was born in Germany and became a professor of psychology and neurology between the two wars.

He developed an interest in the inclination of people towards one mental illness or the other in accordance with their physic and their personality. His researches on human typology and his experiments with the mentally ill directed him into believing that mental diseases were an exaggeration of normal states, particular to each temperament and influenced by it and by the physical constitution.

He published two books: *La Structure du Corps et le Charactère* which was translated into English in 1925, and *Traité Théorique et Pratique de Psychologie Medical.*

He divided people into four categories:

1) The *Pycnic* who is rounded, with short neck and broad chest and who is similar to Hippocrate's *Apoplecticus* (strong, thickset and sanguine) (L.S. or S.L. and similar to Sheldon's *Viscerotonic / Somatotonic*).
2) The *Athletic* who is rather slim and energetic, similar to Hippocrates' B.N. or N.B. and similar to Sheldon's *Somatotonic / Cerebrotonic.*
3) The *Leptosome* who is slim, weak and delicate, similar to Hippocrates' *Phthisicus* (N.), similar to Sheldon's *Cerebrotonic.*

4) The *Dysplasic* which is a pathological state: dwarfs, giants, hairy women, etc. This last group is a category apart.

What interests us is the mental state of the first three categories. We must leave the last one to the experts.

According to Kretschmer his *Pycnic* type was more likely to become a Cyclophrenic (manic depressive); if he were to go mad, than Schizophrenic (Dementia Praecox) which is more the line of the Leptosome. The *Athletic* would be somewhere in the middle (schizophrenic - epileptic).

The two temperamental attitudes progress as follows:

Cyclothymic	- which is a normal state of being of the Pycnic
Cycloid	- which is a "sub-morbid" state.
Cyclophrenic	- which means oscillating between euphoria and depression.
Schizothymic	- which is the normal state of the Athletic and Leptosome.
Schizoid	- which is the sub-morbid state.
Schizophrenic	- which is the dissociation of emotions from reality.

Both *Cyclothymics* and *Schizothymics* are normal, balanced people and, always according to Kretschmer, we all are either the one or the other.

As an oversimplification we can say that: *Cyclothymics* tend more towards extraversion, whereas *Schizothymics* tend more towards introversion.

To sum up:

Pycnic = (similar to Hippocrates' L/S, Apoplecticus and a combination of Sheldon's *Viscerotonic/Somatotonic* types) = rounded and robust, stronger, less lymphatic, less passive than the pure *Viscerotonic.*
Cyclothymic type = manic depressive = oscillating between euphoria and depression.
Predominance of Extraversion.

Athletic = (similar to Hippocrates' BN or NB and a combination of Sheldon's *Somatotonic/Cerebrotonic* types) = also robust, but less than extremely muscular, energetic, rather slim, (the ideal athlete).
Schizothymic type = tendency to schizophrenia (dissociation of emotional trends from necessities of life).
Predominance of Introversion.

Leptosome = (similar to Hippocrates' Nervous or Phthisicus and Sheldon's *Cerebrotonic*) = linear and weak body, slim and delicate.
Schizothymic type = tendency to schizophrenia (as above).
Predominance of Introversion.

Each type has three main subdivisions:

Schizothymics

grades: schizothymic, schizoid, schizophrenic.

types:
- Hypersensitive : introvert, idealistic, touchy
- Aristocratic : introvert, systematic, rigid, cold self control, courageous, stoic, prefers respect to love.
- Anaesthetic : extraversive introvert, little sentiment.

Cyclothymics

grades: cyclothymic, cycloid, cyclophrenic.

types:
- Hypomaniac : cheerful, euphoric, animated, enthusiastic.
- Syntonic : realistic, practical, humorous.
- Soft Depressive : accommodating, rather submissive.

It is an oversimplification to call all Schizothymics introverts and all Cyclothymics extroverts.

E. Kretschmer in graphology

Pycnic - (cyclothymic - cycloid - cyclophrenic)
(manic-depressive)

The writing is : rounded or round. Animated, aerated, fluent, rather rapid but rarely precipitated. In garlands, well nourished, medium to large in size but never large (activity and practical sense dislike large forms). Moderate irregularities (he may be sociable and of happy disposition but he is also practical and prudent sometimes even cunning).

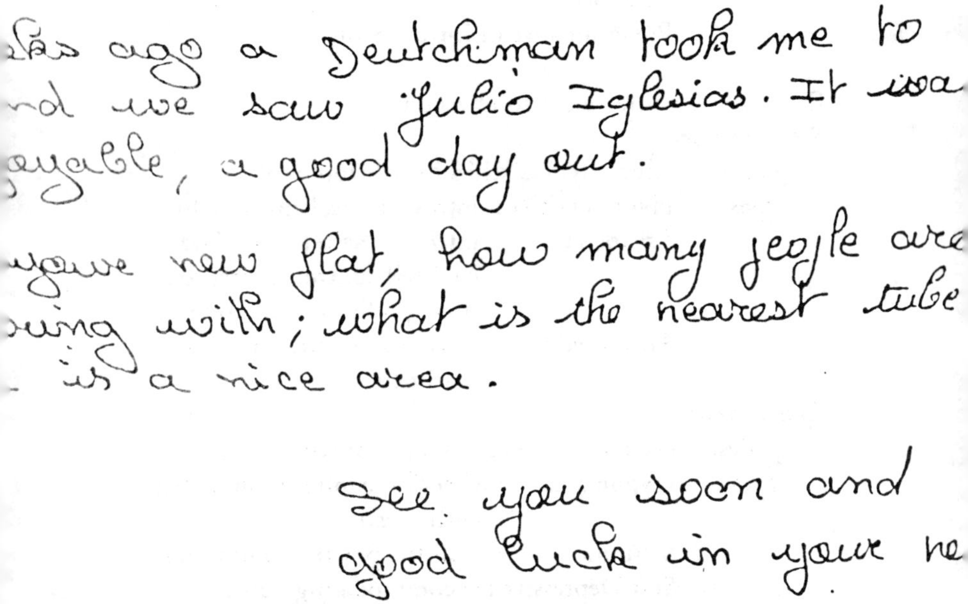
ks ago a Deutchman took me to
nd we saw Julio Iglesias. It wa
ayable, a good day out.

your new flat, how many people are
ing with; what is the nearest tube
is a nice area.

See you soon and
good luck in your ne

Fig. XVII.1
Woman, 30 years

Athletic - (schizothymic - viscous spasmodic)
(epileptoid, epileptic)

The writing is : rather large, firm, more or less heavy (voluntary) and active. Mostly poised with occasional clubs - mainly in the t-bars - or with centripetal final strokes. The connections are oblique (angular) rather than curved and in garlands as in the cyclothymics.

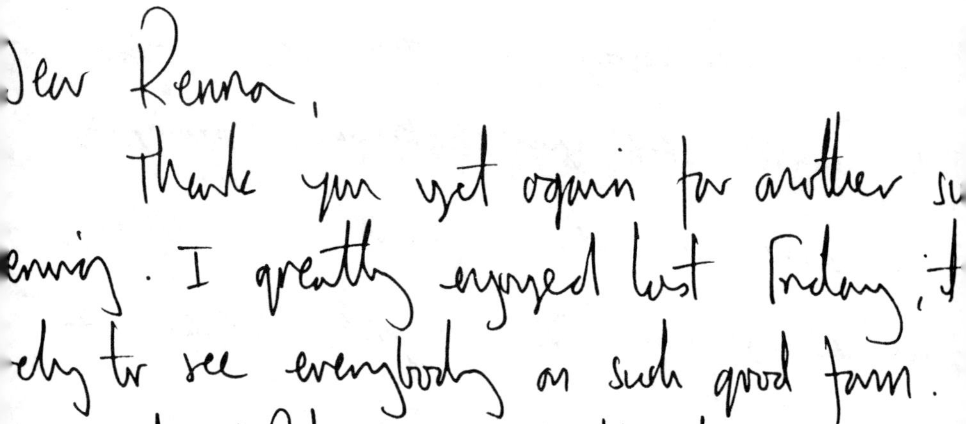
Dear Renna,
Thank you yet again for another su
evening. I greatly enjoyed last Friday, it
ely to see everybody on such good form.
The "Park Lane" food and service
spoils are for real life, but being invited
treat!

Fig. XVII.2
Man, 30 years

Leptosome - (schizothymic - schizoid - schizophrenic)
(dissociation)

The writing is : inhibited and rather regular. More or less small, narrow, occasionally squeezed. Contained if not constrained. Low, angular, often rigid, simple, closed, with irregular pressure. Not rapid, with very slight right slant, horizontal or descending. Leaving a right margin and with a 'sulking' signature, placed on the right with an encircling paraph or signed between two parallel lines and with a full stop at the end.

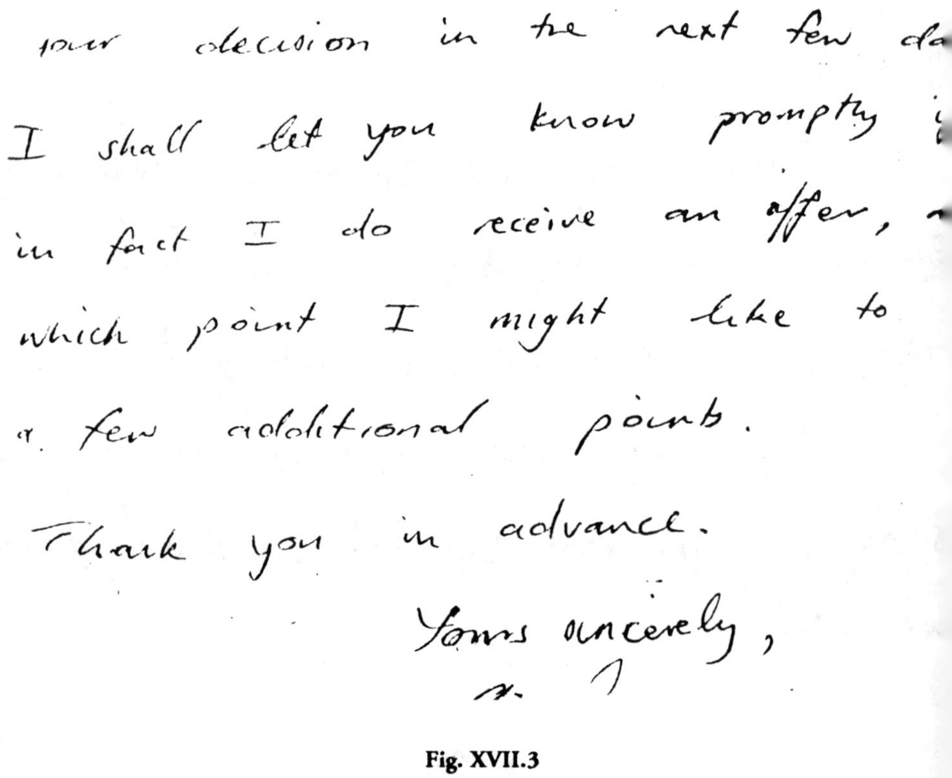
your decision in the next few da
I shall let you know promptly i
in fact I do receive an offer, a
which point I might like to
a few additional points.
Thank you in advance.
Yours sincerely,

Fig. XVII.3
Man, 36 years

WILLIAM SHELDON

William Sheldon was born in the U.S.A. in 1899. He became a professor of Psychology at the University of Chicago and after the 2nd world war he became the Director of the Constitution Laboratory of the College of Physicians and Surgeons at Columbia University.

He wrote two books: *The Varieties of Human Physique* and *The Varieties of Temperament,* both published by Harper in New York in 1940 and 1942.

His researches on constitutional psychology were based on the development of the embryo in the womb. At a certain stage of its development, three constituent parts can be distinguished: the *Endoderm*, which will become the 'visceral' system (the digestive and the glandular systems), the *Mesoderm,* which will become the skeleton and the motor-muscular systems and the *Ectoderm* which will become the neuro-sensory system (the nervous system and the sensory receptors - including the skin).

According to the dominance of one of the three constituent parts of the human body structure, Sheldon classified people into what he called the three main Biotypes:

1) The *Endomorph* or ***Viscerotonic*** (V for short) indicating dominance of the digestive and glandular systems.
2) The *Mesomorph* or ***Somatotonic*** (S for short) indicating dominance of the skeleton and the muscular systems.
3) The *Ectomorph* or ***Cerebrotonic*** (C for short) indicating dominance of the neurosensory systems; skin and all sensory receptors (eyes, ears etc).

The connection of the Biotypes with the Hippocratic Temperaments is as follows: V = L.S., S = B.S., C = N.B.

Everybody is a combination of the three types in different order depending on the dominance of one over the others.

Generally speaking, the *Viscerotonic* is more or less extrovert, sentimental, rather placid and quite often diplomatic, liking comfort and socialising.

The *Somatotonic* is more active, aggressive and competitive. Also mostly extrovert. He can be sadistic, boisterous, with drive for power, which can be constructive or destructive (the majority of criminals are mainly S). He likes taking risks and enjoys loud noises.

The *Cerebrotonic* is mostly an introvert, hypersensitive to noise of any kind, inhibited and often antisocial.

To sum up:

Endoderm = visceral system = digestive and glandular systems. The type is called: *Endomorph* or *Viscerotonic*.
Viscerotonic is a Lymphatic-Sanguine Temperament. V = sentimental extraversion, rather submissive and sentimental, a diplomatic extrovert.

Mesoderm = skeleton and motor muscular system. The type is called: *Mesomorph* or *Somatotonic*.
Somatotonic is a Bilious-Sanguine Temperament. S = is a factor of active, aggressive and competitive extraversion.
Audacious, sometimes sadistic, boisterous, with drive for power, can be constructive or destructive. Often acts before thinking, (majority of criminals are mainly S), love for racing and competing to the point of risking his life, enjoys making noises, i.e. loud car radio etc.

Ectoderm = neurosensory system = the nervous system and the sensory receptors including the skin. The type is called *Ectomorph* or *Cerebrotonic*.
Cerebrotonic is a Nervous-Bilious Temperament.

C = is a factor of introversion, hypersensitivity to noise of any kind.

Possible combinations: V S C S V C C V S
V C S S C V C S V

VS or SV	=	(Kretschmer's Pycnic) cyclothymic - easily adaptable to reality.
SC or CS	=	paranoid personality, rigid, suspicious, aggressive, dogmatic with lust for power.
VC or CV	=	soft, detached introvert, anxious usually with low mental activity.

W. Sheldon in graphology

Viscerotonic - (Lymphatic-Sanguine) Predominance of curves, deep garlands, garland connections. Spread out forms. Dominance of middle zone. Inflated forms (full loops and ovals mainly in middle and lower zones). The writing will have a 'dancing' appearance. The pressure is rather precise and somewhat alive (with some differentiation between up and down strokes). *(Figs. XVII.4, XVII.4b)*

Somatotonic - (Bilious-Sanguine) Elongation of the writing. M/z becomes slightly narrower and the capitals taller. The speed is fast and resolute. Accents, *t*-bars and *i*-dots will be placed high. Occasionally some exaggerated movements (when the Sanguine is stronger). Pressure is strong and firm. In relief. Straight lines (more or less) some swords. *(Fig. XVII.5)*

Cerebrontonic - (Nervous-Bilious) Signs of constraint or control. Spasmodic pressure (sharp pointed). Grouped or juxtaposed. Narrow letters, smaller altogether. Angular, tens, often right slanted. Irregular. Occasionally jerky. Arcades with tension if there is dominance of Bilious. Small and jerky if there is dominance of Nervous. (*Fig. XVII.6)*

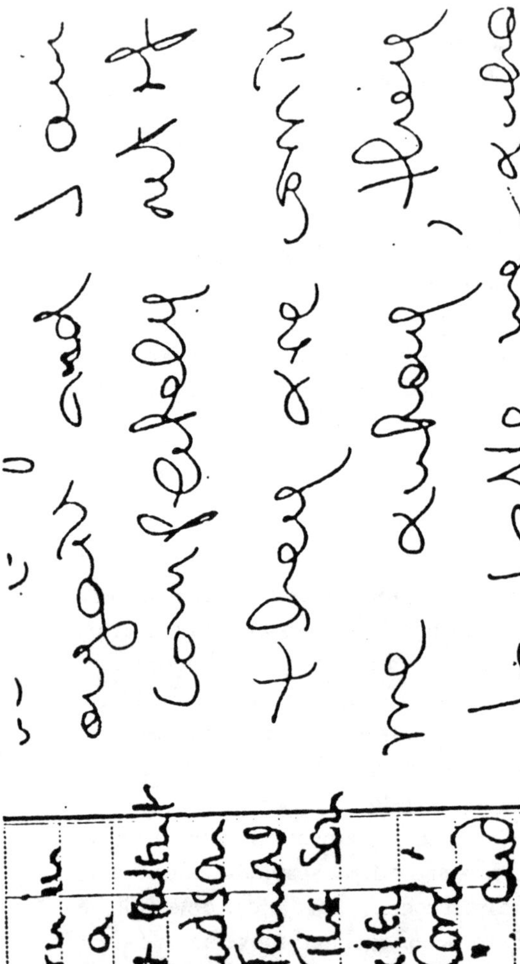

Fig. XVII.4a
Woman, 33 years
Viscerotonic

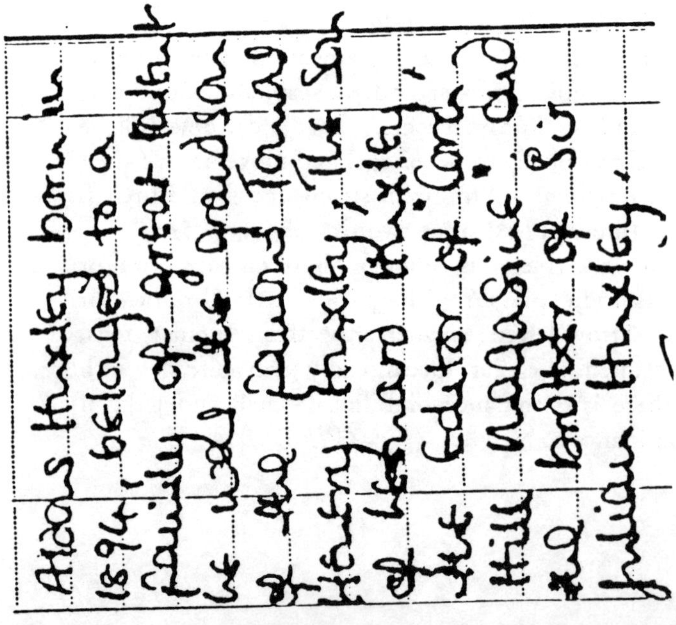

Fig. XVII.4
Woman, 40 years
Viscerotonic

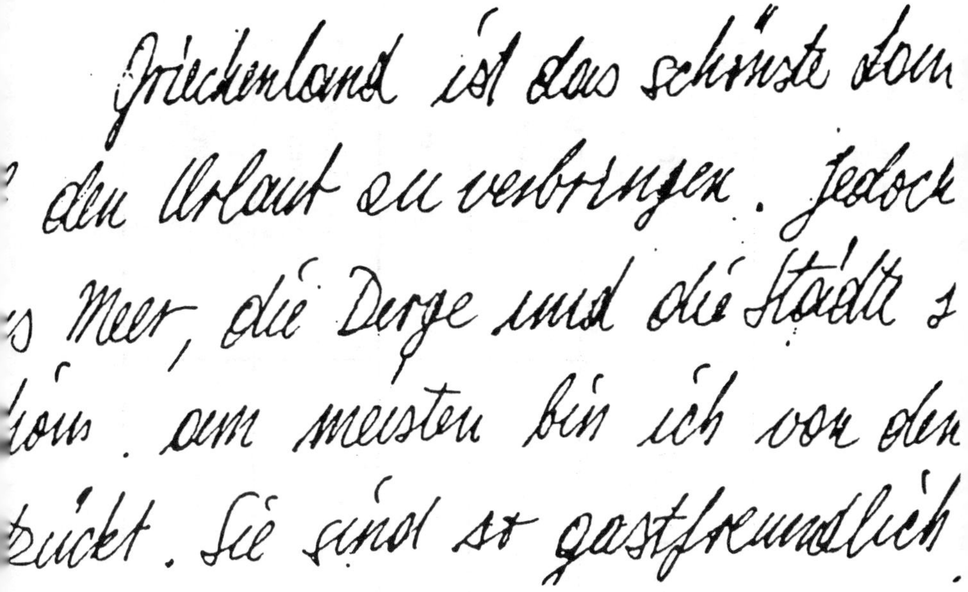

Fig. XVII.5 - Man, 40 years - Somatotonic

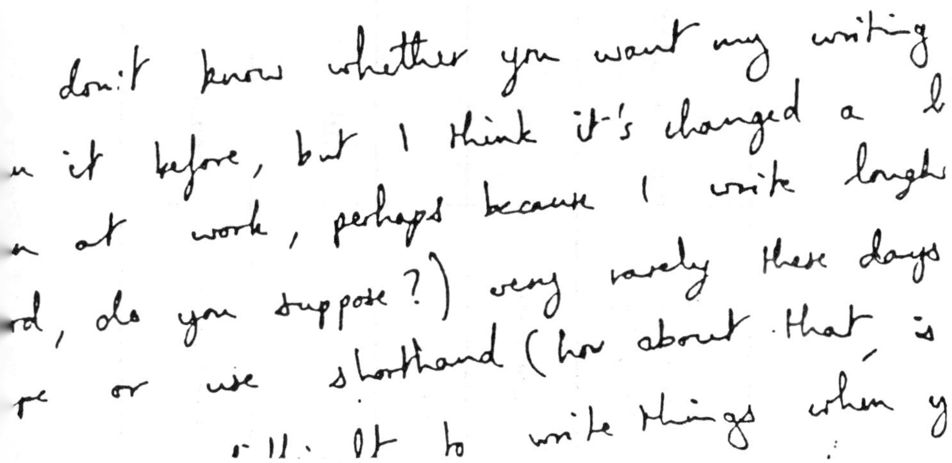

Fig. XVII.6 - Woman, 23 years - Cerebrotonic

SHELDON Somatotype	KRETSCHMER Types	HIPPOCRATES Temperaments	JUNG Attitudes
Viscerotonic	Picnic	L S	Extrovert
Somatotonic		B S	Extrovert
	Athletic	B N	Extraversive introvert
Cerebrotonic	Leptosome	N	Introvert

SOURCES

BOURDEL, L. — *Les Tempéraments Psychobiologiques*, Librarie Maloine SA, Paris, 1961

I.I.R.G. — *Cours de Pratique Graphologique*, ed. I.I.R.G., Paris, 1963.

KRETSCHMER, Dr. E. — *Structure du Corps et Caractère*

MISCHEL, W. — *Introduction to personality*, HRW International, ed. N.Y., 1986

PFANNE, H. — *Lehrbuch der Graphologie*, Walter de Grupter & Co., Berlin, 1961.

TEILLARD, A. — *L'Ame et L'Écriture*, ed. Traditionnelles, Paris, 1966. *translated by Scriptor Books and published 1993 under the title *The Soul and Handwriting*.

LECTURE XVIII

KAREN HORNEY (1885 - 1952)

Karen Horney studied medicine and psychiatry in Berlin. In 1932 she went to America, where she got actively involved with the advancement of the psychoanalytic movement and wrote 6 books.

Her interest was concentrated mainly in the neuroses, their causes and cure. She believed the neuroses are created by the individual himself, unlike Freud who thought that neuroses are born with us, like the instincts.

Conflicts, she said, are the main culprit behind all neuroses, which in turn create more conflict. Neurosis is nothing more than a disturbance in the inner harmony of the personality (inner conflicts), which may eventually cause a psychic or physical illness.

To understand the neurotic character structure we must know that every single neurosis is really a "character neurosis".

Karen Horney's theory, particularly on female psychology, was different to Freud's. After she moved to America she realised that the neuroses there were very different from those she had known in Germany or other European countries. She concluded that the differences in civilisation were the cause. Cultural factors and particularly the style of human relationships were the cause of neuroses in the U.S.A.

This was the point at which Karen Horney realised that Freud's theory of neurosis was fundamentally incorrect. He saw inner conflicts as a battle between repressed and repressing powers and considered the neurosis-producing factors as libidinal, instinctual in all men and women, whereas it was evident to her that this was not so. Neuroses, she discovered were "an outgrowth of disturbed human relationships". The compulsive drives, two of which are, neurotic need for affection and neurotic need for power, spring from feelings of isolation, helplessness, fear and hostility and aim not at satisfaction, but at security.

Compulsive drives, otherwise called "neurotic trends" and their interplay within us, once understood and recognised, can change into constructive and helpful, rather than harmful elements of our personality.

The "neurotic need for affection", together with the "compulsive modesty" and the "need for a partner", represent an attitude towards others and the self, and a particular philosophy of life, which Karen Horney called *"moving towards people"*. Also the "compulsive craving for power and prestige", together with the "neurotic ambition", constitute the factors of what she called *"moving against people"*.

Neurotic trends not only enhance each other, but as we have already seen, they create conflicts.

Through her practice she observed 4 major ways in which people most regularly tried to solve their neurotic conflicts:-

1) One was to repress one part of the conflict and raise its opposite.
2) Second was to *"move away from people"*, to detach oneself from others, thus setting "the conflict out of operation".
3) The third way was that instead of moving away from others, the neurotic moved away from himself. The need for perfection in this case, and the need to be admired became more and more evident as the individual moved further and further away from his reality. The "idealised image" is the most important of all attempts at solving the conflicts, because of its effect on the whole personality, and the gap it creates within.

4) The fourth is the attempt to bridge the gap of the third, which also helps in solving all other conflicts through externalisation.

Other less common attempts at solving the inner conflicts are "rigid self-control which holds together a torn individual by sheer will power", and "cynicism, which in disparaging all values, eliminates conflicts in regard to ideals".

She observed that unresolved conflicts bring about all sorts of fears, waste of energy and deep hopelessness through feeling trapped in an entanglement.

At that point she noticed that sadistic trends are another expression of the individual's despair of ever "being himself". The "all consuming passion" often seen in sadistic practices is an "insatiable need for vindictive triumph", and it is in fact nothing more than another expression of "destructive exploitation".

So Karen Horney developed her theory of the neurosis, at the centre of which is the conflict of the attitudes of "moving towards", "moving against" and "moving away from" people, which she calls "constructive theory" for the following reasons:

1) It abolishes the unrealistic and naive idea that we can resolve neuroses by simple means, i.e. rational decision.
2) It allows us for the first time to tackle and resolve neurotic hopelessness.
3) It permits the actual resolution of the underlying conflicts, thus enabling us to work towards a real integration of personality.

Conflicts can be resolved by changing the conditions within the personality that brought them into being, says Karen Horney in her book, "Our Inner Conflicts".

Freud, not having much faith in human goodness, was very deeply pessimistic when it came to neuroses and their treatment.

"Man is doomed to suffer and to destroy. The instincts which drive him can only be controlled, or at best, sublimated".

Karen Horney, through her observations, grew to believe the contrary. "Man not only has the capacity, but also the desire to develop and become a decent human being, but this deteriorates when his relationship to others and hence to himself is disturbed".

Karen Horney's Theory in Graphology

The 3 attitudes -
1) *Moving towards people*
2) *Moving against people*
3) *Moving away from people*
is what interests us as graphologists.

The first one, *"moving towards people"*, consists as we have seen, of a "neurotic need of affection", "compulsive modesty" and the "need for a partner". This is the compliant type who believes people are generally nice.

This combination is evidently indicative of weakness, therefore the writing will be round, or generally curved, connected with garlands, invading, wide or spread out, with full middle zone letters and simple forms, tangled lines, with more or less light pressure and some filiform tendency and more or less irregular lower zone indicating modesty, dependency and general anxiety and fear of isolation, lack of independent initiative, need for affection and need for approval. *(Fig. XVIII.1)*

The second one, *"moving against people"* consists of the "drive for power, prestige and admiration". This is the aggressive type who believes that people are hostile and that life is a constant struggle against everything and everyone. Socially he may cover up his beliefs with politeness, fair play attitudes and generally suave behaviour (Machiavellian type) or he may well make his attitudes quite evident. Whichever the social behaviour this individual chooses, he will always make sure that others are left in no doubt as to who is in command.

The writing of this type of neurotic will be generally aggressive, rather compact, with heavy pressure, firm, angular, with resolute triangles in all zones, strong and firm *t*-bars, all indicating the attitude of a hard, ruthless fighter determined to rule and to survive in the "jungle", which is what he considers the society in which he lives to be. *(Fig. XVIII.2)*

The third type, *"moving away from people"*, which is the "neurotic detachment" representing an attempt at solving the anxiety through "maintaining emotional distance between the self and others", thus setting the conflict out of operation".

By "neurotic detachment", Karen Horney means the type who feels it is an intolerable strain to associate with people and therefore solitude becomes the only means of avoiding it. This results in general estrangement from people.

The writing of this type will be clear, aerated to spaced out, with a fairly wide right margin and narrow left margin, occasionally with descending lines, narrow forms or thin overall, angles and arcades, with slight right slant or clearly vertical and rather small or medium-to-small. Reduced lower extensions and the overall movement is contained without exaggerations, embellishments or flamboyancy. *(Fig. XVIII.3)*

The writer avoids contact with or commitment to people; he does not wish to get involved in any way - "love, co-operation, fight or competition". His most striking acquirement is resourcefulness; it is his only compensation for his isolation.

Karen Horney wrote six books:
The Neurotic Personality of our time,
New Ways in Psychoanalysis,
Neurosis and Human Growth,
Self-Analysis,
Our Inner Conflicts,
Feminine Psychology.

* * *

SOURCES

(Further reading on Karen Horney's psychological theories)

ENGLER, B. *Personality Theories*
Houghton Mifflin Co., Boston, 1985.

HORNEY, K. *Our Inner Conflicts*
W.W. Norton & Co., New York, London, 1966.

HORNEY, K. *Self-Analysis*
W.W. Norton & Co., London 1968.

HORNEY, K. *Neurosis and Human Growth*
W.W. Norton & Co., London 1968.

* * *

Fig. XVIII.1 - *Moving Towards* type
Woman, 40+ years

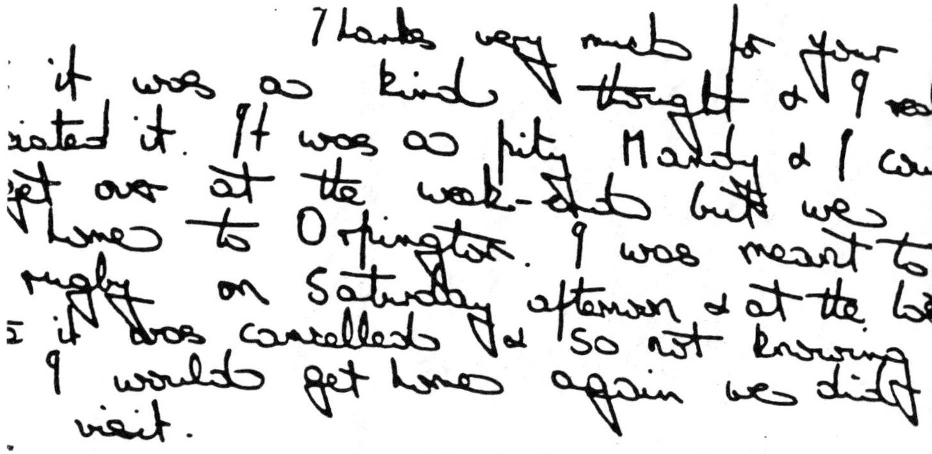
Thanks very much for your
it was a kind thought & I ap
riated it. It was a pity Mandy & I cou
et over at the week-end but we
home to Orpington. I was meant to
rugby on Saturday afternoon & at the la
it was cancelled & so not knowing
I would get home again we didn't
visit.

Fig. XVIII.2 - *Moving Against* type
Man, 40+ years

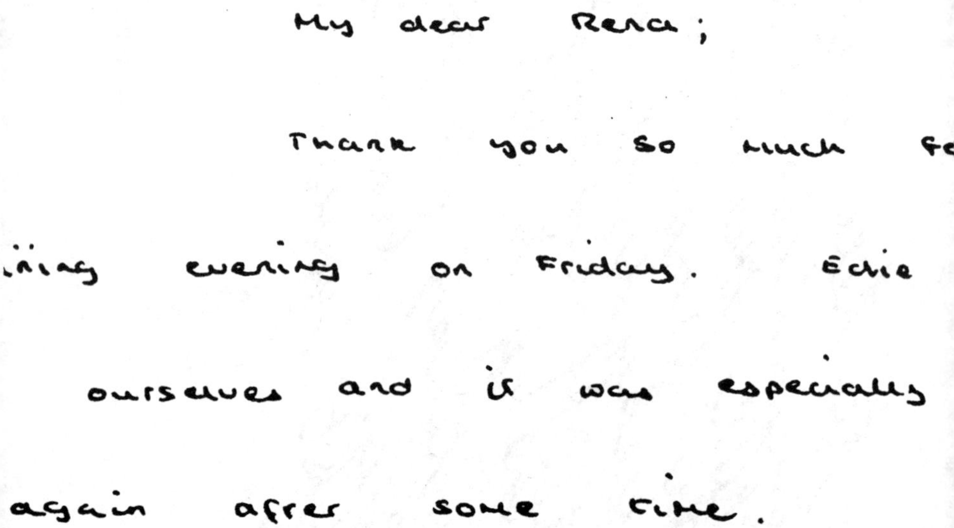
My dear Rena;
Thank you so much fo
ning evening on Friday. Edie
ourselves and it was especially
again after some time.

Fig. XVIII.3 - Moving away type
Man, 35 years

LECTURE XIX

ERIC FROMM

Eric Fromm - a contemporary of Karen Horney - was born in Frankfurt, in Germany. He studied psychology in Munich and Berlin, and moved to America in 1932.

His philosophy and his theories indicate a great concern with man's need to relate - "through attitude and ethic" - to mankind in general, and in a way to himself. He first establishes four basic facts regarding today's man;

1) Man has an essential inborn nature
2) Society is created by man to fulfill this essential nature
3) No society devised by man meets the basic needs of man's existence
4) It is impossible to create such a society.

He points out that the manner of relating is a measure of the individual's inner *productivity*, indicating the pattern of his emotional life, his reasoning his capacity for love and the individual way in which each person relates to material goods.

Productivity in this sense is a life long process which entails realisation of one's potential together with concern for other people's development, holding their welfare as integral to own self-interest and excluding exploitation.

Productiveness is man's use of his potentials.

According to Fromm man relates to the outside world using his productive powers in 2 basic ways:

1. *Reproductively,*
2. *Generatively.*

1. *Reproductive* is the person who perceives the world quite literally as it is. What he creates is a realistic reproduction of what he has perceived; just what he sees in a very unimaginative manner, like a camera. He cannot penetrate beyond the surface into the core, into the essential. He cannot visualise what is not apparent. To him reality is only what is obvious "what has already materialised". This view of reality is unproductive.

2. *Generative* is the person who perceives and recreates the world through "spontaneous activities". In the extreme form, the person who relates to the world in a "generative" way, is a person who has built up his own personal reality and has no longer the ability to perceive actuality. He is unable to relate productively.

Productiveness lies in between these two types; the person who will enrich what he perceives with his own personality. Who is able to relate to the world both reproductively and generatively.

Fromm describes four different types of character with non-productive orientation:

a. **the *Receptive* type** (accepting)
b. **the *Exploitive* type** (taking)
c. **the *Hoarding* type** (preserving)
d. **the *Marketing* type** (exchanging)

Although Fromm calls these four types of orientation *"unproductive"*, each type can have positive qualities, characteristic of his own specific category. Let us see them each one separately.

THE RECEPTIVE TYPE

The *Receptive type* believes that he has nothing of value within him and that all good things are outside - in others. All material goods, such as affection, love, knowledge, pleasure, can only come from others. So, with his orientation, he is unable, for example, to give love; he can only receive. His whole development and attitude revolves around the need to be constantly reassured of being loved, and generally to receive any "donations" of time, affections or material things in order to make up his deficit. He is not too selective in his choice of acquaintances or of loved ones, he does not withdraw or rebuff. In the process he develops an "inviting" personality; he is loyal, responsive, trusting (since he believes that the others are good), idealistic, optimistic, friendly and a good listener (if he is intelligent).

He often has a warm and helpful attitude - thus securing affection.

This attitude - the attachment to others - evidently, does not arise from his interest in them but in himself.

This great will to receive makes him undiscriminating. He tends to say 'yes' to everything and everybody, thus developing conflicts within his loyalties. He expects everything from others and - if he is religious from God as well and will not move a finger to help himself. If he is not intelligent he has no opinions of his own and no principles. He is 'imitative'.

The *Receptive* type people tend to overcome anxiety and depression by eating and drinking.

THE EXPLOITIVE TYPE

The *Exploitive* type believes (like the *Receptive* type) that all good things belong to others, and therefore whatever he needs he will have to take from others. The difference between the Receptive and the Exploitive types is that whereas the Receptive will expect others to give him, the Exploitive does not. So he will take "by force or by cunning".

He cannot imagine anyone wanting to give anything of value. He tends to be attracted to people, for instance, who are otherwise attached and he will do anything "to grab" them. The unattached person is of no interest to him.

Someone else's object of affection is more attractive and more interesting to him than his own. Or someone else's job is always better. This is not because he thinks that the other person is more valuable but because he believes he himself has nothing worthwhile within himself to cultivate.

The Exploitive person, although he is capable of original ideas, will rather steal and copy other people's since they always appear better to his own. (The neighbour's grass is always greener).

He gets quickly tired of people who refuse to be exploited. He is manipulative and hostile, suspicious, envious and jealous. The kleptomaniacs belong to this type os orientation; they will enjoy the stolen good more than if he pays for it (thus making it his own).

THE HOARDING TYPE

The *Hoarding* type is the opposite to the previous two. He has no faith in anything coming from outside. He has nothing to gain from the world. His best chance is to hold on to, and accumulate his own goods, and not to give anything away. His sense of security is based on this attitude, which refers to money and all material things as well as to thoughts, feelings, love (since love is also a possession he does not give love, he only gets it through possessing the person). This extreme tendency of not letting go of anything makes him see all change as a loss. The past appears to him always better than the present, so he holds on to memories, traditions, sentimentalities and experiences. This makes him a person with good memory, and respect for others, tenacious, orderly, punctual, faithful but also pedantic, suspicious, selfish and a cynic ("there is nothing new under the sun").

The Hoarding type is also compulsively clean as a need to wash off the contact with the outside world.

THE MARKETING TYPE

The *Marketing* type is the person who has a special talent to identify himself and his values with whatever is profitable at the time. He has developed the gift of changing and adapting to the rapid changes of supply and demand, in order to survive. He does not trust that to have a skill is enough in order to succeed, he must also be able to put across his personality and to successfully compete with others. His greatest concern is to be "salable" and not his personal life or happiness.

As a result this type loses his identity. He does not develop his potential or any kind of specific relatedness. He is always ready to change. His attitude is versatile. "His feeling of identity becomes as shaky as is his self-esteem; it is constituted by the sum-total of roles one can play: I am as you desire me". (Eric Fromm: *Man for Himself*).

What mostly matters to this type is what sort of family background he has, whether he knows the 'right' people, where he lives, what clubs he belongs to, etc. depending of course, on the special field in which he works and wishes to market himself. As a result, he is unable or unwilling to form any sort of permanent relationship, he has to be constantly free in order to be able to follow the trend of the market. His only permanent quality is the versatility of attitude.

This last type is a modern type; a product of the economic function of the market in modern society.

Each one of the above four types of orientation has his negative and his positive type. For example where the Positive Receptive type will be trusting and accepting, the Negative Receptive will be gullible and passive respectively, and so on.

Eric Fromm's Theory in Graphology

Let us see them separately with their graphic signs;

The Receptive positive type

is loyal, adaptable, responsive, receptive, trusting, modest, idealistic, optimistic, sensitive and polite.

His writing is:

Layout - clear overall, with good distribution of spacing, rather invading - in right and lower margins mainly.

Movement - mostly regular, curved, round, right slant or slight right slant, progressive and often (but not necessarily rising), with extended finals.

Form - rather stylised but simple or simplified (mostly the capitals), medium size, with garland connections, well proportioned in all 3 zones, with open curves.

Pressure - light overall and rather fine with medium or no tension.

Speed - usually poised, sometimes (rarely) effervescent (abandon).

The Receptive negative type

is passive, submissive, without firm principles or opinions of his own, servile, gullible, sentimental, unrealistic.

His writing is:

Layout - irregular spacing between lines and words, narrow margins with wide left margin, often mingling letters.

Movement - mainly curved, mostly round, often slanted to the left or varying, some exaggerations of movements, sinuous baseline, weak down strokes.

Form - no particular style, many irregularities, garlands, arcades and threads, slack and without tension, bow ties, double joined, some prolongments in the upper zone without tension or firmness, weak t-bars, generally low Formlevel.

Pressure - weak or superficial, light, irregular, flat, often blurred.

Speed - slow.

The Exploitive positive type

is active, impulsive, proud, confident, active and able to take initiative.

His writing is:

Layout - usually good layout, good distribution of black and white not very wide spacings.

Movement - generally upright of with slight slant either way, curved or straight, extended and firm final strokes, large and confident movements, some exaggerated movements, some diminishing.

Form - generally medium size writing, some upper prolongments, some exaggerations in forms, overall a simplified writing with irregularities, some curved starting strokes.

Pressure - heavy, mainly firm downstrokes.

Speed - rapid, resolute, occasionally with flying strokes.

The Exploitive negative type

is exploitive, egocentric, arrogant, conceited, seducing, aggressive and rash.

His writing is:

Layout - mostly good lay out, left margin usually progressively diminishing, often messy, with poor distribution of black and white.

Movement - angles and arcades, strong capitals, occasionally with ornamentations, right or left slant, emphasis on the beginning of words or lines.

Form - angular and/or arcade connections, thready garlands with tension, regressive overall or centrifugal finals, negligent forms, inharmonious, any size.

Pressure - light pressure, clubs, sharp-pointed.

Speed - rapid, precipitated.

The Hoarding positive type

is economical, practical, reserved, cautious, patient, orderly, methodical, loyal, with good memory and respect for others.

His writing is:

Layout - regular and fairly straight margins, right margin equal to the left, compact but fair spacing between lines for clarity, clear, neat and legible.

Movement - firm and conscious (deliberate), straight baselines (can be rigid), any slant but regular with very little if any, variation; arcades and narrow garlands, some arcades in upper zone, connected, occasionally rigid, often firmly prolonged upwards.

Form - narrow, simple or simplified, rounded, medium middle zone, stylised, firm *t*-bars, with attention to details.

Pressure - firm, particularly in the down strokes, resolute, occasionally heavy, with medium or no tension.

Speed - slow and deliberate writing.

The Hoarding negative type

is stubborn, pedantic, inactive (lazy), obsessional, possessive, suspicious, unimaginative and full of anxieties.

His writing is:

Layout	-	messy, disorderly, invading, diminishing left margin, widening right margin, inharmonious spacing.
Movement	-	lacking freedom of movement, angular or looped garlands, inharmonious, inhibited, hesitant, occasionally very slanted to the right or the left, either rigid or slack, with interruptions of the flow, regressive movements.
Form	-	narrow, ungraceful, disproportionate,very small or very large, tangled lines, mingling letters, either squeezed or spread out forms (laziness), often disconnected, centripetal end strokes, possible shark's teeth, hooks - mainly in lower zone.
Pressure	-	either pastose and blurred or thin, superficial, deviated on the horizontal movements.
Speed	-	slow to poised, irregular, slack.

The Marketing positive type

is social, curious, witty, intelligent, adaptable, tolerant, generous, efficient, open minded, versatile and purposeful.

His writing is:

Layout	-	aerated, right margin narrow or nonexistent, letters widely spaced but narrow spacing between words.
Movement	-	towards the right overall, progressive, curved, fluent, right slanted, dominance of movement over form, garlands and threads, plastic movements, often rhythmic.

Form - simplified, open ovals, rounded forms, combined letters, mixed connections, fairly - but not too - full loops in upper and lower zones, diminishing letters at the end of words, some wavy *t*-bars, original forms.

Pressure - mostly light with medium tension and firm strokes, occasionally deviated in the up strokes or horizontally in the t bars and the garland connections.

Speed - rapid, occasionally carried away, precipitated.

The Marketing negative type

is overactive but aimless, aggressive, opportunistic, inconsistent, often childish, without firm moral values or principles, he dislikes isolation, he is undiscriminating, truly indifferent, wasteful, superficial and disloyal.

His writing is:

Layout - invading, no definite margins, narrow spacing between words and irregular, confused.

Movement - irregular, curved, slack right slant or vertical, fairly regular, animated, some fullness, sinuous base-line, thready, pull to the right, some ornate movements, negligent movement overall, some regressive movements.

Form - vulgar, wide or narrow, irregular, centripetal, negligent, complicated, diminishing and/or enlarging, disproportionate in all 3 zones, ungraceful, generally low Formlevel.

Pressure - mainly irregular, never robust, occasionally light or weak, weak down strokes, some spindles and/or clubs.

Speed - generally rapid, illegible, occasionally abbreviated.

The Productive type

is the person who fulfills all his potential, who has a healthy and lively concern for the welfare of his fellow men. He is the normal, mature, creative, healthy personality (Freud's "genital" character "who is capable of functioning well sexually and socially"). He is capable of "mature production", capable of transforming the materials at hand, using his reason and imagination; the objective "working .... loving, reasoning" (Eric Fromm).

His writing is : organised, clear, spontaneous, pleasantly laid out on the page, progressive but not necessarily extraverted, grouped or connected, combined, often small or medium to small, very simplified, rhythmic, occasionally harmonious, dynamic, resolute with firm down strokes, in relief, rapid or precipitated.

* * *

SOURCES

ENGLER, B. *Personality Theories*
Houghton Mifflin Co., Boston, USA, 1985.

FROMM, E. *Man for Himself*
Routledge & Keagan Paul, Ltd., London, 1949.

FROMM, E. *Escape from Freedom,*
Rinehart & Co. Inc., N.Y., 1941.

FROMM, E. *Beyond the Chains of Illusion*
Abacus, London, 1983.

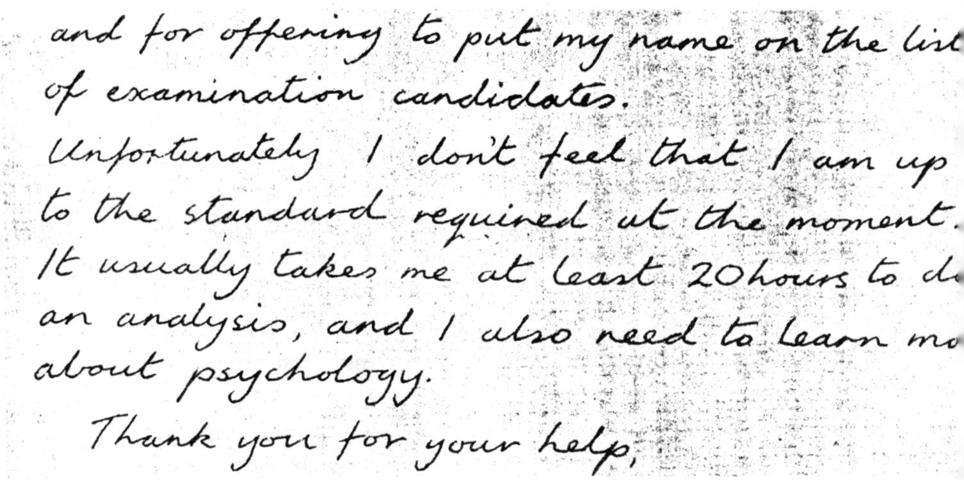
and for offering to put my name on the list
of examination candidates.
Unfortunately I don't feel that I am up
to the standard required at the moment.
It usually takes me at least 20 hours to do
an analysis, and I also need to learn mo
about psychology.
Thank you for your help,

Fig. XIX.1 - ***Receptive positive***
Woman, 50 years.

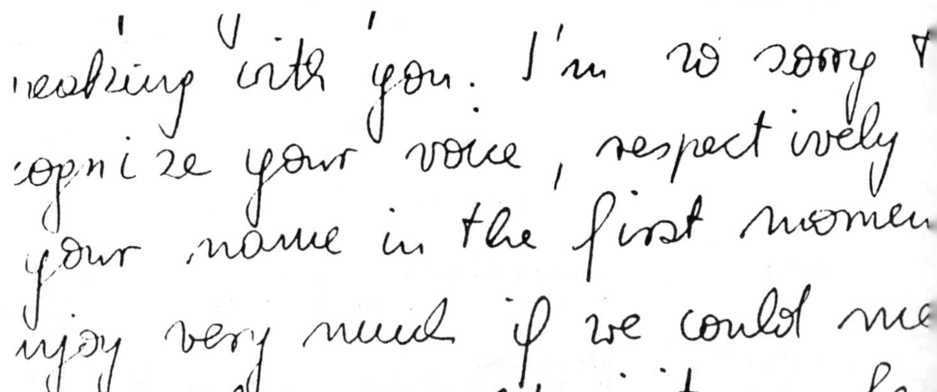
working with you. I'm so sorry
cognize your voice, respectively
your name in the first momen
njoy very much if we could me
at our if you would visit me her
very beautiful too! believe me.-

Fig. XIX.2 - ***Receptive negative***
Woman, 32 years

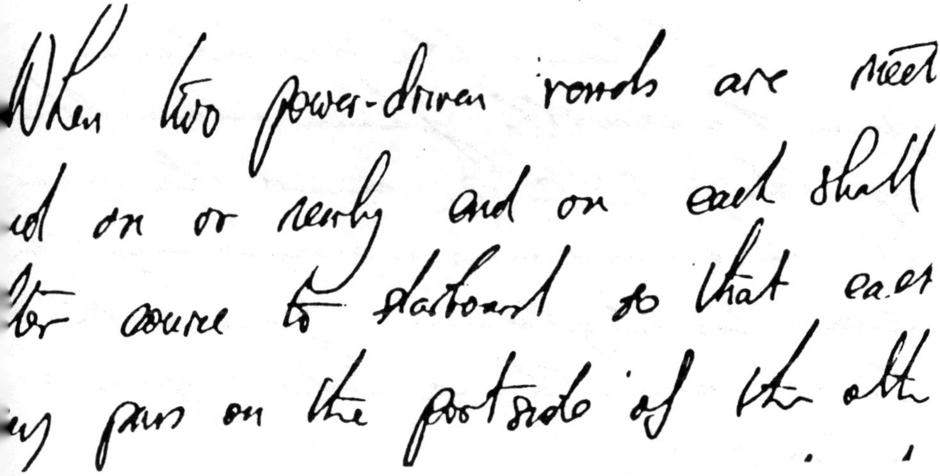

Fig. XIX.3 - *Exploitive positive*
Man, 41years.

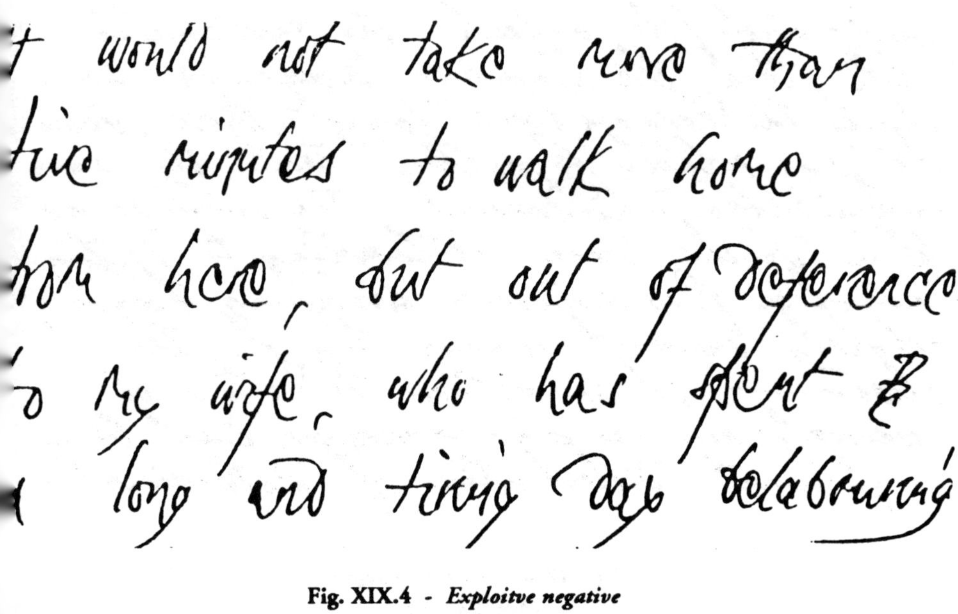

Fig. XIX.4 - *Exploitve negative*
Man, 44 years.

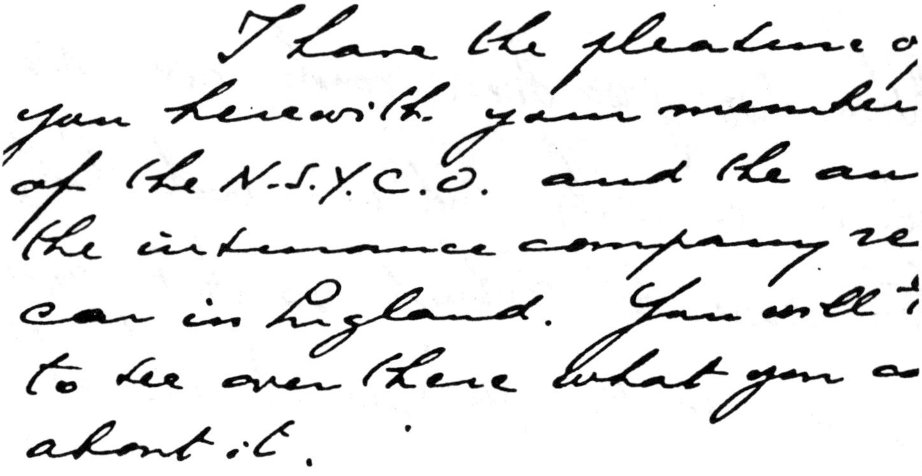

I have the pleasure o
you herewith your membe
of the N.S.Y.C.O. and the an
the insurance company re
car in England. You will
to see over there what you a
about it.

Fig. XIX.5 - ***Hoarding positive***
Man, 59 years.

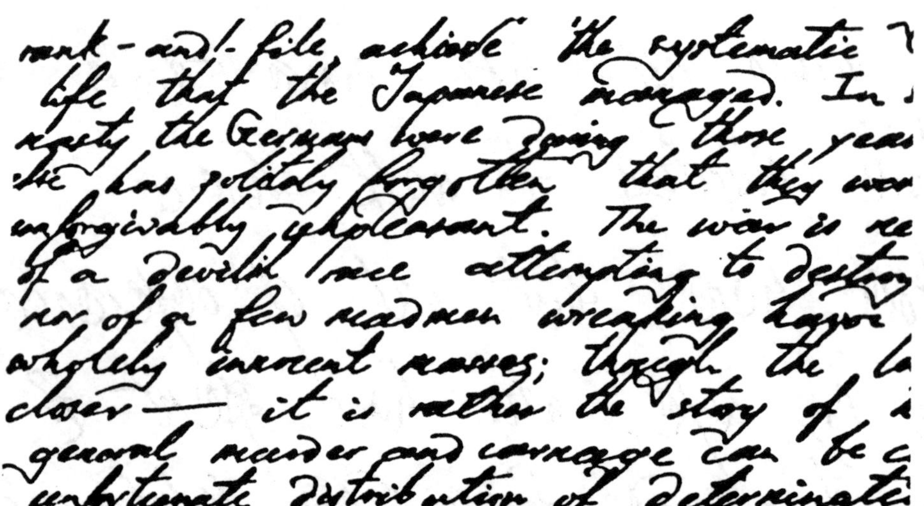

rank-and-file, achieve the systematic
life that the Japanese managed. In
nasty the Germans were doing those years
has solidly forgotten that they were
unforgivably unpleasant. The war is
of a Jewish race attempting to destroy
or of a few madmen wreaking havoc
wholely innocent masses; though the
closer — it is rather the story of
general murder and carnage can be
unfortunate distribution of determinati

Fig. XIX.6 - ***Hoarding negative***
Man, 23 years.

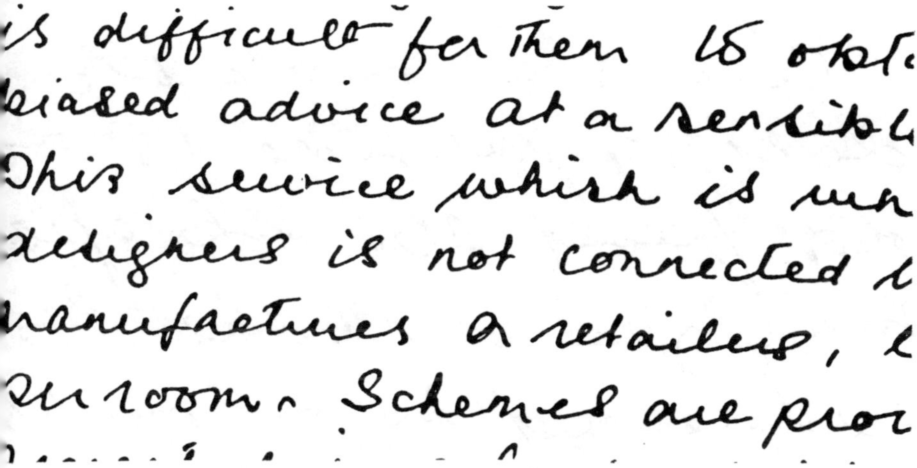

Fig. XIX.7 - *Marketing Positive* - Woman, 38 years.

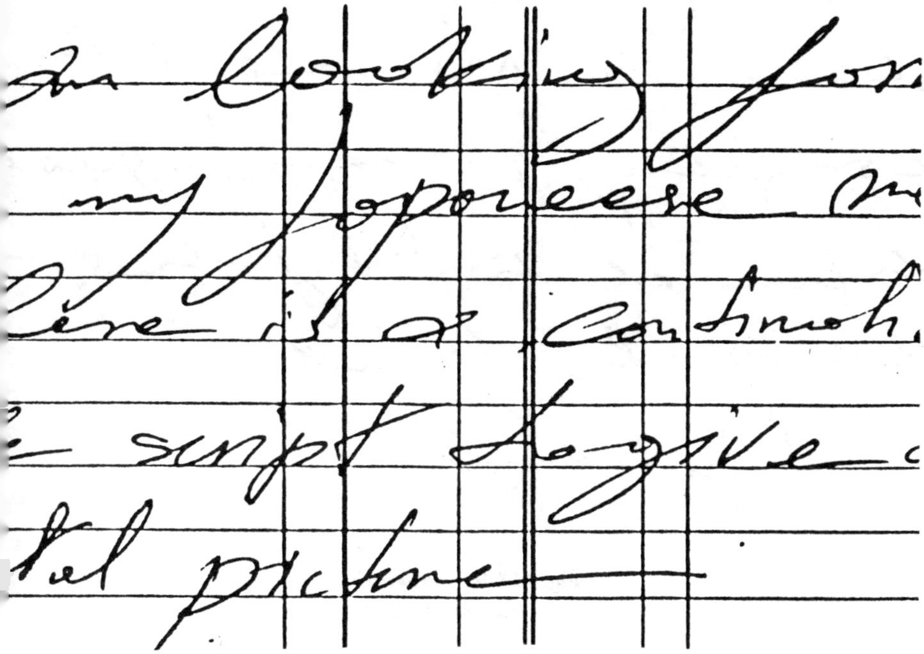

Fig. XIX.8 - *Marketing negative* - Man, 40 years.

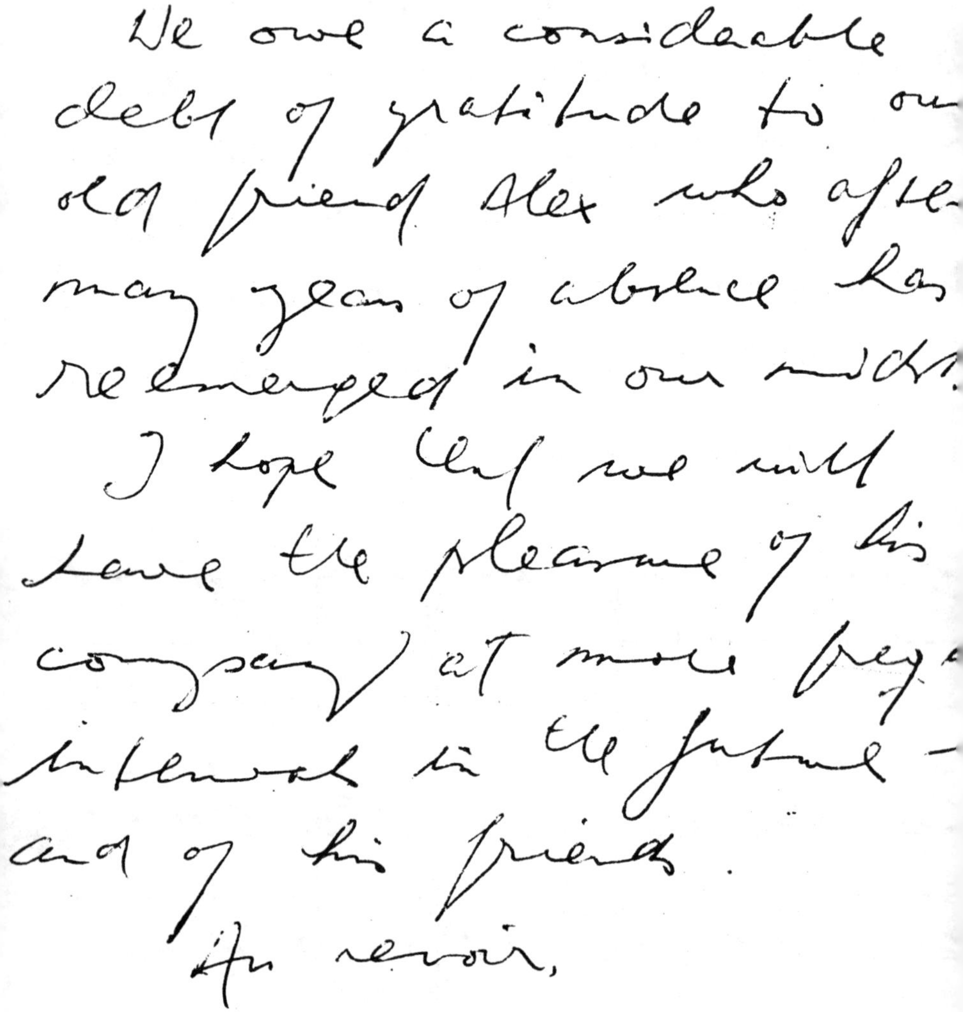

We owe a considerable debt of gratitude to our old friend Alex who after many years of absence has reemerged in our midst. I hope that we will have the pleasure of his company at more frequent intervals in the future — and of his friends.

Au revoir,

Fig. XIX.9 - ***Productive***
Man, 45 years.

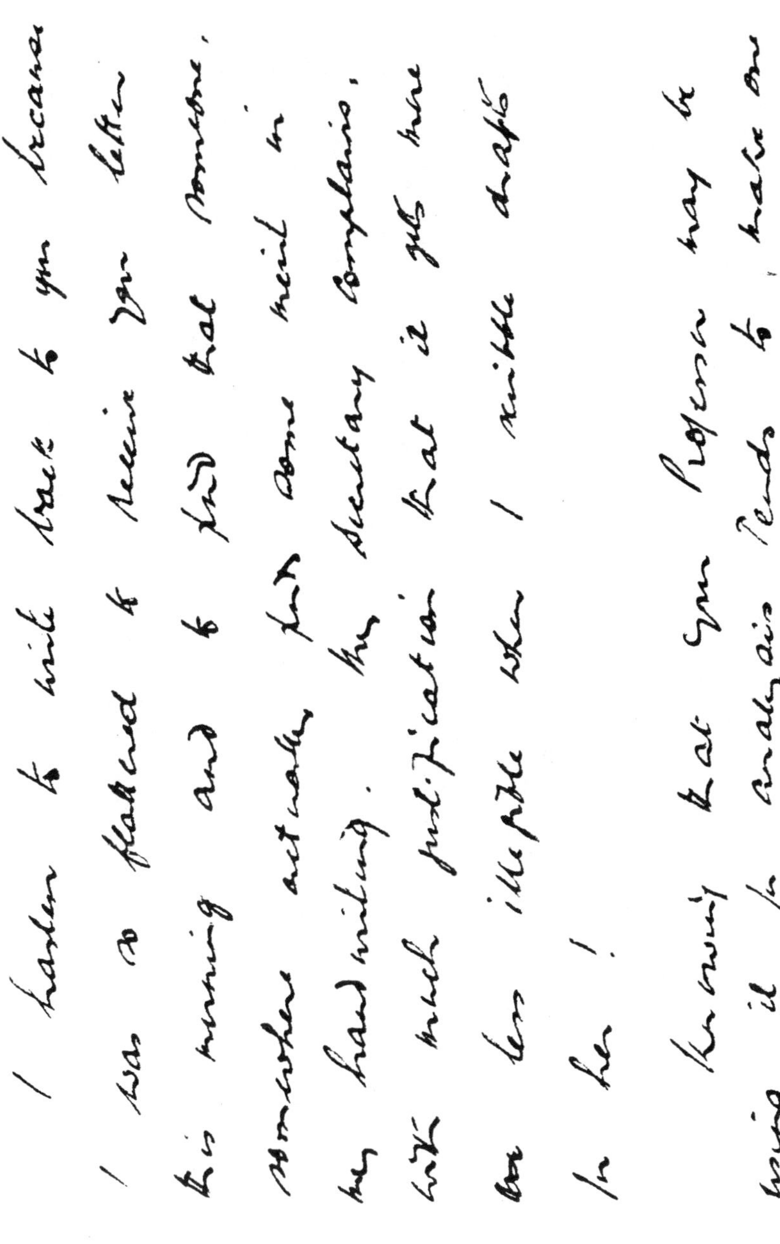
I hasten to write back to you because I was so flattered to receive your letter this morning and to find that someone somewhere actually finds some merit in my handwriting. My secretary complains, with much justification, that it gets more and more illegible when I scribble drafts for her!

Knowing that your profession may be using it for analysis tends to make me

Fig. XIX.10 - *Productive* - Man, 63 years

LECTURE XX

ABRAHAM MASLOW (1908 - 1970)

Graphology, over the years, has involved many psychologists in its practice. Apart from the pioneers - Freud, Jung, Adler - who studied human nature with great insight and made psychology the new science, we have a few contemporary psychologists who have developed new theories through their observation of the modern man.

Some of the best known to us are Erich Fromm, Karen Horney and Abraham Maslow.

Erich Fromm with his 'productive' and ' unproductive' concepts and Karen Horney with her 'drives' and 'attitudes' can be called typologists.

Abraham Maslow was not a typologist, but he was a brilliant theoretician and a keen observer of human nature in all its states. His approach is more Jungian than Freudian. He studied both the healthy and the sick with equal fascination and compassion. Most of all he studied the level of evolution of the individual. And this is of equal interest to any student of human nature, as is the understanding of the character, the temperament, the tendencies and their expression.

It is not enough for a graphologist to be able to say that the writer is an extrovert who likes sports and is a good businessman, easily adaptable to any social circumstance, or that he/she suffers from Oedipus conflict. It is of equal importance to be able to see the stage of his/her evolution. Only when we are able to understand the writer's basic needs shall we be able to see the direction of his aggression, for instance, or of his ambitions, the level of his or her tolerance, the orientation of his desires, his ability to absorb and benefit from experience, the serenity of his behaviour and his productivity in any field.

Maslow noticed and studied the progress and the striving towards self-actualisation in men and women. This is an extremely important process of evolution, towards the highest level of which all the human race strives. Some of us consciously, but most of us subconsciously, look upwards and are never really satisfied until we reach the highest step, which unfortunately only very few do. Jung called this state "individuation" and Fromm called it "productiveness". They all refer to the same thing.

Among all the writings we see in our careers as graphologists, some are healthy and well balanced in all aspects, I but only very few indeed will be samples of self-actualised people. We need to be able to recognise them.

*

Abraham Maslow was born in Brooklyn on 1st April, 1908 and died on 8th June 1970. He was Professor of Psychology at Brooklyn College and President of the American Psychological Association (1967-8).

He was an enthusiastic lover of human nature, a humanistic psychologist and a positive thinker. Through his observations of the human psyche, he was driven to believe that human nature is basically good. He developed a trust in the unlimited beautiful possibilities of a growth of consciousness.

Freud was the first to discover the unconscious through psychoanalysis. All his life was an investigation into the mysteries of the mind and hence the causes of neuroses. This agonising search into the maze of the neurotic drove him towards a pessimistic view of human destiny. "Man is doomed to suffer and to destroy", he wrote.

Jung, at the end of his life, expressed the hope that man, although suffocated by the 'masses' (his own creations, from 'the State' to 'religious confession') would be able to save himself with the help of his inner resources alone, which he considered all-powerful. In his last book, ***Present and Future***, which can be taken as his spiritual testament, Jung expresses his hope by concluding: "Certainly I am not motivated either by exaggerated optimism, or by a solemn ideal. I am simply concerned about the destiny, the well-being and the unhappiness of man, this infinitesimal unity upon which the world depends, the individual being into which - if we understand correctly the Christian message God himself sees his purpose".

Maslow was much closer to Jung in attitude than to Freud. His last book, *Toward a Psychology of Being*, expresses his excitement at the discovery of a new concept of human sickness and health, which he felt held wonderful possibilities for the future.

The basic assumptions of this new concept are similar to those of René, Le Senne and Heymans / Wiersma.

Man is born with an essential basic nature which is "intrinsic, given and unchangeable". This inner nature is not necessarily evil. The basic human needs of food, water, health, warmth, shelter and security, the basic emotions of belonging, respect and approval, and the basic capacity of self-actualisation, are either neutral or positively good. They are pre-moral. Cruelty, malice and destructiveness seem to be violent reactions to the frustration of our basic, intrinsic needs, emotions and capacities.

Since this inner nature is basically good, it is best to bring it out and encourage it rather than to suppress it, because this will lead sooner or later to illness, for instance, through a conflict or an 'identity crisis' or the refusal to conform. Most psychotherapists accept this situation at its face value and try to cure these 'symptoms' without knowing the underlying reasons which caused it. Sooner or later, they will reappear, more severe, more destructive, more difficult to 'cover up'.

'This inner nature is not as strong as the instincts; it is weak, delicate and easily suppressed by habit, cultural pressure and wrong attitudes. But it is enduring and persists underground, "forever pressing for actualisation".

He considered that in order to fulfil our inner nature we had to experience discipline, deprivation, frustration, pain and tragedy. They should be seen in this light, because like steel being tempered in the furnace, we emerge stronger, with heightened self-esteem and confidence. "Unless we conquer and overcome, we never know that we can."

All experiences without exception, are recorded in our subconscious and colour our taste, choice and decisions later on in life. It is those which, together with our inherited attributes, form our definitive personality. The more we know about ourselves, the more we are able to direct ourselves towards good and constructive achievements. We can encourage development and become full human beings, healthy and successful.

Maslow expressed the belief that the ultimate disease of our time is valuelessness and that this state has reached a dangerous level which is creating amorality, emptiness, hopelessness and 'anomie' (Durkheim). New generations are being taught not to trust or to respect the sage, the knowledgeable and the mature.

People's idealism is invested in superficial values such as wealth, prosperity, education, technology and political ideologies, which when they fail to bring serenity and peace exacerbate hopelessness.

He believed that we need a new system of values based on a profound knowledge of human nature and society. This new humanistic approach to psychology - the so-called Third Force Psychology - is the third viable system (excluding Freudianism) after Objective and Behaviouristic psychology, and it goes far beyond the purely descriptive or academic. It is nothing less than a new way of living which satisfies man's inner needs as well as providing a framework for him as a social being.

He went further than this, however, for he considered the Third Force Psychology to be transitional, a preparation for a still higher "Fourth Psychology", which, as he described it, would be "transpersonal, transhuman, centred on the cosmos rather than on human needs and interests; going far beyond humanness, identity, self-actualisation and the like".

These psychologies give promise of developing into a surrogate religion supplying the values which people today are missing.

Maslow was convinced that the best answer to valuelessness lay in the advancement of knowledge, which is the route to self-actualisation. This enrichment of our understanding would encompass love, goodness, beauty and hope, as well as the depths of human nature. Excluding nothing, it would nevertheless be motivated by compassion and love for the human being, not cynicism.

He warned against our foolish tendency to see compassion for the weak as being incompatible with respect for the strong. We must learn to accept feeling virtuous, self-loving and respect-worthy and not fear maturity and the "godlikeness that comes with it".

There are people who have reached that stage the hard way and others who are simply born to it: saints, sages, great and good leaders. It is instructive and rewarding to study their attitude as Maslow did, to find out what distinguishes them from other people.

What does their self-actualisation consist in? Maslow defines it as ".... a development of personality which frees the person from the problems of youth and from the neurotic problems of life, so that he is able to face and endure the real problems of life." This will create health, "openness to experience" (C. Rogers), productivity and creativity.

Such a person is spontaneous, innocent and free. He combines a childlikeness in expression, spontaneity and perception, with a sophisticated mind.

Through a process of fusing together, and resolving into unities, opposites and apparently incompatible characteristics in a sensible and dynamic way (i.e. selfishness and un-selfishness are no longer opposites, "this mutual exclusion is itself characteristic of a lower level personality development", said Maslow), the self-actualised person is not only not frightened by the unknown, but positively attracted to it and sees it as a fascinating puzzle to solve. Play and work are not compartmented off, but are part of a pleasurable whole. Inner contradictions having been resolved, the individual has "more of himself available for use, for enjoyment and for creative purposes" and wastes no time and energy in self defence. His personal goal of health, fulfilment and prosperity merges with the aim of the organisation he works for. When management sets up social conditions with which the individual can identify, the good of society and the good of the individual become synonymous rather than antagonistic.

The self-actualised individual is self-accepting and understands human nature with all its shortcomings, instead of trying to deny them.

The Hierarchy of Needs

The hierarchy of all the basic human needs is only the step ladder towards self-actualisation.

☛ *see oppositve page*

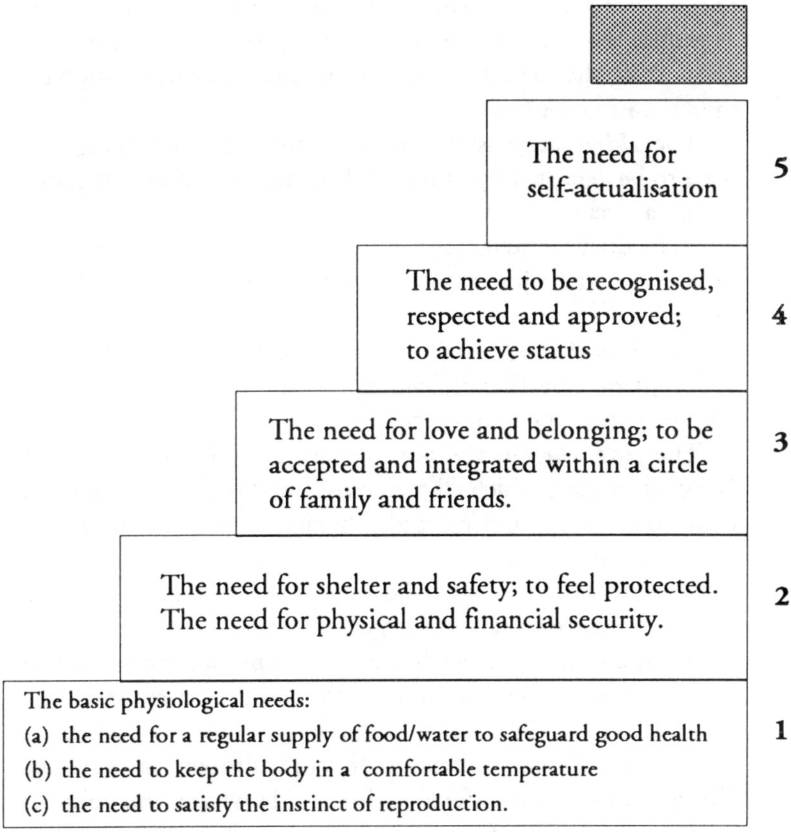

According to Maslow, the hierarchy of human needs starts from the ***physiological, or biological, or basic needs***, which are:

- (a) a steady supply of adequate food and water, resulting in good health,
- (b) keeping the body consistently in a comfortable temperature, and
- (c) satisfaction of the instinct of reproduction.

The ***second stage*** is the need for shelter and safety; the need to feel protected and the need for physical and financial security, as well as the need of others, are more pressing and more vital needs than the need for love, for instance, but less important than the need for food.

The ***third stage*** is the need for love and belonging; the need to be accepted by family and friends and to be integrated within a circle.

Individual, idiosyncratic differences create preferences in relating to others just as cultural differences generate different values.

The ***fourth stage*** is the need to be recognised, respected and approved by friends, colleagues and society; the need to achieve status among one's peers.

The ***fifth stage*** is the need for self-actualisation. This is a "far goal towards which all men strive" and is closely connected with good health and creativity (which is not necessarily the same as productivity).

These basic needs, or basic values, are both goals for each step and steps towards a single goal.

Although the basic needs (*stage 1*) are probably common to all mankind, some will have different priorities based on different values. Personality differences create preferences in relating to self and others. Different cultures also generate different values and different priorities. However, the need for happiness and self-fulfilment, in one way or another, is common to all.

Most people are not aware of the gradation of needs. They strive for security or love and don't realise that once their goal is achieved they will still not be fully satisfied. Such is human nature until it reaches the top step of self-actualisation and self-fulfilment.

This notion of self-actualisation or *individuation* might seem obscure to people who are not familiar with analytical psychology. It is, however, the central point of Jung's work too. The symbols, the world of dreams, the repeated references to the oriental religions, to alchemy, etc., all correspond to a very simple concept.

During the educational years, an individual will only develop a certain amount of his personality. The rest will remain neglected for varying reasons, such as indifferent education, too strict a discipline during the tender years, or total lack of it, imposed inhibitions and prohibitions through a prejudiced religious (or other) education, all of which will bury three quarters (in some cases even much more) of the individual's abilities and natural tendencies in the 'Shadow'.

If we were able to develop the totality of our possibilities, we could become "who we are" and achieve our "total personality". This can happen (only sometimes, not always or often) during the second half of our life, or occasionally, during psychoanalysis.

"The process of *individuation* is a reality. Its discovery and the description of its phenomenology constitute the true glory of Jung who, with it added a dimension to our psycho-analytical understanding of man" (Jean-Charles Gille-Maisani).

The first stage of individuation is the confrontation between our attitude and our inferior function.

Jung's 'Shadow' is that part of ourselves where all our dark sides are gathered: not what is evil, rather, what has remained uncultured, unused, unseen, unacknowledged, uninvestigated, unventilated and savage. "We all trail behind us the tail of the lizard", Jung liked to say.

The existence of this Shadow is not pleasant for our conscious to admit. When it is rejected, it causes brutal disturbances of the activity of the conscious Self. But it is potentially positive. If, or when, the individual acknowledges its proper existence, confronts his Shadow, the energy of the latter will be liberated and used in a constructive way. The old "destructive" Shadow will contribute positively to the enlightenment and growth of the personality.

The inferior function resides in the Shadow. Its disruptive influence upon the principal f unction, the instinctive reactions, the neurotic symptoms, are all indications of the influence of the Shadow.

The first step towards a total personality is therefore to know and accept this inferior function, and to accept and live its influence on its own different level: not to try to replace the principal function with it. The inferior function will always retain its primitive character, but its influence will be beneficial and constructive.

Graphology plays a double role in this chapter. First, it allows us, through the handwriting, to see the hierarchy of a person's needs and values; secondly, it offers the graphologist a way towards self-actualisation through knowledge and positive thinking.

The human personality is seen in the handwriting through the *synthesis of orientation,* the *dominants of the 7 categories* and the *signature.*

The following may be seen as the graphological validation of Maslow's theory.

Graphology is not only for practising. In fact, this is its most vulgar task. Graphology is for learning, for opening the mind and the soul. It is for increasing understanding, compassion and tolerance. First and foremost, graphology should be for the graphologist's own education and growth and only through this, for the benefit of humanity.

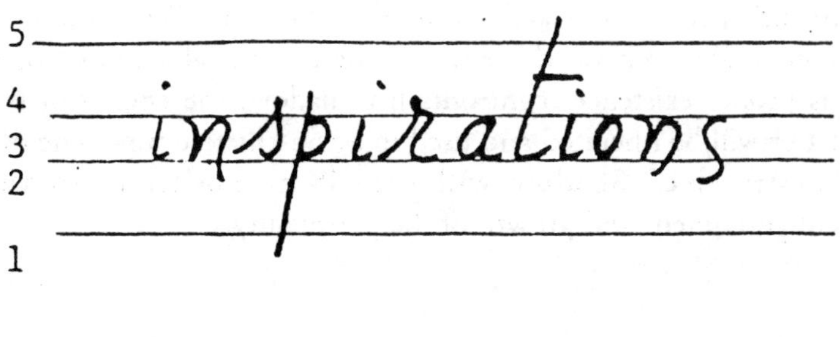

1. ***Lower Extensions prolonged**: (see Figs. XX.1 and XX.2)*

Dominance of primitive forces. Need to satisfy the basic needs. Need for possessions. Need for territorial occupation, to establish roots. Preoccupation with want. Target-oriented activity. Strong intuition (with fine irregular writing and often sharp-pointed). Strong unconscious. Unexplained agonies. Premonitions. Difficulty in adapting. Possibly selfishness, narrow-mindedness (with supporting signs).

2. ***Middle Zone prolonged downwards:** (see Figs. XX.3 and XX.4)*

Need for physical or financial security. Need for others. Cunning selfishness (usually if the prolongations curve to the left or end with a leftward hook). Calculated amiability (if supported by looped garlands). Materialistic ambitions for want of security. Often also uncontrolled instincts, impulsivity (if supported by other signs) and generally psychic exitation.

3. ***Dominance of middle zone**: (see Figs. XX.5 and XX.6)*

Need to belong and to be accepted by friends and family. Need to be part of a circle. Preoccupation with everyday life and with matters of the heart. Egocentricity, selfishness, narcissism (particularly with full movements). Maladjusted emotionality.

4. ***Superelevations**: (see Figs. XX.7 and XX.8)*

Need to be approved by society, friends and colleagues. Need for status. Pride, pretention, ambition and the like. Independence. Creativity. Activity (with supporting signs). Possible exaltation. Egocentrism. Overestimation of self. Touchiness (if the superelevations are caused by an elevation from the base of the letters:  = L

5. ***Upper Extensions prolonged**: (see Fig. XX.9)*

Need to achieve, to make a mark. Idealism. Need for self-fulfilment. Rich imagination. Active intellect. Also, occasionally strong physical activity (when supported by other signs). Aspirations. Enthusiasm. Mystical tendencies. Illusions. Lack of judgement. Lack of order. Possible paranoiac tendencies (with supporting signs). Possibly overcompensation of inferiority complex with pride and arrogance. Possible stupidity.

As a final note, although not all *nuancée* (that is, subtly differentiated writings) indicate an integrated personality, most integrated people tend to have nuancée writings. *(Fig. XX.10)* Some sublimated writings may indicate self-actualisation. The most likely Le Sennian characters to attain self-actualisation are, EAS, nEAS or EnAS. It is more difficult for Primary characters to reach such a state. A person with any Jungian function can be individuated, though in the cases where this occurs it is mostly where all four functions are equally developed on a high level. Any Hippocratic Temperament and any Planetary Type may become self-actualised.

* * *

SOURCES

Maslow, A. — *Toward a Psychology of Being*, Van Nostrand Reinhold Co., 1982

Maslow, A. et al — *New Knowledge in Human Values*, Gateway Edition, 1959

Gille-Maisani, J.-Ch. — *Types de Jung et Temperaments Psychobiologiques*, ed. Maloine, 1978

Jacobi, J. — *La Psychologie de C.G.Jung*, Delachâux & Niestlé, 1950

Jung, C.G. — *Present et Avenir*, Buchet/Chastel, 1962

Jung, C.G. — *Dialectique du Moi et de l'Inconscient*, Gallimard, 1964

Jung, C.G. — *L'homme à la découverte de son âme*, Mont-Blanc, 1970

HANDWRITING SAMPLES of LECTURE XX

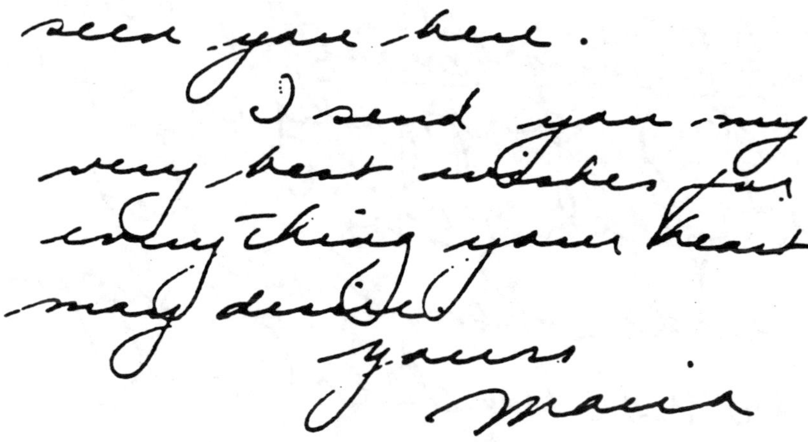

Fig. XX.1 - ***Domance of lower zone***
Maria Callas, 35 years. - She was famous for her 'target-orientated activity' which is also evident in the cadence of her writing, the relief of her stroke and the overall strong rightward pull.

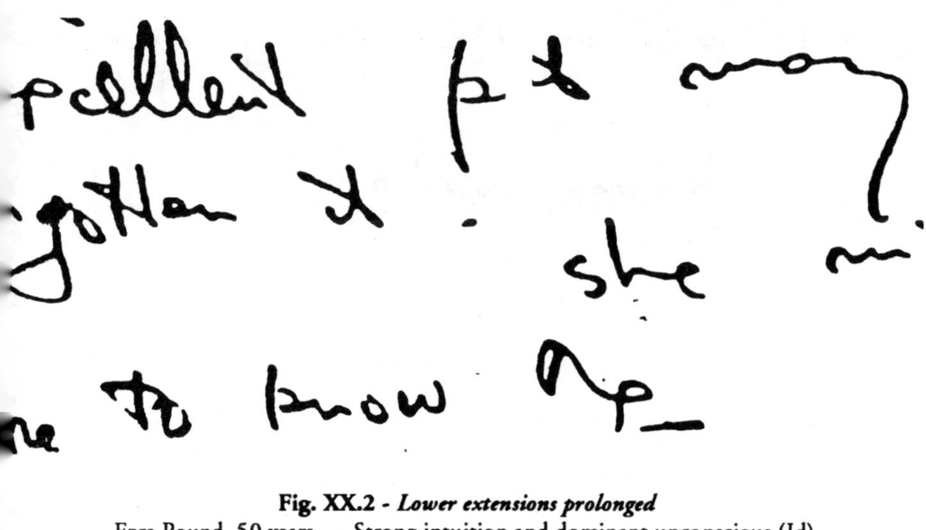

Fig. XX.2 - ***Lower extensions prolonged***
Ezra Pound, 50 years. - Strong intuition and dominant unconscious (Id). Unexplained agonies and premonitions marred his life.

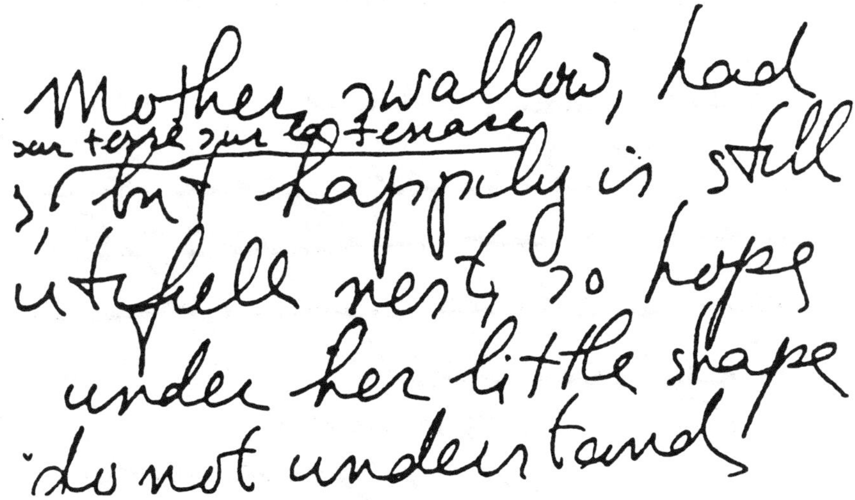

Fig. XX.3 - Man, 40 years

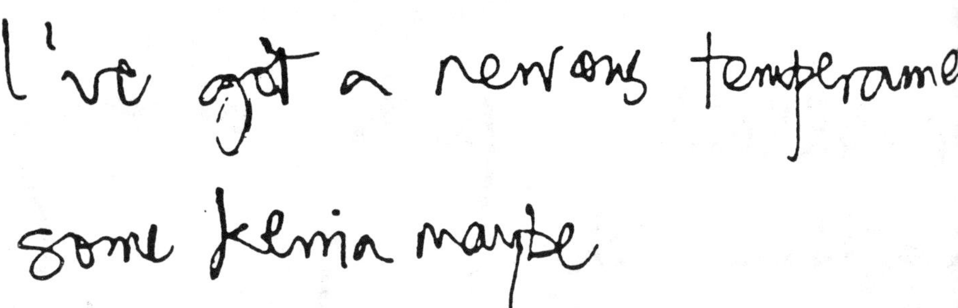

Fig. XX.4 - Woman 42

Two writings (Figs. 3 & 4), with middle zone letters handing down into the lower zone. In both cases there is need for others and need for security. Both writings clearly express the impulsity and excitation of the writer, and the cunning selfishness with which both (partiuclarly the first) are manoeuvering to achieve their satisfaction.

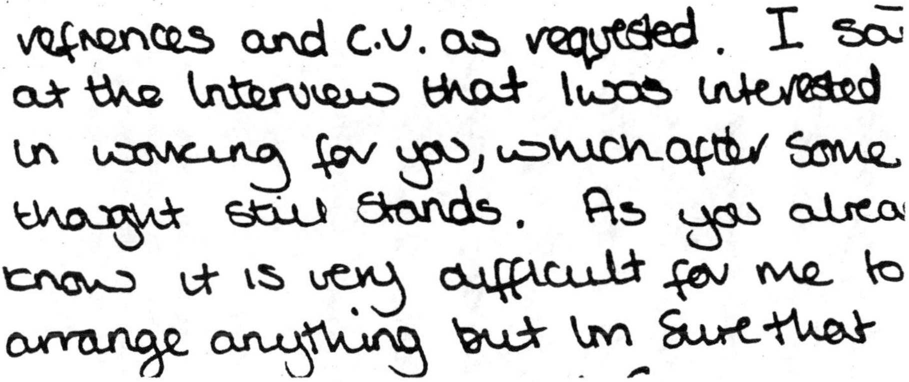
vefrences and C.V. as requested. I sa
at the Interview that I was interested
in working for you, which after some
thought still stands. As you alrea
know it is very difficult for me to
arrange anything but Im sure that

Fig. XX.5 - Woman, 22 years.

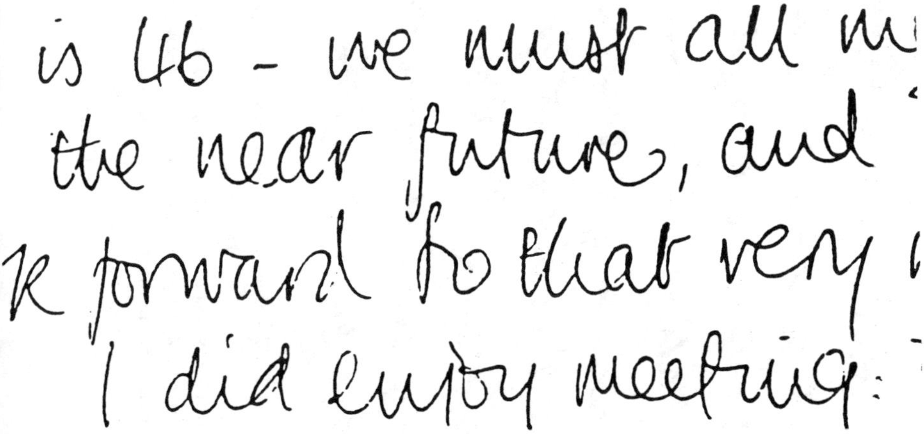
is 46 - we must all m
the near future, and
k forward to that very
I did enjoy meeting

Fig. XX.6 - Woman, 23 years.

The need to belong and to be accepted by friends and family are very important. These two young ladies (*Figs. 5 and 6*) are both very preoccupied with matters of the heart and of everyday life. Emotions here are the order of the day. Every day!

They are both egocentric, selfish and very narcissistic. In *Fig. 5*, the middle zone is not only dominant, it is also very full. This young girl is very pretty and rather spoiled. Her emotivity is not very well adjusted. The second one (*Fig. 6*) is freer. There is some tendency towards rhythm - eventually - and some movement and some life in it, too.

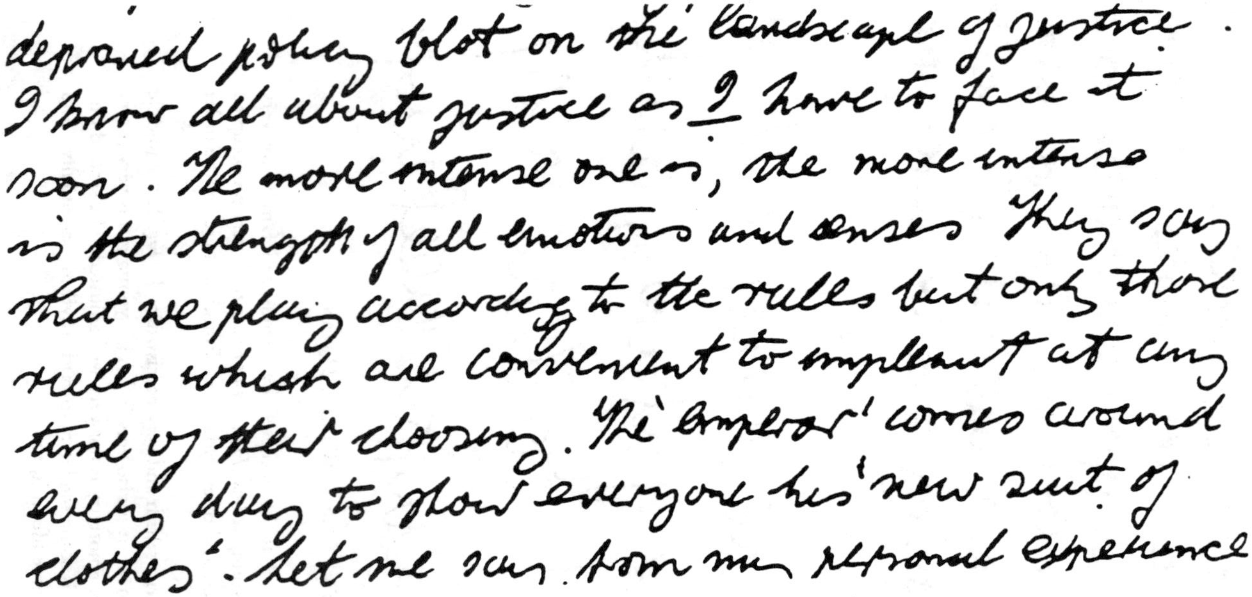

Fig.XX.7 - *Domance of the middle zone and superelevations*

Daniel Nielsen, 33 years

Dominance of the middle zone and many, many superelevations. His strong need to belong, to have friends who would not go away in the morning, drove him to kill sixteen young men in two years. He left their bodies in front of the television set so that he could be sure to find them there in the evening upon returing from work. (There is brutality in the writing, too). He is egocentric and selfish. There is exaltation and touchiness. There are also some middle zone letters digging down into the lower zone; these show uncontrolled insticts, cunning selfishness and need for others.

Fig. XX.8 - ***Domance of the middle zone and superelevations***

Woman, 27 years. - The almost total lack of substance in the lower extensions here, shows concentration of interests in matters of the heart and a negation of materialistic interests. But they also show a feeling of unfulfilled sensuality, creating strong neuroses and fantasies. She needs to belong and to be part of a circle. She is egocentric but not at all selfish. She is generous and loving.

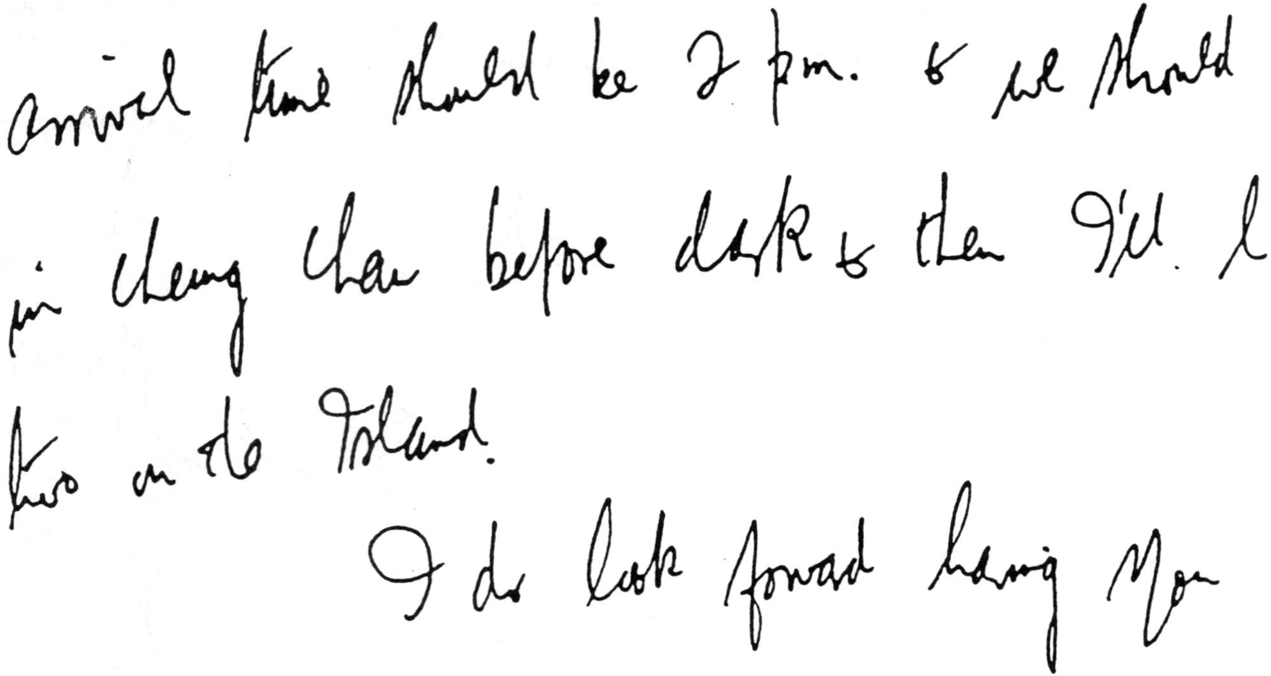

Fig. XX.9 - Man, 47 years

Superelevations galore! He is a famous lawyer. He needs to be at the top; to be approved by society, friends, etc. He needs high status. He needs to achieve (there are also a lot of polonged upper extensions). He is proud, pretentious, egocentric and very, very ambitious. He is a brilliant criminal lawyer. He is in the best books of the best crooks! There is plenty of imagination and enthusiasm, but also lack of order (his office is in a permanent mess. He has four P.A.s).

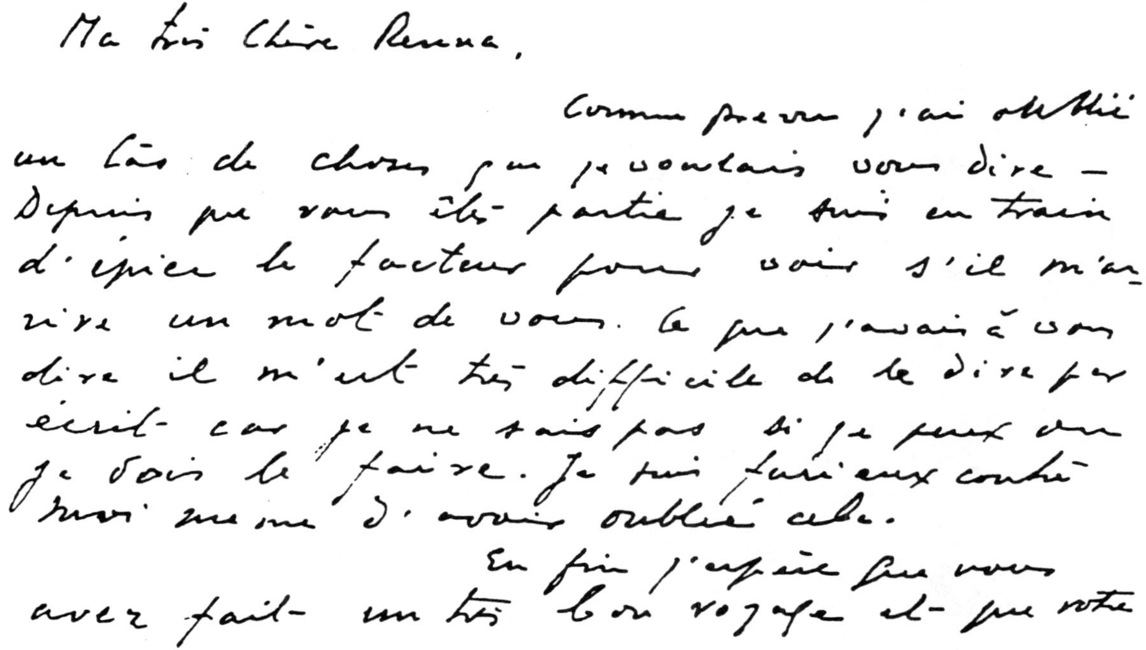

Ma très chère Renna,

Comme preuve j'ai oublié un tas de choses que je voulais vous dire — Depuis que vous êtes partie je suis en train d'épier le facteur pour voir s'il m'amène un mot de vous. Ce que j'avais à vous dire il m'est très difficile de le dire par écrit car je ne sais pas si je peux ou je dois le faire. Je suis furieux contre moi même d'avoir oublié cela.

Enfin j'espère que vous avez fait un très bon voyage et que votre

Fig. XX.10 - Man, 66 years - Psychologist. Graphologist. Philosopher. Writer. Teacher. A Sage.
An actualised personality, delicate and extremely evolved. There is total liberation from the division of self, the dark and the light, and absolute integration of the interior function. The opposites are reconciled into wholeness. The religious needs have found fulfilment in the continuous exchange between the conscious and unconscious mind. The motivations are purely allocentric. Tolerance and serenity are spontaneous. Calmness, positive thinking and good sense are second nature to him.

A FINAL WORD OF ADVICE

We must not forget that graphology has quite a few limitations. There are many personality elements that ***cannot be seen through the handwriting***. These are:

- The age and gender of the writer
- The quantity of his intelligence (we can only see the quality of it, such as analytical, synthetic, deductive, generalising, particularising, etc.)
- stupidity
- the profession (we can only see what the writer would be better at doing, not what he/she is actually doing)
- looks
- financial status (we can only see how the writer feels about his/her financial status)
- destiny
- specific physical behaviour
- specific physical malfunction
- honesty - which is not a personality element as such. (*Dishonesty*, however, is and the absence of any signs indicating dishonesty should point towards *honesty*).

What we can see in a handwriting

- ability to accelerate pace when needed
- ability to give and/or take orders
- ability to keep cool under pressure
- ability to work with others
- adaptability
- ambition
- attention to detail
- authority
- backbone
- clarity of judgement
- clarity of thinking
- common sense
- communication
- complicated way of thinking
- concentration
- confidence
- confused ideas
- conscientiousness
- consideration of other people's feelings
- consistency
- courage
- creativity
- critical mind
- cunning
- curiosity of mind
- decisiveness
- deductive thinking
- diplomacy
- discretion
- dishonesty
- dynamism
- egocentricity
- energy
- equilibrium
- evasiveness
- extroversion
- flair
- flexibility
- generalising intelligence
- goal orientation
- harmony
- hypocrisy
- imagination
- imbalance (mental/ emotional)
- independence
- inhibitions
- informed judgement
- introversion
- leadership ability
- logic
- lying
- mental agility
- methodical approach
- meticulousness
- modesty
- moral priorities
- motivation
- narcissism
- nervousness
- order
- organisation
- originality of ideas
- particularising intelligence
- perception
- perseverance
- practicality
- pride
- prudent
- receptivity
- reliability
- rigidity
- self-affirmation
- sense of priorities
- sensitivity
- sincerity
- speed of thinking
- stability
- stubbornness
- suppleness of mind
- tenacity
- versatility of ideas

and probably quite a few other elements, always on those lines.

EUROPEAN CODE OF ETHICS

01 The object of this European Code of Graphology is to define the rights and duties of graphologists wishing to exercise their profession in accordance with common professional ethics.

02 Graphology, a human science and a technique of observation and interpretation, enables the personality to be studied through the examination of handwriting.

03 The graphologist is expected to maintain and develop his specialised skills.

04 The graphologist studies the personality of the writer. He works exclusively on authentic handwritten documents. He carries out this work of analysis and synthesis in response to a request of a professional or private nature.

05 The graphologist shall undertake to use only methods relating to his practice, and to work within the limits of his knowledge and experience.

06 The graphologist shall abstain from issuing diagnoses in fields reserved to the medical profession.

07 Any graphologist signatory to this Code shall not display his graphology qualifications on professional documents if these are associated with an activity concerned with the occult or divination. He shall abstain from publishing or advertising in periodicals related to the above activities.

08 The work undertaken by the graphologist concerning the human person imposes the respect of moral and professional values. The graphologist must safeguard at all times his independence, integrity and sense of humanity. He must not be influenced by any prejudice in respect of sex, race, politics, social class or religion.

09 In every analysis, the graphologist shall remain tactful and discreet. In work concerned with the selection of personnel, he shall avoid touching upon those aspects of the writer's personality which are not related to the criteria of the position to be filled. His language must remain clear, prudent and unambiguous. In his work, he must be completely impartial and refuse to provide any analysis of 'accommodation'.

10 The graphologist shall undertake not to use the documents or the information in his possession for the purpose of causing harm to others. Being the sole judge of the worth of the documents submitted to him, he shall be able to refuse to provide an analysis without having to give any reason for doing so. He shall refuse to express an opinion on a document he knows to have been stolen. He shall refuse to work on documents transmitted by fax or photocopied, because these processes alter the quality of the handwriting trait.

11 The graphologist shall respect the laws of his country regarding the human person and, in particular, professional secrecy, which must be respected verbally as well as in the circulation of documents.

12 The legitimate owner of a document shall be the sole person responsible for the subsequent use of the analysis. The results shall be exclusively sent to the person who made the request.

13 The graphologist shall not divulge the name of his clients without their prior consent. He shall not communicate or publish texts, or analyses thereof, without the agreement of the interested party or the owner of the document. In education, teachers shall respect the anonymity of the writers of documents used.

14 Each association or grouping of graphologists, having signed this Code of Ethics, shall undertake to ensure that it is respected and applied by all their qualified members. Offences shall be dealt with by the disciplinary board of each association or grouping of the co-signatory countries.

The present Code consists of 14 articles and came into force on the 1st January 1992.

FOUNDER MEMBER SIGNATORIES

- President of the Groupement des Graphologues-Conseils de France
  Mrs J. THIBONNIER
- President of the Société Française de Graphologie
  Mrs J. PEUGEOT
- President of The British Academy of Graphology
  Mrs R. NEZOS-IATROU
- President of the Berufsverband Geprüfter Graphologen/Psychologen e.V.
  Mr HELMUT PLOOG
- Vice-President of the Société Belge de Graphologie
  Mrs A. VERBIST
- Honorary President of the Association de Graphologie Italo-Française
  Mrs J. ROSSI-LECERF
- President of the Association Italienne de Recherche Graphologique
  Mrs N. BOILE